THE WORLD CITIES

THE WORLD CITIES

THIRD EDITION

Peter Hall

Weidenfeld and Nicolson
London

© 1966, 1977, 1984 Peter Hall

First edition 1966
Reprinted 1971
Second edition 1977
Third edition 1984

George Weidenfeld & Nicolson Limited
91 Clapham High Street
London SW4 7TA

British Library Cataloguing in Publication Data
Hall, Peter, *1932-*
    The world cities.—3rd ed.
    1. Cities and towns—Case studies
    I. Title
    307.7'64'0722   HT151

ISBN 0 297 78237 1 (cased)
ISBN 0 297 78238 x (paperback)

Printed in Great Britain by
Butler & Tanner Limited
Frome and London

Contents

Tables

Figures

Maps

Acknowledgements

For help during the writing of the first edition of this book, my grateful thanks are due to: Professor W. Gordon East and Professor Michael J. Wise, on London; Dr G.B.W. Huizinga, on the Netherlands; Mr Kunihiro Omori, on Tokyo; Messrs Stanley J. Tankel, Ernst Hacker and Joseph Leper, on New York; and Mr Rodric Braithwaite. I want especially to thank Birkbeck College for their generous grant which made it possible to study New York at first hand. Miss Ursula Stoksa typed the manuscript with great speed and efficiency. For the second edition of the book I am equally indebted to Professor Claude Chaline, on Paris; Mr Stephen Hamnett, on the Randstad; Dr Norman Perry, on Rhine Ruhr; Dr Ian Hamilton, on Moscow; Mr Boris Pushkarev, on New York; and Professor William Robson, on Tokyo. For the third edition, my debts are to the Information and Documentation Centre for the Geography of the Netherlands, and the Netherlands Embassy in London, for Randstad Holland; Hong Kong Government Office, for Hong Kong; and Dr Timothy Campbell, for Mexico City. My secretaries - Mrs Monika Wheeler, Mrs Linda Hoskins and Miss Linda Tarrant - also deserve my best thanks, as do Hilary Walford and Linden Lawson for their advice and help in preparing the third edition for publication.

My thanks are due to Mrs Kathleen King who designed the maps, and to the following sources for providing material: Standing Conference on London Regional Planning; Her Majesty's Stationery Office; PADOG; IAURP; J. Winsemius; Het Rijksdienst voor het nationale Plan; Siedlungsverband Ruhrkohlenbezirk; Regional Plan Association, New York; Tokyo Metropolitan Government; Hong Kong Government.

1 The metropolitan explosion

There are certain great cities in which a quite disproportionate part of the world's most important business is conducted. In 1915 the pioneer thinker and writer on city and regional planning, Patrick Geddes, christened them 'the world cities'. This book is about their growth and problems.

World cities: a unique phenomenon

By what characteristics do we distinguish the world cities from other great centres of population and wealth? In the first place, they are usually major centres of political power. They are the seats of the most powerful national governments and sometimes of international authorities too; of government agencies of all kinds. Round these gather a host of institutions, whose main business is with government; the big professional organizations, the trade unions, the employers' federations, the headquarters of major industrial concerns.

These cities are the national centres not merely of government but also of trade. Characteristically they are the great ports, which distribute imported goods to all parts of their countries, and in return receive goods for export to the other nations of the world. Within each country, roads and railways focus on the metropolitan city. The world cities are the sites of the great international airports: Heathrow, Charles de Gaulle, Schiphol, Sheremetyevo, Kennedy, Benito Juarez, Kai Tak. Traditionally, the world cities are the leading banking and finance centres of the countries in which they stand. Here are housed the central banks, the headquarters of the trading banks, the offices of the big insurance organizations and a whole series of specialized financial and insurance agencies.

Government and trade were invariably the original *raisons d'être* of the world cities. But these places early became the centres where professional talents of all kinds congregated. Each of the world cities has its great hospitals, its distinct medical quarter, its legal profession gathered around the national courts of justice. Students and teachers are drawn to the world cities: they

1

commonly contain great universities, as well as a host of specialized institutions for teaching and research in the sciences, the technologies and the arts. The great national libraries and museums are here. Inevitably, the world cities have become the places where information is gathered and disseminated: the book publishers are found here; so are the publishers of newspapers and periodicals, and with them their journalists and regular contributors. In this century also the world cities have naturally become headquarters of the great national radio and television networks.

But not only are the world cities great centres of population: their populations, as a rule, contain a significant proportion of the richest members of the community. That early led to the development of luxury industries and shops; and in a more affluent age these have been joined by new types of more democratic trading: by the great department stores and the host of specialized shops which cater for every demand. Around them, too, the range of industry has widened: for the products of the traditional luxury trades, forged by craftsmen in the world cities of old, have become articles of popular consumption, and their manufacture now takes place on the assembly lines of vast factories in the suburbs of the world cities.

As manufacture and trade have come to cater for a wider market so has another of the staple businesses of the world cities - the provision of entertainment. The traditional opera houses and theatres and concert halls and luxurious restaurants, once the preserve of the aristocracy and the great merchant, are now open to a wider audience, who can increasingly pay their price. They have been joined by new and more popular forms of entertainment - the variety theatre and revue, the cinema, the night club and a whole gamut of eating and drinking places.

The staple trades of the world cities go, with few exceptions, from strength to strength. Here and there, a trade may wither and decay: thus shoemaking in nineteenth-century London, diamond-cutting in twentieth-century Amsterdam, shirt-making in twentieth-century New York. In the long view, even the world cities may themselves decline. Where now is Bruges - a world city of late medieval Europe? But so far in history, such cases are conspicuous by their rarity. Nothing is more notable about the world cities, taking the long historic view, than their continued economic strength. Not for them the fate of depressed regions which see their staple products decline: regions like the coalfields of Northumberland–Durham in Great Britain or Pennsyslvania–West Virginia in the United States, or remote rural regions like the Massif Central of France or the south-east uplands of the Federal Republic of Germany. True, one disquieting note is that, during the 1970s, some great world city regions - London, New York - for the first time recorded declines in population, while in others - Paris, Tokyo - the rate of growth notably slowed. But this should be seen, in large measure, as the continuation of a

2

long process of economic adaptation and of outward deconcentration; the statistical trends suggest that the official definitions of these city regions, big as they are, are no longer big enough.

As the economies of the advanced nations become steadily more sophisticated, and as those of the newly industrializing nations strain to catch them up, so in all world cities does the economic emphasis shift to those industries and trades most aptly carried on in the metropolis: industries and trades dependent on skill, on design, on fashion, on conduct with the specialized needs of the buyer. Associated with these trends, white-collar jobs grow faster than blue-collar ones; for every producer of factory goods, more and more people are needed at office desks to achieve good design, to finance and plan production, to sell the goods, to promote efficient nation-wide and world-wide distribution. So it is not surprising that, as they gain such new jobs, the world cities shed those activities that can be as readily performed elsewhere - mass production of standardized goods, space-consuming docking and warehousing, routine paper-processing in factory-like offices: such processes of economic invasion and succession are no novel event for the world cities.

These trends, at least down to the 1970s, have helped to swell the populations of the world cities. Table 1.1, based on United Nations data, shows that around 1980 there were twenty-eight metropolitan centres in the world each with a population of over 5 million; ten with over 10 million; and three with over 15 million. Not all these are world cities: even among the real giants, urban complexes like Osaka-Kobe, Chicago and Los Angeles have a regional, rather than a national or international significance. And conversely, some city regions that do not even appear in table 1.1, like the Dutch Randstad, play a world role - as centres of trade, of finance, of culture - that is far greater than a mere total of population might indicate.

This book therefore will study six centres among these twenty-eight - plus two others too small to include in table 1.1, but nevertheless world cities by any standard. Four of them are among the ten greatest urban agglomerations in the world. First we look at two west European capital cities - London and Paris - which have tended until recently to grow at the expense of the provincial regions of their respective countries, giving rise to very similar problems of congestion at the centre, economic decline and underemployment in the peripheral regions. Now, however, the London region is in decline and its inner city areas are suffering serious problems of industrial closure and loss of jobs; the growth of Paris has greatly slowed down, and there also industry is beginning to desert the inner city.

Then we turn to an urban complex - the Randstad, or Ring City, of the Netherlands - which is a world city of a very special kind. (Another example, the Rhine-Ruhr region of Germany, has been omitted from this edition of the book for reasons of space.) Instead of concentrating all the metropolitan

3

Table 1.1 Population of the world's metropolitan areas, c. 1980

		Population (thousands) c. 1980
1	New York-Northeastern New Jersey	20,383
2	Tokyo-Yokohama	20,045
3	Mexico City	15,032
4	São Paulo	13,541
5	Shanghai	13,410
6	Los Angeles-Long Beach	11,676
7	Peking	10,736
8	Rio de Janeiro	10,653
9	London	10,209
10	Greater Buenos Aires	10,084
11	Paris	9,907
12	Osaka-Kobe	9,496
13	Rhine-Ruhr	9,275
14	Calcutta	8,822
15	Seoul	8,490
16	Greater Bombay	8,343
17	Chicago-Northwestern Indiana	8,314
18	Moscow	7,757
19	Cairo-Giza-Imbaba	7,464
20	Jakarta	7,263
21	Milan	6,603
22	Manila	5,664
23	Bogotá	5,493
24	Delhi	5,414
25	Madras	5,406
26	Istanbul	5,162
27	Baghdad	5,138
28	Karachi	5,005

Source: United Nations, *Patterns of Urban and Rural Population Growth* (*Population Studies*, 68), New York: United Nations, 1980.

functions into a single, highly centralized giant city, such agglomerations manage by accidents of history to distribute them among a number of smaller, specialized, closely related centres. This 'polycentric' type of metropolis has special interest for planners and citizens in those countries that have to grapple with the centralized city.

We look then at the Soviet Union, where Moscow proves to be a rapidly growing, multi-million metropolis with many of the problems of its western European counterparts. In North America the gigantic New York City urban complex, biggest in the world in terms of population, presents many of the basic problems of the great metropolitan city in a particularly acute form: it shows that a high degree of affluence, not shared by the whole population, is compounded by problems of industrial out-movement and economic decline to produce unique problems for the planner. Tokyo stands as the most advanced example of the fast-growing cities of eastern Asia. Its rate of population growth – high by the standards of other cities of the advanced world, modest in comparison with those of the developing world – helps to demonstrate many of the potential problems in store for those latter cities; its peculiar difficulties of physical planning offer a warning for countries whose financial and technical resources are still limited.

Finally we look at two emerging world cities from the newly industrializing countries themselves, chosen to point up both parallels and contrasts. Hong Kong is a city-state where British traditions of colonial administration have married with Chinese entrepreneurship to produce one of the most dynamic economies on earth, packed on to one of the most constricted physical sites on earth: a fact that might have proved its undoing, had not the administrative tradition overcome the resulting problems by powerful and sweeping plans. Mexico City in contrast serves as the archetype of the ex-Spanish Latin American capital which has been all but overwhelmed by explosive growth in the short period since the Second World War, making it potentially the biggest city the world has ever seen. Its experience offers a chastening lesson to similar third world cities.

Forces behind metropolitan growth

Most of this book is an examination, in detail, of these eight city-complexes: of the causes behind their growth, the problems which result, and the attempts to solve those problems. But because the book is mainly about the particular problems of particular cities, it is important to understand at the outset the general forces which all over the world are contributing to growth and change in the world cities. In this chapter, therefore, we try to provide a preliminary overview. In the final chapter, on the basis of our knowledge of the case studies, we shall return to this problem of generalization.

There are three principal forces behind urban growth. The first is that population has increased, is increasing and threatens to go on increasing in most countries of the world. True, throughout the period after 1970 many developed and some developing countries have been recording drastic reductions in population growth as compared with the levels of the 1950s and 1960s, when birth-rates peaked. But modest growth is still expected in most of these countries – while in the developing world, where a large and increasing number of the greatest world cities are now found, the increase is explosive.

The second factor is the continued shift of mankind off the land, and into

5

industry and service occupations in the cities. This is a trend observable in all advanced countries since the industrial revolution, which has now spread to almost every country in the world; progressively, more and more of the world's population is becoming urbanized.

The third factor, and the most problematic, is that a large part of this total urban growth is being concentrated into the great metropolitan city regions. It is difficult to generalize about this: though most world cities are attracting a progressively greater share of the populations of their respective countries, some of the most important and prestigious – London, Randstad, New York – are losing ground while others – Hong Kong, Mexico City – are still showing explosive growth. Overall, however, most (not all) of the world cities are still increasing; and this alone creates enormous problems of land-use competition, transportation, urban renewal and local government. And even when overall growth has turned into decline, the resultant problems of outward deconcentration create many of the same problems.

In the rest of this chapter we will look at these forces in statistical terms. First, because it is fundamental, is the general growth of population.

Population growth: the mid-twentieth-century revolution

Between 1970 and 1975, according to the United Nations, the urban population of the less developed world overtook that of the more developed world. And at about that time, a majority of the greatest urban complexes in the world – as shown in table 1.1 – came to be located in these less developed countries: or, to be precise, in that sub-group called the Newly Industrializing Countries (NICS). So it is important first to understand the very different demographic trends, in recent decades, in the developed and the newly industrializing nations.

Back before the Second World War the population texts, like Sir Alexander Carr-Saunders' *World Population*, gave no hint of what was to come. Then, it appeared that population in every country followed a fairly simple pattern of evolution. In primitive countries, and in all the world until about 1750, a high 'natural' birth-rate was offset by high infantile mortality, arising from malnutrition and lack of medical knowledge, and a high adult death-rate caused by wars, epidemics and famines. Later, rapid medical advance and better diets caused a big reduction in the death-rate, while the birth-rate remained high, resulting in a rapid natural increase of the population; this condition prevailed in western Europe and North America between 1750 and about 1900. Later still, the spread of contraceptive knowledge caused a fall in the birth-rate in advanced countries of western Europe and North America; but the death-rate had already been cut so low that it could not fall as fast as the birth-rate, so that the rate of population growth in such countries declined, and by the 1930s in some cases was approaching zero. The population experts

6

in most advanced countries were therefore convinced that soon in the future population would decline. But after the Second World War, in almost every one of these countries, the demographic experts were confounded by a sudden upturn in births: a veritable baby boom. In some, it peaked early and began to decline in the 1950s; in others, as in Great Britain, there was a second and more sustained baby boom from the mid-1950s to the mid-1960s.

For this post-Second World War era, table 1.2 tells the story. It shows both *total* population change (including migration into and out of each country) and *natural* population change (the balance of births and deaths) alone. The two generally move together. From the late 1950s in the United States, from the mid-1960s in much of western Europe, birth-rates again turned down – and in the 1970s they plummeted. By 1979–80 the Federal Republic of Germany recorded natural decrease; Britain's natural increase was near zero. True, there are still important differences here – above all those resulting from age structures: Belgium's ageing population produces a natural decrease while Canada's young immigrant population still shows notable natural increase. But overall, in the developed countries there is a sharp contrast between the demographic dynamism of the 1960s – when official projections typically showed increases of between 15 and 30 per cent over two or three decades – and the stagnant early 1980s, when the same projections showed negligible increases or none at all. We are back, it seems, in the 1930s.

The experts could of course be confounded again; the decision, whether or not to have children, is one of the least predictable confronting the social scientist. But, in the early 1980s, the most reasonable expectation is for very modest growth. True, this is powerfully modified by the fact that, in most advanced countries, a near-static population is dividing itself up into more and more, smaller and smaller households – a result of rising numbers of older people, of social changes that lead younger people to desert the paternal home sooner than they did formerly, and of rising divorce rates. Thus a static population can still produce a rising demand for homes. Nevertheless, there is no doubt that the sharp decline in natural increase has been one of the most potent forces in the sudden lack of growth – and, in some cases, actual decline – in some of the world cities during the 1970s.

In the developing world, as everyone knows, the story is different. After the Second World War, sudden and dramatic advances in medical knowledge eliminated many traditional diseases, such as malaria, tuberculosis and small-pox, that had ravaged these countries. Improvements in agricultural tech-niques – the so-called green revolution – similarly reduced, though they could not entirely prevent, the horrendous famines that had periodically killed millions of third world people. The result was a remarkable fall in death-rates coupled with continuing high birth-rates, producing a population boom with-out precedent in world history; the rapid nineteenth-century growth of

Table 1.2   Increase of population in advanced and newly industrializing countries, 1950-80

	1950	1960	1970	1980
a	*Total increase (per cent per year)*			
Advanced countries				
Canada	1.97	2.13	1.51	1.06
USA	1.67	1.60	1.08	0.90
Belgium	0.29	0.54	0.31	0.10
Denmark	0.97	0.75	0.61	0.00
France	0.81	0.99	0.89	0.43
Germany (Fed. Rep.)	1.61	1.11	1.43	0.35
Italy	0.64	0.63	0.94	0.22
Netherlands	1.59	1.18	1.16	0.07
Norway	0.96	0.84	0.78	0.49
Sweden	0.83	0.35	1.00	0.24
Switzerland	1.19	2.12	0.96	0.16
United Kingdom	0.58	0.73	0.32	0.02
Japan	1.37	0.83	1.19	0.79
Newly industrializing countries				
Mexico	2.76	3.14	3.52	3.65
Brazil	2.31	4.82	2.89	3.69
Korea	N.A.	2.88	1.92*	1.85
Hong Kong	N.A.	3.64	2.59	3.47
b	*Natural increase (per cent per year)*			
Advanced countries				
Canada	1.80	1.91	1.00	1.16
USA	1.39	1.41	0.88	0.71
Belgium	0.44	0.40	0.23	−0.02
Denmark	0.94	0.70	0.46	0.03
France	0.78	0.66	0.61	0.47
Germany (Fed. Rep.)	0.44	0.63	0.17	−0.15
Italy	0.98	0.88	0.71	0.15
Netherlands	1.52	1.36	1.00	0.45
Norway	1.00	0.82	0.64	−0.24
Sweden	0.64	0.37	0.37	0.07
Switzerland	0.80	0.70	0.69	0.23
United Kingdom	0.44	0.60	0.44	0.10
Japan	1.73	0.96	1.20	0.75
Newly industrializing countries				
Mexico	2.68	3.45	3.25	3.41†
Brazil	2.93	2.90	2.85	2.82†
Korea	0.50	2.86	2.11	1.82
Hong Kong	2.13	2.99	1.49	1.15

Sources: United Nations, *Demographic Yearbooks*.
*1970-1
†1975-80 average

populations in the advanced countries, which foreshadowed it, was nevertheless miniscule in comparison.

Such an explosion of population could hardly be contained on the peasant farms, which down to the Second World War represented the basis of subsistence for the great majority of people in these countries. So, driven by a combination of necessity and hope, they flooded off the land and into the cities. The result, since 1950, has been the greatest flowering of cities and of urban life in world history. Some undoubtedly would not care to call it a flowering; the predictable consequences have all too often been squalid housing, marginal jobs, collapsing or non-existent public services and epic congestion. But few could deny the exuberant vitality of the economies and the societies of these burgeoning metropolises.

The results of the population boom are clearly seen in the figures for both urban and rural populations for the 1950s in table 1.3. But what is also evident from this table is the less publicized fall in rates of increase during the 1970s. This is particularly marked in the most advanced and most prosperous of the third world nations: the group now commonly distinguished as the newly industrialising countries. And in these countries, the move to lower birth-rates was led by the city-dwellers – including the many millions that had migrated there from the land. City life, it seems, leads to city folkways – and among these are smaller families. The Asiatic city-state of Hong Kong, a classic example of a NIC, neatly illustrates this trend in table 1.2.

The world pattern of urban growth

In 1899 Adna Ferrin Weber, a young graduate of Cornell University, published a thesis on *The Growth of Cities in the Nineteenth Century*. He manipulated with great skill a mass of statistics from different countries to show that urbanization had been one of the most distinctive, and most universal, features of the nineteenth century. Thus, in England the percentage of the total population that was urban had risen from 16.9 in 1801 to 53.7 in 1891; in the United States from 3.8 in 1800 to 17.6 in 1890; in France from 24.4 in 1846 to 37.4 in 1891; in Prussia from 25.5 in 1816 to 40.7 in 1895.

Since Weber wrote, the process has continued unabated. It is now recorded by the United Nations Statistical Office in their *Demographic Yearbook*, on which figure 1.1 has been based. This makes it clear that, with variations, the most highly developed industrial nations are the most highly urbanized. (And conversely: in 1971, Nepal recorded 3.7 per cent urban; in 1976, the Solomon Islands recorded 7.4 per cent.) It is notable, too, that the countries which undergo the most rapid economic development also record a rapid increase in urbanization – as in Japan, which went from 18 per cent to 75 per cent urban in the half-century from 1920 to 1975 (as shown in figure 1.1). Indeed there is a close relationship between the statistics of figure 1.1 and the figures for the industrial structure of the labour force, which Colin Clark published for various dates in his book *The Conditions of Economic Progress*. England and Wales stand at one extreme, with 40 per cent of their labour force in manufacturing and 78 per cent of their population urbanized. Experience in Norway, Sweden and Switzerland shows that industrialization *can* take place on a largely rural basis, especially with the aid of hydro-electric power; but these countries prove exceptions to a very general rule. The indication is that

Table 1.3   Urban populations, in continents and their subdivisions, 1950-80

	Urban population (as per cent of total population)		Rates of population growth (per cent per year)			
			urban	rural	urban	rural
	1950	1980	1950-60		1975-80	
World	29.0	41.3	3.4	1.1	2.9	1.3
More developed	52.5	70.2	2.4	−0.1	1.7	−0.8
Less developed	16.7	30.5	4.7	1.4	4.1	1.7
Africa						
Eastern	5.5	16.1	5.4	2.0	6.9	2.2
Middle	14.6	34.4	4.1	1.5	5.0	1.1
Northern	24.5	43.8	4.3	1.7	4.6	1.6
Southern	37.2	46.5	3.5	1.7	3.6	2.3
Western	10.2	22.3	5.0	1.8	5.3	2.1
America						
Northern	63.8	73.7	2.3	0.9	1.5	−0.2
Caribbean	33.5	52.2	3.2	1.2	3.4	0.6
Middle	39.8	60.8	4.7	1.8	4.4	1.6
Temperate South	64.8	82.2	3.1	−0.7	1.9	−0.7
Tropical South	36.3	64.9	5.4	1.3	4.2	0.7
Asia						
China	11.0	25.4	6.8	0.7	3.3	1.0
Japan	50.2	78.2	3.4	−1.6	2.0	−1.6
Other East	28.6	58.9	4.2	0.6	4.0	−0.4
Eastern South	14.8	23.1	3.9	1.9	4.3	2.3
Middle South	15.6	22.5	3.0	1.8	4.2	2.2
Western South	23.4	55.8	5.8	1.2	5.2	1.1
Europe						
Eastern	41.5	59.3	2.3	−0.3	1.7	−0.8
Northern	74.3	85.1	0.8	−0.5	0.9	−1.9
Southern	41.0	59.4	2.4	0.3	2.3	−0.3
Western	63.9	78.1	1.7	−0.6	0.9	−0.3
Oceania	61.2	75.9	3.0	0.8	2.6	−0.1
USSR	39.3	64.8	3.9	0.0	2.2	−1.1

Source: United Nations, *Patterns of Urban and Rural Population Growth* (*Population Studies*, 68). New York: United Nations, 1980.

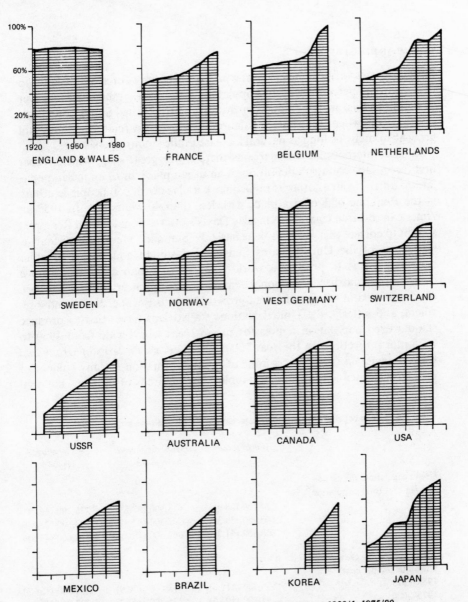

Figure 1.1 *Percentage of population in urban areas, selected countries, 1920/1-1975/80.*
As industrialization proceeds, the urban population rapidly increases as a percentage of the total,
typically from as low as 20 per cent to 80 per cent and more. At an advanced stage of development,
however, the urban percentage may decline as people leave the cities for rural areas. This diagram, based
on United Nations data, suffers from inconsistency of urban definition from one nation to another.

11

most countries will continue to shift a part of their work-force off the land, so that the urban percentage of the population will grow; that there will however be a limit to this, as the examples of Britain and the United States now show; but that even when the urban population does not grow relatively it may still grow absolutely, as long as natural increase in the country persists.

In such international comparisons there is one great snag, which Weber first faced. One country's definition of an urban place, or of an urban population, differs from another's: in Denmark a place with 250 people is urban, in the Republic of Korea a place with less than 40,000 is not. In 1959 an American research team, Dr Kingsley Davis's International Urban Research, sought to correct this. They took as basis the Standard Metropolitan Statistical Areas of the United States Census, and sought equivalents in other countries, so as to provide a world-wide list of urban areas based on a common, standardized, functional definition. Their pioneering work has been much imitated in studies of urban growth made in Europe, Japan and elsewhere; and latterly, the United Nations statisticians have tried to produce standardized population figures for urban areas world-wide from 1950 to 1975 plus projections to the year 2000. Their report, *Patterns of Urban and Rural Population Growth*, is a mine of basic information for any student of urbanism. Dependent on figures supplied by hundreds of different national

Table 1.4   Urban populations and population changes, actual and forecast, 1950–2000

	World total	*More developed regions*	*Less developed regions*
Urban population (thousands and per cent total population)			
1950	724,100 (28.9)	448,900 (52.5)	275,200 (16.7)
1975	1,560,900 (39.3)	767,300 (67.5)	793,600 (28.8)
2000	3,208,000 (51.3)	1,092,500 (78.8)	2,115,600 (43.5)
Urban population, changes (absolute and per cent)			
1950–1975	836,700 (118.3)	318,400 (70.9)	518,300 (188.3)
1975–2000	1,647,200 (105.5)	325,200 (42.4)	1,322,000 (166.6)
1950–2000	2,483,900 (343.0)	643,500 (143.3)	1,840,300 (668.7)
Urban population, changes (per cent world)			
1950–1975	100.0	38.1	61.9
1975–2000	100.0	19.7	80.3
1950–2000	100.0	25.9	74.1

Source: United Nations, *Patterns of Urban and Rural Population Growth* (*Population Studies*, 68), New York: United Nations, 1980.

statistical offices, it cannot emulate the attempt of Davis and his successors to define rigorously comparable functional urban regions – but it is the best approximation we have (table 1.4). It shows that the world's urban population grew from 724 million in 1950 to 1,561 million in 1975 and is expected to grow to 3,208 million in 2000, an increase of 34 per cent. But while in the more developed regions the projected growth over the entire half-century is from 449 million to 1,092 million – 143 per cent – in the less developed parts of the world it is a staggering 275 million to 2,115 million – 669 per cent. In other words, of the world's entire urban population in 1950, a mere 38 per cent were in the less developed countries; by 2000 this figure could be as much as 66 per cent.

Some of the resulting figures of city growth, shown in table 1.5, are almost mind-boggling. Mexico City, still an amiable post-colonial capital with a notably relaxed way of life, numbered about 1.8 million people in 1940 and some 3.0 million in 1950, when the United Nations figures start. The figure for 1960 was 5.1 million, for 1970 9.0 million and for 1980 an estimated 15.0 million. By the year 2000, according to projections, the population will be 31 million – making Mexico City the biggest urban area the world has ever seen. São Paulo in Brazil, in the half-century from 1950 to 2000, is expected to grow from 2.5 to 25.8 million; Shanghai from 5.8 to 22.7 million; Peking from 2.2 million to 19.9 million; Rio de Janeiro from 2.9 million to 19.0 million. By the year 2001, of the world's thirty largest urban agglomerations, no less than twenty-one will be in the nations we now term the less developed countries.

Table 1.5 Population of the world's biggest urban areas, actual and forecast, 1950 and 2000

	Population (thousands) 1950		Population (thousands) 2000
1 New York–Northeastern New Jersey	12,300	Mexico City	31,000
2 London	10,400	São Paulo	25,800
3 Rhine–Ruhr	6,900	Tokyo–Yokohama	24,200
4 Tokyo–Yokohama	6,700	New York–Northeastern New Jersey	22,800
5 Shanghai	5,800	Shanghai	22,700
6 Paris	5,500	Peking	19,900
7 Greater Buenos Aires	5,300	Rio de Janeiro	19,000
8 Chicago–Northwestern Indiana	4,900	Greater Bombay	17,100
9 Moscow	4,800	Calcutta	16,700
10 Calcutta	4,400	Jakarta	16,600
11 Los Angeles–Long Beach	4,000	Seoul	14,200
12 Osaka	3,800	Los Angeles–Long Beach	14,200

Source: United Nations, *Patterns of Urban and Rural Population Growth* (*Population Studies*, 68), New York: United Nations, 1980.

Thus the cities of the third world overtake those of the advanced capitalist first world and the communist second world. Indeed, evident from table 1.5 is a decided slowing-down in the growth rate of many of the older world cities. What appears to be happening is indeed some kind of urban ageing process. In the first stages of rapid industrialization – stages experienced in Europe and North America in the nineteenth century, and in Japan during the period down to 1960 – people pour off the land and into the cities: the great metropolitan centres, which spearhead the process of industrialization, are the chief beneficiaries. Later, two major changes occur: first, the central cities in the more advanced countries tend to export population and then jobs to their suburbs; secondly, bigger urban agglomerations show a decided slowing-down, and even stagnation, in comparison with smaller ones. Taken together these trends spell actual contraction and economic decline for the older, bigger central cities. By the 1970s London, Paris and New York were all recording losses of population and employment from their central city areas. The American geographer Daniel Vining, noting losses of urban population and increases in rural population, has labelled this a clean break with the classical farm-to-city migration trends that have been observable ever since the Industrial Revolution; the same break now seems to be observable in Great Britain.

The resulting trends of world urban growth represent an intriguing set of paradoxes. On the one hand, in the advanced industrial countries, decentralization and deconcentration – from city to countryside, from inner city to suburb, from big metropolis to smaller city – that result in actual decay of the older, central cities that constitute the heart of the world's great metropolitan areas. On the other, the burgeoning growth of the cities of the third world and above all of the NICs; but there also, in the 1970s, the rapid growth of the suburban zones outside the boundaries of the formal city – often unplanned, unserviced, chaotic. These are the principal themes of any study of the world cities that looks forward into the last years of the twentieth century.

The growth of the giant metropolis

For every major country of the world it should be possible, with the aid of the standardized United Nations figures plus certain supplementary data for each country, to distinguish a metropolitan region: a single dominant metropolitan area, surrounding and growing out from a world city. But, precisely because the world city regions are so large and so complex in internal organization, this is far from easy. As already seen, geographers and demographers in the past have sought to measure city regions on the basis of functional criteria, such as commuter fields; but there are presently no such standardized figures world-wide, and the United Nations data refer to smaller, physically-urbanized and densely-populated areas. Thus, even in the case of fairly simple monocentric regions such as London or Paris, we find important differences of definition. For London, UN data show an estimated 1980 population of 10,209,000; the British Office of Population Censuses and Surveys shows a 'Metropolitan Area' around London with a 1981 Census population of 12,113,000, which includes the commuter fields of some medium-sized towns just outside the London orbit. For Paris, similarly, the UN shows a 1980 population estimate of 9,907,000; the French *Institut National de Statistique et des Études Économiques* shows a 'Région Île de France' with a 1982 Census population of 10,060,000. For New York, the UN figure of 20,383,000 compares with a 1980 United States Census figure for the 'New York–Newark–Jersey City Standard Consolidated Statistical Area' of 16,120,000. For Tokyo, the UN figure of 20,045,000 for Tokyo–Yokohama compares with Japanese figures that range from 11,472,000 (for the Tokyo Metropolitan Government in 1980) through 20,356,000 (for 'Densely Inhabited Districts' in 1980) to an epic 35,702,000 (for the 'National Capital Region'). Those who enjoy entering a competition to identify the world's biggest city clearly have some room for dispute here.

The difficulties, however, increase when the administrative capital of a nation is not its largest commercial city – as is the case of the United States (where in 1980 the New York–Newark–Jersey City population of 16,120,000 compared with a population for the Washington, DC, Standard Metropolitan Statistical Area of only 3,060,000) or of Australia (where in 1980 the Sydney population of 3,022,000 compared with only 197,000 for the Commonwealth capital of Canberra). In a number of European countries – the Netherlands, the Federal Republic of Germany and Italy – there is no one dominant city: political, commercial and other forms of power are shared among a group of leading cities. And in the first two of these, to compound the difficulty, a number of these leading cities in effect form a complex polycentric urban agglomeration: Amsterdam, Rotterdam and the Hague are part of what the Dutch call Randstad (Ring City) Holland, with an approximate population – depending very much on definition, and so difficult to establish – of about 3.8 million in 1980; Bonn, Cologne, Düsseldorf, Essen and Dortmund are part of the vast Rhine–Ruhr agglomeration numbering about 9.3 million at the same date.

Definitions thus will differ, and academics will dispute them; we present alternative figures for most of the areas in this book. What does matter is that, in most cases, the differences are ones of degree; they mainly have to do with the inclusion of peripheral towns having some degree of linkage, but often a weak one, with the economy of the core city. In time, as world city regions grow and spread, this degree of linkage may become stronger; so, in a study concerned with planning implications, there is a case for a wider view.

However defined, during the century and a half down to 1960 most of the world city regions have seen continuing and even accelerating growth. Since then, in the advanced industrial countries, their core cities tend to have declined; and in a number of cases this has slowed, and even reversed, the growth of the entire metropolitan region (table 1.6). The forces behind this long growth, and its recent retardation, form one of the main themes of the case studies in this book.

One critical factor in this extraordinary growth was suggested as early as 1915 by a visionary pioneer of town-planning theory, the Scotsman Patrick Geddes, in his book *Cities in Evolution*. The first industrial revolution, Geddes pointed out, was based on inventions like Darby's coke-smelting process for iron (1709), Crompton's mule (1779) and Cartwright's power loom (1785); these inventions harnessed coal and they produced the age of coal and iron, of heavy industry dependent on coal and rooted to the coalfields, of black-country landscapes like those of the Birmingham district in England, Lille in France, the Ruhr in Germany, Pittsburgh in the United States. But after 1850, a whole series of further inventions created a new technology, which passed into general industrial use after 1900 and ushered in a new era: the 'neotechnic era'. They included the electric circuit (Siemens, 1850), the telephone (Bell, 1876), the power station (Edison, 1882), the oil well (Drake, 1859), the petrol motor (Daimler, 1833), the radio (Marconi, 1896) and many others. The new technology, and the industry it created, were almost the obverse of those of the first industrial age: instead of heavy crude products, light and increasingly complex ones; instead of coal, electricity; instead of the universal railway, increasing dependence on the motor vehicle; instead of concentration in congested centres, freedom of location through improved communications.

Industry, it could now be argued, was free to locate almost anywhere, provided that blind inertia did not multiply new industrial plants in old industrial regions: the logical pattern of neotechnic industry was almost complete decentralization. This was Geddes's thesis, and it was the thesis of writers who followed and developed his ideas: Lewis Mumford in the United States, after the First World War, and Jean-François Gravier, in France, after the Second. Unfortunately, as was all too clear to Mumford and to Gravier as they wrote, something very different was occurring: instead of decentralization, the neotechnic era was resulting in new concentrations of industry and services and population away from the coalfields, in the great metropolitan regions. Both writers tried to explain this by artificial reasons of policy: in Mumford's view the modern megalopolis was the product of finance capitalism and of imperial bureaucracies bent on war; in Gravier's analysis the growth of Paris was a simple consequence of the policy of ruthless centralization pursued by every French government from the Revolution of 1789 onwards. Now it is fairly evident that deliberate policies have affected

Table 1.6   Growth of the world cities, 1800-1980

Area*	Population (thousands) 1800	Per cent of national total
London	865	8.2
Paris	547	2.0
Randstad	416	22.1
Moscow	238	0.7
New York	63	0.2
Tokyo-Yokohama	492	1.7
Hong Kong	20	?
Mexico City	128	0.5

Area†	Population (thousands) 1950	Per cent of national total
London	10,369	21.2
Paris	5,525	12.9
Randstad	2,773	27.7
Moscow	4,841	2.9
New York	12,340	8.1
Tokyo-Yokohama	6,736	8.1
Hong Kong	1,747	86.7
Mexico City	2,967	11.5

Area†	Population (thousands) 1980	Per cent of national total
London	10,209	18.3
Paris	9,907	18.4
Randstad	3,666	25.9
Moscow	7,757	2.9
New York	20,383	9.0
Tokyo-Yokohama	20,045	17.2
Hong Kong	4,085	80.6
Mexico City	15,032	20.9

Sources:
* T. Chandler and G. Fox, *3000 Years of Urban Growth*, London, 1974
† United Nations, *Patterns of Urban and Rural Population Growth* (*Population Studies*, 68), New York: United Nations, 1980.

the *rate* of metropolitan growth in certain countries and at certain times. But it is equally clear that the *phenomenon* of growth is universal. It has occurred alike in centralized and decentralized countries, and also in both capitalist and communist states. A more general, and perhaps a more complex cause must be sought.

Even before the general application of neotechnic technology a very significant revolution occurred, during the 1860s and 1870s, in the organization of industrial and commercial enterprises. Up till 1850 and even later, almost all enterprises – alike in industry, trade, mining, shipping, finance – had been one-man or family firms or partnerships, financing themselves out of profits or the savings of their owners, or at most borrowing on a modest scale from local banks. But it then became evident that this form of small-scale organization was quite unsuited to new and expanding types of activity like mining, railways or gas supply. The result was the joint-stock company with limited liability: between 1855 and 1870 England, France and Germany all made it relatively easy to form this sort of company. From then on, a critical split developed: the actual productivity process was still in the hands of the industrialist, but the more important decisions – what to produce, how much, for what markets – were henceforth in the hands of individuals remote from the factories, who held controlling interest in the new companies. In that era, these men were characteristically financiers, who at that time were uniquely fitted to decide whether a new company was worth floating, an idea worth supporting, an existing firm worthy of short-term credit.

Thorstein Veblen in 1904 pointed out a most important consequence of the change: costs were cut, not so much in manufacturing as in manufacture and selling. For the change was associated with a revolution in marketing. The popular consumption market was expanding rapidly, with rising living standards. More and more purchases were being made by corporate institutions, and (because of the increasingly complex nature of industry) by industrialists. The processes of consumption were speeded up, obsolescence became more rapid, style achieved popular singificance for the first time in history. And the financiers could take advantage of these trends as the old-style manufacturing capitalist could not. The period after 1870 is one of rapid developments in marketing: of speculative production in advance of demand; of advertising to create new wants and shift existing ones; of the conscious manipulation by industry of style and fashion.

Contemporary observers of these changes – Marx and later Hobson in England, Sombart in Germany, Veblen in the United States – rightly described them as a shift in *capitalist* organization, from early capitalism to high or finance capitalism. But that was because the characteristic and universal mode of production was the capitalist one; we cannot say how any other system of industrial organization might have changed as it matured. The real change was deeper, deeper perhaps than the change in the identity of the people who wielded the power, took the decisions and drew the lion's share of the proceeds. It was a shift of interest away from the physical process of production, and towards questions of financing, decisions to produce, and marketing: in other words, from the factory to the office. In these years, an extraordinary concentrated set of inventions created the modern office, which might indeed be called the first characteristic product of neotechnic technology: commercial shorthand (Pitman's, 1837), electric telegraphy (also 1837), cheap universal postage (1840), the lift or elevator (1857), the typewriter (1867), the skyscraper (c. 1875), the telephone (1876), the adding machine (developed commercially 1872-88), the electric light (1880), the steel-frame skyscraper (1883), the mimeograph and the dictating machine (1887), carbon paper (applied to typewriting c. 1890). And, between 1849 and 1893, another whole series of developments in printing and photo-reproduction made modern advertising possible. It was logical, then, that these years also saw the very beginning of the dramatic shift towards white-collar employment associated with the rapid entry of women into the labour force, which has been especially characteristic of the twentieth century. In the United States, total white-collar employment rose from 5.1 million in 1900 to 21.6 million in 1950, or from 17 to 37 per cent of the total United States labour force, and women white-collar workers alone increased from less than one million to 8.6 million.

These changes had a critical effect on urban development. For, while neotechnic industry might be decentralized, the neotechnic office was not. Under finance capitalism, the new types of office - the headquarters of railways, of public utilities, of industries, of foreign investment trusts - developed next to the financial institutions in the traditional banking centres. Soon, ancillary offices sprang up to provide specialized services for the new headquarters offices: accounting, law, advertising, management consultancy. Around the turn of the century, the increasing role of government in economic and social life manifested itself in a big increase in office employment in the political capital of each country - which, in many cases, was the commercial metropolis also. Increasingly, formal organizations grew up to represent economic or professional interest: trade unions, employers' federations, professional institutes. These needed to have the ear of government and of government officials, and so they naturally gravitated to the administrative capital or the administrative quarter of the metropolitan city. (A little later, in communist countries, headquarters offices of productive and transport organizations were grouped near the government offices, from which overall economic plans came.) The new communications industries, which combined factory and office functions - newspapers, magazines, radio, television - naturally located in the centres of affairs. For all these activities, the transmission of news was all-important; and it could most readily and economically be obtained in the metropolitan centre. The twentieth century saw a great expansion of higher education, especially in scientific and social-scientific research; this too tended to develop in the metropolitan centres, which were the traditional seats of education in most countries and which were close to important sources of research funds. And developments in transportation technology – the electric tram or streetcar, the electric train, the underground train, the motor bus – allowed increasing numbers of workers to be concentrated close together right in the centres of the great metropolitan cities.

The growth of white-collar occupations of all kinds, then, is without doubt the most important single explanation for the growth of the world cities in the period since 1850. But there are many other contributory causes. Retail trade grew in most metropolitan cities faster than did the demand of the immediate population; for these centres provided a shop window for national and even international markets. Certain types of manufacturing industry – women's fashions, men's bespoke tailoring, jewellery and precious metals, high-class furniture – had always been distinctively metropolitan trades. In the twentieth century they were joined by a host of new industries, which were the creations of neotechnic technology, and which for one reason or another needed to be close to the centre of affairs. Most characteristic of all is the manufacture of expensive, complex, custom-built electronic apparatus for scientific purposes, much of which goes into metropolitan business houses or laboratories or hospitals, or is ordered by the metropolitan offices of government departments. Such goods, like the bespoke suits and dresses of an older industrial age, have to be made in close and immediate contact with the final purchaser and specifier.

In the light of these features of modern technology and economic organization, the rise of the giant city appears natural, even inevitable. In the words of the American economist, R.M. Haig, who studied the forces behind the growth of cities in 1926:

> Instead of explaining why so large a portion of the population is found in the urban areas, one must give reasons why that portion is not even greater. The question is changed from 'Why live in the city?' to 'Why not live in the city?'

In 1926, Haig could find few possible technological trends which would substantially diminish the role of the metropolis in the future. And, for many years after he wrote – down to the end of the 1960s – most metropolitan cities tended to grow notably faster than the countries of which they formed a part. More recently, though, in the advanced industrial countries – as already seen – their rate of growth has sharply turned down; in terms of population and economic activity, they have tended to stagnate, even to decline. The reasons are not hard to find. On the one hand, the hearts of great cities are no longer optimal locations for most kinds of manufacturing or for goods-handling service activities such as ports and harbours, warehousing or transport. On the other, routine paper-handling activities also move out in search of lower rents and salary costs at the periphery of the metropolitan area and beyond – from London to such places as Southend on Sea, Harlow and Reading, from New York to Greenwich and Stamford, generally between 50 and 80 kilometres (30 and 50 miles) distant. What remains are the highest level, highest paid national and international functions where face-to-face contact, and good communications, are at a premium. And workers in these occupations can afford generous houseroom near the centre, thus creating the problem of 'gentrification', whereby upper-income house-buyers displace lower-income renters – again contributing to the depopulation of the city as lower- and especially middle-income residents are squeezed out to the metropolitan fringe.

World city problems

Oddly, therefore, the cities of the developed world may suffer simultaneously from decline and from continuing congestion. The outward movement of population and industry may engender a crisis in the city's finances, as in New York City in the mid-1970s. But, at the same time, the continued presence of low-income, low-skill inhabitants – now, often, displaced from their traditional jobs and unable to find new ones – increases the burdens on the city's older, poorer housing stock and on its social services. And meanwhile, rising car ownership and the declining quality of public transport service may contribute to increasing paralysis on the city's streets and to increasing frustration on the part of the city's remaining industrialists. Meanwhile, with more people moving farther out to ever more far-flung suburbs, the strain on the metropolitan area's entire commuting system may become intolerable as constantly rising fares interact in a vicious spiral with constantly declining levels of service.

The cities of the developing world do not share these problems of decline. But they too face the consequences of the apparently inexorable trend to outward movement. The new arrivals, too often, cannot find shelter in the slums close to the city centre. So they seek housing – and often themselves build it – on vacant land, often illegally occupied, at the edge. The results, in city after city of the third world, are identical, and predictable: lack of basic services, and strains imposed on those that are available; inadequate housing; dangers to public health; lack of access to jobs, meaning long, expensive and exhausting journeys to work and, too often, unemployment masked by membership of the subsistence economy on the city's streets. And, as a result, the

21

third world metropolis shares with the first world metropolis one final problem: that of devising an effective and economical system of local government, which can organize those services – transportation, infrastructure, strategic planning – that must be handled metropolis-wide; which can ensure effective delivery of those other services that must be provided locally, ranging from refuse collection to schooling of children; and that can secure the necessary public finance to do these things in an efficient and equitable way.

The rest of this book is an examination, in depth, of the growth of eight of the world's greatest cities, of the problems that this growth brings in train, and of the attempts being made to solve some of these problems.

2 London

Even Londoners find it difficult enough to know what they mean by London. Because there has hardly ever been a decade of recorded history when London was not growing physically, it has never been easy to determine with any finality where London ended and the rest of Britain began. Paradoxically, in recent decades it has become both easier and more difficult than ever before. Easier, because since 1945 the outward growth of London has been limited by one of the most powerful systems of land-use planning ever introduced in any country. More difficult because, though the intention was to stop the growth of London altogether, in fact the metropolis has gone on growing and spreading – but in subtler and more complex forms than ever before (map 2.1). And by the 1970s this process has gone so far that, for the first time, the whole vast region around the capital was in aggregate losing population to more distant areas.

London growing greater

By 1938, aided by extensions of the underground railways system and suburban electric railways, the suburbs of London had sprawled out to a temporary limit roughly 19 to 24 kilometres (10 to 15 miles) from the centre. In that year, the temporary limit became permanent: an Act of the British Parliament, the Green Belt Act, created the means to fix a girdle of permanent open countryside round the existing sprawl, thus preventing further erosion of the countryside. And in 1947, when the Town and Country Planning Act introduced at last a complex system of machinery to control the land use of every hectare of land in Britain, the preservation and even extension of the Metropolitan Green Belt became a major policy objective. It happened that the built-up areas of 1938 coincided fairly neatly with a definition of London commonly used for statistical purposes: the Greater London conurbation. And, since 1 April 1965, following major reform of London's government, this unit has become the territory of the Greater London Council (GLC), which administers the broader functions appropriate to the conurbation as a

23

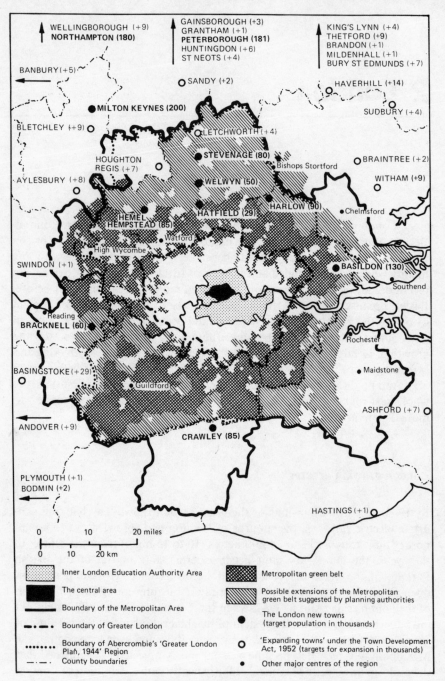

WELLINGBOROUGH (+9)
NORTHAMPTON (180)

GAINSBOROUGH (+3)
GRANTHAM (+1)
PETERBOROUGH (181)
HUNTINGDON (+6)
ST NEOTS (+4)

KING'S LYNN (+4)
THETFORD (+9)
BRANDON (+1)
MILDENHALL (+1)
BURY ST EDMUNDS (+7)

BANBURY (+5)

SANDY (+2)

HAVERHILL (+14)

MILTON KEYNES (200)

SUDBURY (+4)

BLETCHLEY (+9)

LETCHWORTH (+4)

HOUGHTON
REGIS (+7)

STEVENAGE (80)

Bishops Stortford

BRAINTREE (+2)

AYLESBURY (+8)

WELWYN (50)

WITHAM (+9)

HATFIELD (29)

HARLOW (90)

Chelmsford

**HEMEL
HEMPSTEAD (85)**

Watford

SWINDON (+1)

High Wycombe

BASILDON (130)

Southend

Reading

BRACKNELL (60)

Rochester

BASINGSTOKE (+29)

Maidstone

Guildford

ANDOVER (+9)

ASHFORD (+7)

CRAWLEY (85)

PLYMOUTH (+1)
BODMIN (+2)

HASTINGS (+1)

| 0 | 10 | 20 miles |
| 0 | 10 | 20 km |

Inner London Education Authority Area

Metropolitan green belt

The central area

Possible extensions of the Metropolitan
green belt suggested by planning authorities

Boundary of the Metropolitan Area

The London new towns
(target population in thousands)

Boundary of Greater London

Boundary of Abercrombie's 'Greater London
Plan, 1944' Region

'Expanding towns' under the Town Development
Act, 1952 (targets for expansion in thousands)

County boundaries

Other major centres of the region

Map 2.1 *The London region.* For local government, London means Greater London, an area
roughly between 20 and 30 kilometres (12 and 15 miles) from the centre. Outside this is the
green belt, and then the new towns created after 1945. The London region (Metropolitan Area)
recognized for planning purposes stretches up to 65 kilometres (40 miles) from the centre, while
some towns receiving London's overspill are even farther out.

24

whole, and the thirty-two London boroughs which together with the ancient City of London administer the more local functions. Thirteen of these boroughs constitute 'inner London': the inner, more densely-built-up mass that was developed before the First World War. The others make up 'outer London': the more spacious suburbs of outer London, built in a frenzy of speculative development in the twenty-one years between the First World War and the Second. The GLC – ironically threatened with abolition in 1986, under current government proposals – is responsible for an area of 1,580 square kilometres (610 square miles) which in 1981 had a population of 6,713,165. So – pending the GLC's disappearance – in London a situation obtains that is rare in any world city: physical reality, statistical reality and administrative reality are all approximately the same.

The difficulty is that there is another, deeper, sort of reality than the physical one: the economic and social reality of people's jobs and homes and the way they travel between them. Even at the point when it came into being as a unit of government, Greater London was becoming less great: between 1961 and 1971 it lost 540,000 people or 7 per cent of its population; between 1971 and 1981 another 739,000, 9.9 per cent. By 1981, indeed, it had nearly 2 million less people than a similar area – slightly different in size and shape – had in 1939. Yet in one sense this is an illusion. In fact, since 1945 London has continued to grow, and grow rapidly; but, because the planners would not let it sprawl, because it has been hemmed in by the green belt, it has grown in new ways. In the zone beyond the original green belt, 8 kilometres (5 miles) wide, that is in a wide ring between 30 and 65 kilometres (20 and 40 miles) from central London, existing towns have swelled; and new towns have grown out of villages, or on virgin fields, into major centres. Altogether this 'Outer Metropolitan Area' added nearly one million to its population in the decade 1951-61, representing two-fifths of the net growth of the British population; another 650,000 from 1961 to 1971; and finally, as the wave of growth moved even farther afield, a mere quarter of a million from 1971 to 1981 (map 2.2).

Of course, not all these people look to Greater London for a living; but many – over half a million at the time of the 1971 Census – travel across the green belt into London's centre or its suburbs, each workday morning, to earn their daily bread. So, in an important sense, towns 30 to 50 kilometres (20 to 30 miles) out, like Guildford, Reading, Chelmsford and Maidstone, have become parts of London too. But in another sense, they have not: they remain – thanks to planning – separate physical entities, and the majority of their people find work locally.

In consequence a new sort of London has been appearing since 1945, a London so complex in form and function that it is difficult to describe or delimit it: an increasingly polycentric region, in which the great working and servicing mass of central London is just the leading centre among many

25

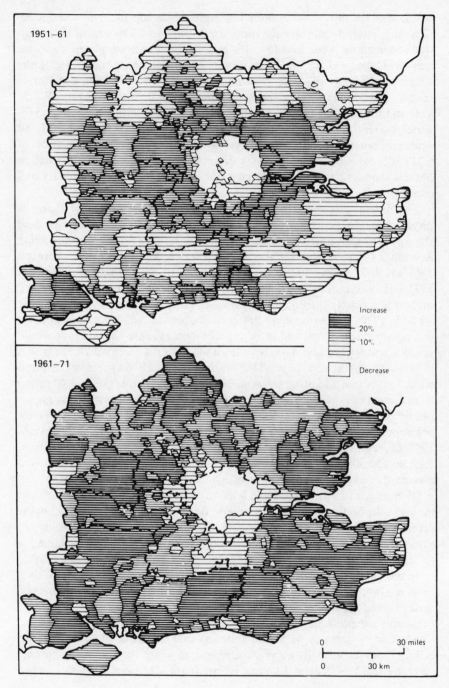

1951–61

1961–71

Increase

20%

10%

Decrease

0   30 miles

0   30 km

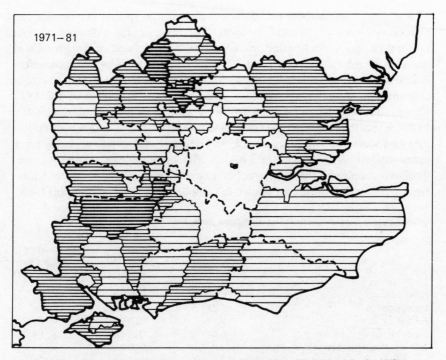

Map 2.2 *The London region: population changes, 1951-61, 1961-71, 1971-81.* In the 1950s, while Greater London lost 165,000 people, the surrounding Outer Metropolitan Area gained nearly one million. During the 1960s Greater London's loss accelerated, to over half a million; the Outer Metropolitan Area gained 800,000, and the zone of fastest growth moved farther from London. During the 1970s Greater London lost nearly three-quarters of a million people, while growth in the Outer Metropolitan Area slowed dramatically; the fastest growth was now beyond the London region, in isolated areas at the edge of south-east England, more than 80 kilometres (50 miles) from London.

others, and in which more and more people work as well as live outside the continuous mass of Greater London. The most useful definition of this London region is the London Metropolitan Area defined in British official statistics: it embraces an area of 11,427 square kilometres (4,412 square miles) bounded by a roughly circular line with a radius 65 kilometres (40 miles) from Charing Cross; and it contained a population of 12,112,917 at the 1981 Census. But this figure marked a loss of over half a million people during the 1970s: a loss that reflected the continued outward drift of London's population and work-force. Just as after 1945 Greater London was an inadequate definition, so after 1971 is the London Metropolitan Area. The same undoubtedly applies to the much smaller area defined by United Nations statisticians. These definitions are shown in table 2.1. Greater London plus Outer

Table 2.1 The London region and its constituent parts, 1981

	Area (square km.)	Population (thousands) (1981)	Population change (per cent) (1971–81)
Inner London	321	2,498.0	−17.6
Outer London	1,259	4,215.2	− 4.6
Greater London	1,580	6,713.2	− 9.9
Outer Metropolitan Area	9,848	5,399.8	+ 4.8
Metropolitan Area (London region)	11,427	12,112.9	− 3.3
(UN definition)		10,209.0	− 3.6

Sources: Census, 1981; United Nations, *Patterns of Urban and Rural Population Growth* (*Population Studies*, 68), New York: United Nations, 1980.

Metropolitan Area, therefore, equal Metropolitan Area or London region. These are the important definitions. But even within Greater London there are important social and economic distinctions between one ring and another. It is necessary to look now at the problems of the different parts of London in more detail; and the most logical place to start is the centre.

Congestion at the centre

Most of the least tractable of London's problems stem from the centre, whether or not they manifest themselves there. It is not merely a question of the increasing volumes of traffic on an inadequate street system, or of the increasing congestion of people in streets, cafés, restaurants, pubs; for the problem of the congestion expresses itself also in the ever increasing crush on the suburban trains from Maidstone to Reading, the traffic congestion in the morning rush hours in Lewisham or Croydon or Leytonstone, and the problem of the isolated wife in the 'commuter country' of Camberley or Three Bridges or Chelmsford, 50 kilometres (30 miles) or more from London.

The office centre

As defined for the 1971 Census – a definition not repeated in 1981 – London's 'conurbation centre' is rather bigger than that of most other world cities. It covers just under 27 square kilometres – 10.5 square miles – mainly on the north bank of the Thames within a ring bounded by the main terminal railway stations, but stretching also about 2 kilometres (1 mile) south of the river as far as the Elephant and Castle where government and other new office blocks began to go up in the early 1960s. With a resident population in 1971 of some 230,010, the central core had a daily work-force of some 1,241,000 – just over one-fifth of the 6,029,000 workers in the London region. Counts of commuters into the central area show a steady fall, from 1,264,000 in 1961 to 1,165,000 in 1971 and 1,054,000 in 1981 – a fall of nearly 17 per cent in twenty years.

Over 80 per cent of these central area workers were in the tertiary sector, and about 60 per cent were in office occupations. This in turn reflects the concentration of commercial office floorspace there, which rose from 7,627,000 square metres (82,000,000 square feet) in 1967 to 10,488,600 square metres (112,000,000 square feet) in 1980 – this last figure representing some 64 per cent of all commercial office floorspace in Greater London and nearly 25 per cent of the total for England and Wales.

The overall decline in central area employment in the 1960s and 1970s was dominated by falls in manufacturing jobs – including associated offices. There were also declines in routine clerical jobs. But there was a pronounced increase in high-grade office and other work in specialized financial and professional services. Central London, in other words, is becoming steadily more specialized.

The new offices have powerfully changed the London skyline since 1950. The planners have eased the old rigid regulations which for centuries limited the height of London buildings, and the traditional landmarks of London are becoming lost amongst the office towers. Yet London's skyscrapers represent only a physically different expression of a very old phenomenon. Office employment in Britain has been traditionally concentrated in central London ever since the first offices were built by the government and the banks in the eighteenth century. But, until the last decades of the nineteenth century, office employment was limited in scope. It was mainly restricted to the government offices in Westminster and the traditional commercial and financial functions of the City. Then, as the economy became more sophisticated, all sorts of new office functions multiplied: head offices of manufacturing organizations, concerned with sales; ancillary services like advertising, consultancy and operations research; non-profit organizations like trade unions, higher education research and professional organizations; journalism and broadcasting. The new functions colonized new areas; especially parts of the West End, which changed within a few decades from the home of the rich to office quarters, as deserted at night as the City. This was a change paralleled in other cities, for in the same decades offices took over from residences in the Grands Boulevards of Paris and in the Midtown district of New York.

Traffic and commuting

The growth of offices has brought problems, of which the most obvious is traffic congestion. But here caution is necessary. Londoners are fond of saying that London's traffic is grinding to a halt: they have been saying it for at least a century, and probably since the Middle Ages. Though traffic volumes in central London have increased, according to police censuses, many times between 1904 and 1983, the evidence is that improvements in traffic control, and in the speed and flexibility of vehicles, have just kept pace. No major street works were undertaken in central London between the creation of Kingsway in 1900 to 1910 and that of the Hyde Park Boulevard in 1962; but the capacity of the existing streets was expanded enormously by increasingly complex systems of traffic-light control, waiting restrictions, parking meters – which already by 1965 extended almost right across the central area – one-way street systems, and then after 1973 computer-controlled traffic lights. Nor is it necessarily true that conditions for pedestrians or the ordinary worker and traveller have deteriorated. Few now remember the horrors of noise and smell which were the inevitable accompaniment of horse-drawn traffic on cobbles or wooden paving. Nevertheless, in 1963 an officially-sponsored report appeared with the revolutionary suggestion that, in terms of civilized urban life, to keep pace was not enough. *Traffic in Towns*, the report of a working party under Professor Colin Buchanan, was published by the Ministry of Transport with government blessing in autumn 1963. The report's central argument was that it was possible to define an environmental standard for any street or street network – a standard in terms of noise, fumes, danger and inconvenience – and that this standard would then automatically determine the amount of traffic which could be allowed to pass through the system. Once given the standard and the existing system, the amount of traffic could be increased only by comprehensive reconstruction.

For central London, the implication of this approach would be a very costly reconstruction. Here, it is clear that congestion and regulations have long kept traffic flows well below potential maximum. Annual traffic counts over the period 1961–81 have shown that, during the morning peak period (07.00–10.00 hours), the proportion of passengers entering the central area by private transport rose from 14 to 19 per cent. Still, in 1981, over 71 per

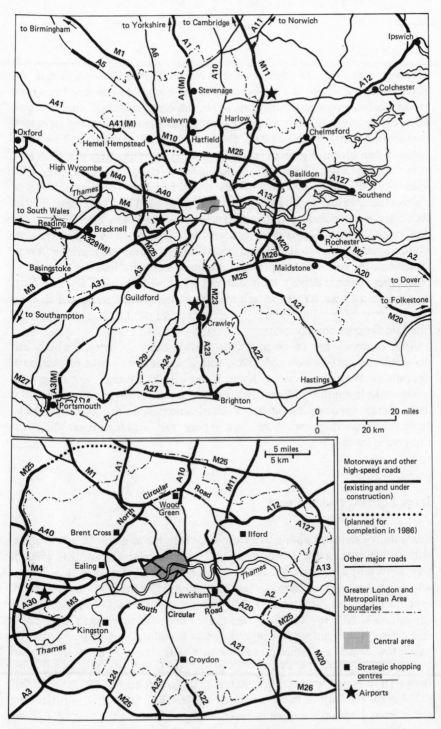

Map 2.3 *The London region: transport improvements.* The map shows the mid-1983 position. Since the Greater London Council abandoned its ambitious urban motorway plans, the conurbation lacks circumferential access except for the North Circular Road, which is being slowly upgraded. Farther out the M25 Orbital Motorway, through the green belt, will be completed in mid-1986, providing a fast circumferential link between the main radial highways from London to major provincial cities.

cent were using rail transport – either London Transport underground, or British Rail trains into the major terminal, or both. The London Transportation Study shows that the majority of the vehicles on central London streets on working days are carrying people rather than goods; but they represent commercial traffic, which can be displaced only with difficulty. The other critical effect of office growth is on the journey to work. Between 1966 and 1980 total commuting into central London fell by over 13 per cent, from 1.21 million to 1.05 million. But, within these totals, London Transport passengers – almost all coming from within Greater London – fell by 28 per cent; British Rail travellers – including longer-distance ones – fell by less than 10 per cent. And of the British Rail travellers, fewer were coming from within Greater London, more from outside. These long-distance commuters represent a new element in the social geography of London. Like their New York counterparts, they make relatively long journeys on express trains every morning, and then must transfer at the terminals to buses or tube trains which take them to their offices. Their journeys may take up to two hours each way; their fares are proportionately heavy.

And, if money has to be found to provide extra capacity – which has occurred during the 1960s and 1970s, with electrification works on the main lines out of Waterloo, Euston, Kings Cross and St Pancras, and expensive track works in south London – then, even with central government aid in the form of grants and writing off accumulated deficits, some money may have to be found from commuters themselves. Indeed, rail fares have risen steeply in this period (map 2.3).

Inner London: east and west

Surrounding central London in a close-built belt, 8 kilometres (5 miles) wide, is the inner ring of the London region. Together with the central area, it represents the physical growth of London before 1914, before electric railways allowed the suburbs to sprawl. The 321 square-kilometre (117 square-mile) inner London area contained 2,497,978 people at the census of 1981: 7,782 to the square kilometre (20,155 to the square mile), compared with only 3,350 (8,670) in outer London. But inner London is still built up to an extraordinarily low density by international urban standards: its 7,782 to the square kilometre compares with 15,180 (39,338 per square mile) for Manhattan and Brooklyn (a bigger unit of 3,658,000 in inner New York) in 1980, or 20,700 (53,600) for the City of Paris (population 2,169,000) in 1982. The difference stems from London's unique development since medieval times. As Steen Eiler Rasmussen points out in his book *London the Unique City*, London grew rapidly outside its medieval city walls, establishing a tradition of low-density suburbs for almost everyone, which has persisted ever since. London did not build apartment houses to accommodate its enormous nineteenth-century influx of population, as almost every other city of the world did; up to 1914 and in large areas up to the present day, the commercial core of London gives way immediately to separate houses with gardens, or at least small yards. Alike in the tiny, two-storey labourers' cottages of the East End, in the solid bourgeois houses occupied by city clerks and professional men in the streets and squares of Islington, and in the great stuccoed terraces of the rich in Kensington, this pattern persisted. It makes London, to this day, the airiest and least oppressive, and in summer the greenest, great city of the world.

Within inner London, for centuries the classic distinction has been between east and west. In 1662 William Petty wrote that London was growing westwards to escape 'the fumes, steams and stinks of the whole easterly pyle'. The east, lying alongside the busy river port downstream from the city, was then already the home of London's poor, while the suburbs of the rich spread westwards and north-westwards from the court in Westminster. In the nineteenth century, the East End took in many of the poorest of the new arrivals in London, as an industrial revolution occurred in industries like clothing and furniture and as hundreds of thousands of Jewish immigrants fled here from persecutions and privations in eastern Europe between 1880 and 1910. In the late 1880s and early 1890s Charles Booth conducted the first large-scale modern social survey here: 12.45 per cent of East Enders were found to be 'very poor', who 'live in a state of chronic want', and another 22.79 per cent were 'poor', 'living under a struggle to obtain the necessaries of life and make both ends meet'. In the years after Booth, conditions improved slowly. The population of inner East End – the modern London borough of Tower Hamlets – fell from 597,000 in 1901 to 308,000 at the outbreak of the Second World War in 1939; then, evacuation and bomb destruction reduced the population still further to 231,000 in 1951. By 1981, the figure had fallen to 143,000 – less than one-quarter the level of eighty years earlier.

Reconstruction and decay

The bombing gave a unique chance for London to rebuild the East End; and London seized the chance. In the middle of the war, in 1943, appeared London's blueprint for reconstruction: the County of London Plan, prepared by the notable town planner Sir Patrick Abercrombie, in association with the planners of the old County of London which gave way to the GLC in the reform of 1965. This plan devoted much space to the problems of rebuilding bombed and blighted areas like the East End. Its analysis concluded that, if the majority of East Enders were to be given housing suitable for family life, with houses and gardens on the traditional London pattern for the bigger families, then some people would have to move out of the area. Thus two important concepts were born, which have governed London planning ever since: the *net residential density* of 136 persons on each residential acre (or, in metric, 336 on each hectare) which was to be applied to areas like the East End (and, in the event, to most of inner London), and the associated concept of *overspill* into new and expanded communities far from the congested redevelopment areas.

Working from this plan, even before the war ended, London took powers to designate a huge area within the modern borough of Tower Hamlets as an area of comprehensive redevelopment, which meant that all reconstruction would be carried through according to a master plan prepared by the planning authority. In the 1950s and 1960s this area of nearly 3 square kilometres (2 square miles) was still the biggest area of comprehensive development in Britain. The plan involved nothing less than the creation of a new town within the heavily built-up area of inner London, to hold close on 100,000 people – compared with over 100,000 in 1951 and over 200,000 in 1939. It was not quite finished by the early 1980s, and it has already been joined by two other schemes on the northern flank which will increase the total area under comprehensive reconstruction by nearly one-fifth as much again. The result, in the mid-1980s, is dramatic for anyone who recalls the old East End. Huge areas are already transformed into totally new neighbourhoods, dominated by tall blocks of flats and by the lower terraces of three- and four-storey apartments, standing in spacious landscaped areas. Only a few yards away stand the reminders of the past: the long, squat rows of cottages inhabited by dock labourers or Jewish tailors. But most are gone; and the remaining ones invariably already have the air of waiting for the demolition men.

The biggest comprehensive developments are concentrated east of the City: north of the river within the borough of Tower Hamlets, south of it in the Bermondsey area within the Borough of Southwark. These schemes were in large part conceived in the late wartime years of 1943 and 1944, to deal with the slum problems of the London of 1939. They are well on the way to completion; and, for the generation of planners of the 1980s, London's biggest housing problem lies in a different quarter. It is the west, home of London's rich; and paradoxically, the problem stems from that fact.

Though the landscape of inner London is almost everywhere still dominated by houses built for occupation by single families, these houses are very different in east and west. In the east, they are the small terraced cottages built in the 1840s and 1850s for the labourers who fled from the countryside into London's docks and industries; in Chelsea and Kensington and Paddington, they are the town houses of the rich and comfortable middle class of the mid-Victorian era, built on three or four floors above their basement kitchens. But progressively, as land values have risen in inner London after the First World War, and as the trek to more distant suburbs has taken place, the big houses of west London have been broken up into separate apartments or flats. Thus, in an area like North Kensington, middle-class houses have become working-class flats; they are occupied by people who drive buses or vans, or wait in restaurants and bars in central London and who have to live near their work. These people have been paying low rents for rather poorly equipped and poorly maintained property, and, since rents were frozen as a result of two world wars, the maintenance has got worse and the property has deteriorated. In other areas, like Earls Court, houses have been fragmented into 'bed-sitters' for students and secretaries without families, who can pay relatively high uncontrolled rents to be near their work in central London. As the growth of the central London economy has swollen the ranks of these people, so they have displaced others unless rent control provided a barrier. Now, as a result of partial decontrol of rents and the constant pressure of demand for owner-occupied housing, many working-class families are finding themselves displaced. In some cases their homes pass to new immigrants, from the West Indies or other parts of the Commonwealth, who are willing to pay high rents because of colour discrimination elsewhere. Others pass, perhaps after a spell in the occupation of black immigrants, to professional and executive workers who are willing to pay high prices to buy and re-convert them to one-family occupation. Yet others are converted by property developers into luxury apartments. The process has made big profits for those who bought cheap and sold dear; but here, the professional speculator finds common cause with the middle-class owner-occupier, whose infiltration of working-class areas gave a new word to the English language in the 1970s – gentrification. It is this process, above all, that has caused a catastrophic loss in the population of several inner London boroughs between 1961 and 1981; 100,300 or 38.4 per cent in Islington, 99,700 or 36.5 per cent in Kensington and Chelsea (map 2.2).

The Milner Holland report on London housing, published in March 1965, was a milestone in the systematic statistical analysis of inner London's hous-ing problems. It identified the worst areas of housing stress: they formed a wide arc surrounding central London on its north and west sides. And it found a systematic association between overcrowding, lack of basic facilities (like exclusive household access to kitchen and bathroom), multi-occupation of housing, and rented housing – especially in the furnished lettings. Nor has this situation altered subsequently. The 1981 Census showed that, though 93 per cent of all households in Greater London had exclusive access to fixed bath and inside w.c., for furnished tenants this proportion fell to 63 per cent. And though only 1.4 per cent of all households lived at more than $1\frac{1}{2}$ persons per room, for furnished tenants it was 6.9 per cent.

But there is no simple answer to the problem of 'multi-occupation' of former one-family houses in areas like west London. The local authorities have already been given considerable powers, under the Housing Acts, to prevent mismanagement of rented housing. But a problem is bound to remain as long as population in London grows by natural increase and by rapid immigration; as long as coloured immigrants suffer prejudice and are so driven to offer high rents for cramped, insanitary accommodation; as long as London continues to attract disproportionate numbers of well-paid professional and executive workers who can afford high prices to buy houses near the centre. To build outwards is no necessary answer, for the pressure of people on space near the centre will remain; and no government could seriously contemplate the abandonment of the green belt policy. Yet to build higher and more densely in inner London is no necessary answer either: it will make at best a partial contribution because much of inner London does not need replacement; it will probably be more expensive, in real terms, than the present density standards for rebuilding; and as the housing authorities have stressed, it will almost certainly be less satisfactory for children. At bottom, the problem is not capable of solution; it may be relieved by giving people the maximum possible opportunity, incentive and help to move out of inner London, and even out of the crowded south-east of England altogether.

The decline of the inner city

The problem is complicated by the fact that by the middle and late 1970s inner London was in demographic and industrial decline. Total employment began to fall from the early 1960s: from 1966 to 1971 Greater London lost 263,000 factory workers, or 18.5 per cent; from 1971 to 1976 another 233,000, or 20 per cent. And, of a total employment loss of 583,000 in the period 1966–76, 246,000 was in central London, 257,000 was in inner London outside the central area (table 2.2). Manufacturing employment in inner London, in fact,

Table 2.2   Greater London: employment change, 1966–76

	(thousands)	(per cent)	(thousands)	(per cent)	(thousands)	(per cent)
	1966–71		1971–6		1966–76	
Factory workers	−263	−18.5	−233	−20.0	−496	−34.8
Office workers	−8	−0.5	+5	+0.3	−3	−0.2
Other workers	−75	−5.1	−9	−0.6	−84	−5.7
Total	−346	−7.8	−237	−5.8	−583	−12.1
Central London	−90	−6.7	−156	−12.5	−246	−18.4
Inner London	−188	−14.8	−69	−6.4	−257	−20.2
Outer London	−68	−3.7	−12	−0.7	−80	−4.4

Source: Standing Conference on London and South East Regional Planning, 1981.

fell by over 30 per cent during the five years from 1971 to 1976 alone. By the mid-1970s, 70 per cent of London's jobs were in services. The reasons for the decline of inner city manufacturing are complex: economic recession, rationalization associated with take-overs, redevelopment and clearance of the areas that included many small factories and workshops, labour supply problems. Certainly, since the loss of factory jobs in London was four times as rapid as in the country as a whole, a 'London factor' was at work: the metropolis is now an unfavourable location for manufacturing. But the resident labour force has fallen even faster, with a net outflow of 100,000 people a year – mainly from the inner boroughs.

The experts are not in entire agreement as to whether this decline really represents a major problem. On one hand, the Greater London Council and the inner boroughs argue that it is producing an ill-balanced population, with many rich and many poor and too few middle-income workers, and that it is putting an increased strain on local authority finance as the rateable value (local tax) base is eroded. On the other, some experts think that London and Londoners can only benefit from the thinning-out process. The official inner area study of Lambeth in south London, commissioned by the Department of the Environment from consultants and published in 1977, suggests that many Londoners would like to leave the city but are prevented by housing problems. It argues that efforts to provide more jobs in Lambeth should be matched by training schemes to upgrade the skills of the local labour force and – more controversially – by measures to help those who wish to leave to do so. Certainly the right answer to inner city decline – in London, Birmingham, Liverpool and other large British cities – was not clearly in sight when the inner area studies appeared.

Outer London: Greater London's interwar suburbs

About 8 to 11 kilometres (5 to 7 miles) from the centre of London, the outward-bound traveller passes, quite abruptly, from the more densely built inner ring to the suburbs built between 1918 and 1939. During the period 1921–39 the population of Greater London grew by about 1.2 million or 16.6 per cent; but the built-up area grew over three times. By 1939, the zone between about 8 and 20 kilometres (5 and 12 miles) from the centre was almost uniformly built up with housing at an average density of 30–5 per hectare (12–14 per acre). The new houses were not only much more widely spaced than ever before; they were also built in much freer patterns, for it was everyone's ambition to own a house slightly different, in design or position, from his neighbour. The frequent corner shops of the old London were replaced by shopping parades, often built around the electric railway stations which took commuters into central London.

The interwar suburbs, in fact, were built on good communications – better than London had known before. Ironically, in the mid-1980s perhaps the chief problem they present is the problem of getting about. Between 1918 and 1939 the underground railways took their lines far into what was then open countryside, opening up the suburban ring to the commuter in areas like Hendon, Edgware, Wembley, Harrow or Ruislip; south of the river, the Southern Railway electrified its suburban lines and built some new ones, with the same result. Underground or Southern suburban lines stretch, on average, some 24 kilometres (15 miles) from central London. They have frequent stops so that journeys – especially on the underground – are relatively slow. Because of considerable overloading on the inner stretches, again especially on the underground, they are also often rather uncomfortable. Those suburbanites who earn their living outside the centre – the majority, in most suburban areas – may travel by car, and many suburbanites travel exclusively by car in the evenings and at weekends; the 1981 Census shows that in outer London, 64 per cent of households (as against only 41 per cent in inner London) owned cars. But here, too, their journeys are far from smooth. The arterial roads which sweep through the suburbs are now fifty years old, and are congealed with a volume of traffic for which they were never conceived. They are bad traffic carriers, with frequent side-road access and frontage developments, including some major shopping centres. Some few have been relieved by new motorways (freeways), while others have been reconstructed as motorways. But it looks as if extensive improvements and new roads would have been needed to cope with rising traffic volumes; and these were not forthcoming (map 2.3).

Despite these disadvantages, it does not yet appear that the interwar developments are losing favour with commuters in competition with the newer suburbs farther from the centre, as may be happening in New York. Like the Bronx, many interwar suburbs of London are now experiencing slow population decline as their original inhabitants grow old and their children move away. The suburban zone as a whole has lost population since 1951 (map 2.2); most of the individual boroughs were losing population in the decade 1971–81. Many of the houses are already being bought by a second generation of occupants. These young people do not appear to find the houses of the suburbs obsolescent by the standards of the 1970s, possibly because fewer own cars than their New York counterparts, and even fewer own two cars. And to London suburbanites, the more distant suburbs appear less attractive because the green belt puts them so far away. So without any firm evidence, it would be wrong to suppose that the interwar suburbs will suffer rapid obsolescence. Pockets of older, smaller suburban housing, near to factory areas, may pass into the hands of coloured immigrants escaping from the overcrowded multi-occupied housing of the inner ring: a process observable in the immigration of factory workers from the Indian sub-continent into Southall. By 1981 indeed an outer London borough, Brent, had the highest proportion in all London of population living in households headed by people from the so-called New Commonwealth countries and Pakistan: 33.0 per cent of the total population. (The next highest, Haringey with 29.4 per cent, is geographically in outer London but is technically included in the inner London group.) But this will make relatively little impression on the suburbs as a whole. Overall, change is likely to be very gradual.

The Outer Metropolitan Area: the green belt and the new towns

London is the city of a thousand suburbs, but that perhaps is no longer the most remarkable fact about it. The unique thing is that the suburbs suddenly stop, to be replaced by open countryside. London's physical growth, some local rounding and infilling apart, has been stopped by the planners' edict at the point it happened to reach in the summer of 1939. The green belt has even grown. There is now the agreed belt, between 8 and 16 kilometres (5 and 10 miles), generally wider than the belt shown in Abercrombie's Greater London Plan of 1944 – his second great plan for London; around it is a much wider penumbra of land that the local authorities have held for many years as an extension of the belt. But it is now certain that the belt will not be extended beyond its present limits of 2,300 square kilometres (900 square miles); indeed, in 1983 the government suggested that some incursions in green belts might be possible and desirable.

In the period of rapid building in south-east England since the mid-1950s, the green belt has been subject to intense commercial pressures; for the planner's decision to re-zone an area, from agriculture to housing, can put astronomical fortunes into private pockets. In the face of these pressures, successive governments have reiterated that the belt is to be rigidly preserved. But in successive policy statements, from 1963 to 1973, governments have admitted the principle that areas of doubtful agricultural or landscape value might be re-examined, to see if their inclusion in the green belt served any useful purpose. A frequently quoted example is the area of abandoned glasshouses in the horticultural district of the upper Lea Valley north-east of London. The strong argument is that, if land must be found for housing, it is preferable to take this sort of land than better land farther out.

This, though, is unlikely to make more than a marginal difference to the size and form of the belt. The South East Study published by the government

39

in 1964, and the later Strategic Plan for the South East, published in 1970, specifically reject more radical solutions such as the replacement of the present belt by a series of green wedges running in less developed land between the main transport lines. Though this form is almost certainly preferable for a rapidly growing metropolis like London, these studies point out that London has been planned on the basis of a green belt for nearly twenty years and that the green belt is now an accepted part of the structure of the London region. But this does not at all weaken the force of the criticism that the function of the belt needs re-thinking. The Scott Report on Rural Land Use in 1942, and the Abercrombie Greater London Plan of 1944, could not have anticipated the postwar explosion of population in Britain, and especially in the south-east - or the impact of mass motor-car ownership. In wartime, and against the background of agricultural depression in the 1930s, it was natural that planners of 1942-4 should have been influenced by the need to preserve farming above all. But in the Britain of the 1980s, it is arguable that the needs of the city dweller should take first place, and his rights of access to the countryside should be greatly strengthened. It seems anomalous, to say the least, to find from David Thomas's careful study that in 1960 only 5.4 per cent of the green belt was used for recreation - and only 3.4 per cent was open to the public for their enjoyment. Country parks, opened by local authorities and private bodies with government grants following the Countryside Act of 1968, may remedy this to a limited extent; a bigger hope is to incorporate them in larger regional parks, such as the Lea Valley Park in east London - well advanced in the mid-1980s - and the proposed Colne Valley Park west of London.

Strategically sited, at the outer edge of the original Abercrombie green belt or a few miles beyond, are the eight London new towns (map 2.1), a comple-mentary part of Abercrombie's grand strategy for Greater London. Aber-crombie proposed, and government and local planners accepted, that London should be developed at relatively low densities of population - 336 per hectare (136 per acre) of residential development - over much of inner London, rising to 500 (200) in a very small area at the centre but falling to 250 (100) or less at the periphery of the inner ring. The inevitable consequence was a huge overspill population - 1,033,000, in the calculation of the Greater London Plan - who must be rehoused elsewhere by public action, with perhaps another 250,000 moving privately of their own accord. A central feature of Abercrombie's plan was that these people should not be housed in outgrowths of the existing suburban sprawl; the green belt was to stop that. But as a complement to this restrictive policy, there was to be a positive programme of new, fully planned communities to receive the overspill beyond the green belt: the new towns in a ring, 32 to 56 kilometres (20 to 35 miles) wide, the expansions of existing small towns in the same ring and farther afield. Here people and jobs would move together, so that there would be no additional commuting problem.

The new towns represent a uniquely British solution to a universal problem of metropolitan growth. They are communities of a finite size – generally 60,000 or less in the first conception, since increased to up to 200,000 – built according to the English tradition at fairly low densities of 6 to 7 houses to the hectare (14 to 16 to the acre) with relatively few people housed in multistorey blocks of flats. By 1981 the eleven London new towns – the eight original ones plus three designated in the mid-1960s – had reached a combined population of 878,949, almost exactly two and a half times their original population at designation and nearly four-fifths of the way to their original target populations.

The new towns have on every criterion been a triumphant success. They have proved phenomenally attractive magnets to industry, so that out-commuting has been kept to a minimum; their shopping centres, better adapted to the motor age than those of the older towns, have attracted shoppers from far afield; as examples of comprehensive and humanist planning they have attracted admiring visitors from all over the world. Their most serious limitation perhaps is that, dominated as they are by skilled and semi-skilled factory jobs, they have failed to attract substantial porportions of the lower income groups who remain trapped in poor housing within inner London.

Yet curiously, their very success reflects a deeper failure of the Abercrombie policy. In his concept, they were instruments of a once-for-all planning operation – the removal of hundreds of thousands of Londoners from congested surroundings to new communities set among open countryside – within a London region which was no longer attracting jobs and people from outside. These postulates have not been fulfilled. Industry has grown rapidly in the new towns partly as a reflection of the rapid growth in the south-east as a whole; people, especially skilled workers, have come to the new towns not only from London but from the rest of Britain; the rise in the birth-rate is causing unexpected growth both in the new towns and in London where it creates a new and a continuing overspill problem. Thus the problem of the growth of London, which the overspill policy was designed to solve once for all, has been exported to the new towns and the ring of countryside within which they lie.

This belt – the outer ring of the London region, between 30 and 65 kilometres (20 and 40 miles) from Piccadilly Circus – has, however, witnessed even more radical and disquieting departures from the orderly planned development which Abercrombie foresaw. The ultimate effect of the Abercrombie Plan would have been to give this ring a population of 4,224,000 – 1,166,000 above the level of 1938. Of this increase, all but about 250,000 would have been accommodated in fully planned communities. The postwar

41

reality has been very different. By 1981, the original new towns' programme was largely completed and the programme for planned town expansions – the other important instrument of Abercrombie policy for the outer ring – was more than half-way advanced to its target figures with a combined overspill population of about 170,000 already housed in towns up to 160 kilometres (100 miles) and more from London. Yet by 1981 the population had reached 5,400,000 or more than 1 million above the 'ultimate' Abercrombie level; and the increase of population in the period 1961–81 had been 1,055,000, some 35 per cent of the net increase of the whole British population. The explanation lies of course in continued growth of population in the London region through natural increase, and in 'spontaneous' migration into privately built houses, on a scale that Abercrombie never contemplated. Every one of the major towns in this ring – Reading, High Wycombe, Luton, Bishop's Stortford, Chelmsford, the Medway towns, Maidstone, Guildford – was ringed by a maze of new speculatively built estates in the 1960s and 1970s. Further, the ring of strongest population growth has moved steadily farther out from London: whereas in the 1951–61 decade it was on average 25 to 60 kilometres (15 to 35 miles) from London, by 1961–71 it was 50 to 100 kilometres (30 to 60 miles) away and by 1971–81 more than 100 kilometres (60 miles) distant (map 2.2). This is London's new 'commuter country', inhabited by people who make long journeys of 50 to 80 kilometres (30 to 50 miles) to the London termini each morning. One point though needs stressing: these long distance commuters, in most cases, form only a small minority of the total working population of the Outer Metropolitan Area. Though their total numbers are rising, the areas where they live – the areas round such towns as Reading, Guildford, Maidstone or Chelmsford – are quite self-sufficient labour markets in themselves. Thus the London region is becoming a more polycentric city region; though, it must be said, the new towns are considerably more self-contained than other towns at similar distances from London.

There is an important difference between these new suburbanites and their New York counterparts. London's new commuters live in separate self-contained communities separated from each other by open land, because the green belt policy is being applied in practice around most of these towns. They also live at higher densities than the 10-houses-per-hectare (4-houses-per-acre) American commuter, densities on average about the same as those of the interwar suburbs of London, but which the government planners are trying to raise still further in the future. London and New York commuters, however, suffer the same problems of the rising cost, discomfort and uncertain future of their commuter rail services; their children face the prospect that, when their turn comes, the house they buy may be 15 or 30 kilometres (10 or 20 miles) down the line.

So finally, this tour of the London region brings us round in full circle. The problem of the new commuter estates is also the problem of the centre. In London since 1945, the central set of problems has been the same as that of the decades before 1939: the continued growth of London, the dynamism of its economy, and in particular the attraction of the small area at the very centre for new jobs, especially the white-collar jobs which form an increasingly important part of the British economy.

But the very success of the new suburbs, ironically, was attracting unfavourable attention by the late 1970s – for the simple reason that the suburbs were continuing to drain the inner city of people and jobs. One possible government answer, announced in the spring of 1977, was to scale down the future growth of the new towns' programme – which meant particularly the three latter-day new towns started long after the rest, in the mid-1960s: Milton Keynes, Northampton and Peterborough. Yet in fact the new towns were together a small and insignificant part of the whole decentralization process – most of which was as fully spontaneous as its North American counterpart.

People and jobs in London: past, present and future

The Abercrombie plan of 1944 started from the simple and comfortable assumption that there would in future be no extra jobs and no extra people within the London region. This belief, incredible in retrospect, was not then entirely unreasonable. For one thing, the official forecast was that the population of Britain, 46.6 million in 1940, would be only 47.2 million by 1960; so plans could be made on the assumption of virtually no natural increase of population. (The actual 1981 population was 54.3 million.) For another thing, migration into London could also be discounted, because the Barlow Commission on the Distribution of the Industrial Population in 1940 had concluded that steps could, and should, be taken to control the establishment or extension of factory industry in the London area, thus stemming the inter-regional drift of population at source.

But after 1945 the planners were overtaken by two events. The population increased in every region because of a high (and, from 1955 to 1964, an increasing) birth-rate. Between the 1951 and 1971 Censuses the population of the London region rose by over 1 million but all of this represented natural increase – the excess of births over deaths. In fact, after 1961 the London region was losing population by migration to the rest of the country; after 1971, it began to lose population overall, by half a million in the 1970s. Secondly, employment increased also. It was true that, as the Barlow Commission had recommended, an elaborate apparatus of control was established after 1945 to limit the growth of factory jobs in the London area. But this

43

apparatus did not concern itself with shop and office jobs, which were the hard core of the London problem. Within the London region, a high proportion of the new jobs were in service industries, the location of which was subject to no central control until the Office Development Permit (ODP) procedures were introduced in 1964–5. And even in factory industry, small-scale extensions fell outside the control net. Between 1963/4 and 1979, some 160,000 jobs were moved out of central London, an average of over 10,000 a year, aided by the propaganda efforts of the Location of Offices Bureau and the ODP controls. But of these 51,000, or 32 per cent, moved only within Greater London while another 44,600, or 28 per cent, moved less than 64 kilometres (40 miles) from central London.

The continued strength of the London regional economy reflects structural trends in the British economy as a whole. Certain types of job – the services mentioned above, and manufacturing industries like electrical goods and vehicles – are increasing very rapidly. They have always been strongly concentrated in London and the south-east, and it is very hard to break an established pattern of industrial location, because the existence of an industry in an area automatically tends to foster its further growth there. In addition, certain of these trades, especially the services, are extremely sensitive to the so-called 'external economies' which stem from the close concentration of many firms in the same area. These external economies now seem to work over a larger area than before, so that not only factory and routine jobs but even headquarters' offices are now able to move 60 to 80 kilometres (40 to 60 miles) from London, to centres like Southend, Reading and Basingstoke.

Plans for London and its region

Thus it is not likely that the future growth of the London region, either of people or jobs, will be easily stemmed. This is the background to three major plans for the future of London and its region: first, the Government's South East Study of 1964; second, the statutory Greater London Development Plan (GLDP) for London produced by the GLC, on which a panel of inquiry gave critical views to the central government in 1973; third, the Strategic Plan for the South East, produced by a joint team of central and local government planners, published in 1970 and accepted by the government a year later as the future framework for planning the growth of the whole region down to the century's end. Of these, the last two are both, in a sense, still in force, though greatly overtaken – as we shall see – by subsequent events. The relationship between these two plans – one covering an area of 1,605 square kilometres (620 square miles) and a population at that time of 7.4 million, the other extending outwards to take in over 25,000 square kilometres (10,000 square miles) and 17 million people – is crucial for the future of both areas. And in vital respects, the two plans are in conflict.

The South East Study, 1964

In 1964 the official government South East Study caused controversy by recommending acceptance of a population increase of 3.5 million over the period 1964–81 in south-east England (including East Anglia) with a second generation of new towns and cities, at greater distances from London than the first round, to house the growth (map 2.4). Such a scale of population growth had come to seem inevitable by the early 1970s – if only because it represented the natural increase of the region's own population. The much debated 'drift south' became a myth in the early 1960s; in fact the entire south-east region records a modest net loss of population by migration each year. So the expected scale of population growth – in 1970 estimated at over 4.5 million for the south-east during the period 1966–2001, but later scaled down drastically – does not necessarily rob the development areas of northern England, South Wales or central Scotland of their populations. What it may do is compete for scarce footloose industry – which is a more serious matter.

The Greater London Development Plan, 1969

The GLDP is a general plan setting the broad guidelines for London's development; within these, local plans will be made by the ancient City of London and the thirty-two London boroughs. During the prolonged 237-day inquiry into the plan, the great bulk of the 28,000 objections were into one aspect only: the controversial plan for a £2,000 million motorway network for London (map 2.3), which was accepted in part by the inquiry panel and then by the government but was then rejected by the GLC itself in 1973 after a change of administration at County Hall. But more basic than this, and more important, is the controversy that has taken place only among the professional planners and their critics: on the interlinked questions of London's future size and patterns of economic activity.

At the time of Abercrombie's 1944 plan, and for long after, planners at both national and local level agreed on the need to limit London's growth: hence the green belt and the planned overspill programme into the new and expanded towns. But, as we have seen in this chapter, since 1945 London has lost people at accelerating speed; while since 1960 it has also lost employment. From 8.5 million at its peak in the late 1930s, Greater London's population was down to just over 6.7 million by 1981, well below the GLC's original 7.3 million target for 1981. Jobs, too, have fallen catastrophically – by more than three-quarters of a million between 1966 and 1975 alone, with especially big

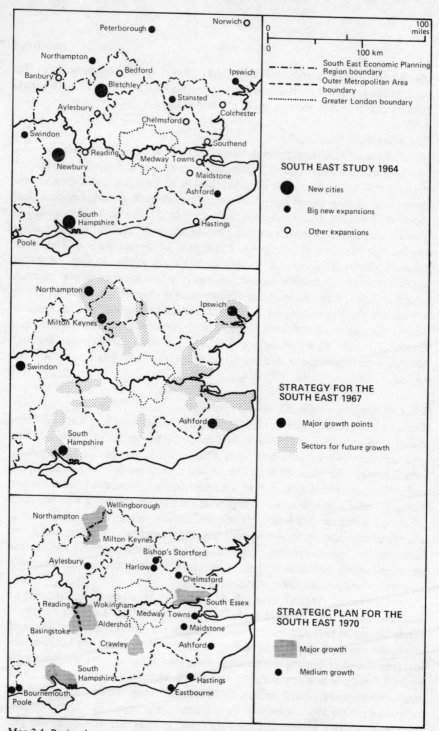

Map 2.4 *Regional strategies for South East England.* The South East Study (1964), based on a projected population increase of 3.5 million to 1981, provided for three new cities at more than 80 kilometres (50 miles) from London. The Strategy for the South East (1967) developed 'growth points', linked back to London via partially-urbanized sectors along major transportation corridors. The Strategic Plan for the South East (1970), accepted by government, provided for five major growth centres plus a number of medium growth centres; this was reduced in 1976 to adjust to falling population projections, but the main strategic features survived.

declines in manufacturing, in dock employment (due to the shift of the Port of London downstream towards Tilbury) and in routine office jobs. (It should be noticed that this was a time of declining employment nationally and in the south-east.) Further, it was mainly the middle-income jobs – the skilled and semi-skilled factory jobs, the routine office jobs – which moved out; increasingly, the jobs that remained were either high-paying (senior management or professional jobs) or low-paying (service jobs in transportation, hotels and bars, associated particularly with the tourist explosion). Thus the outward movement was associated with a danger of social polarization, with London divided increasingly into rich and poor. And the loss of both people and jobs contributed to be a progressive erosion of the GLC's tax base; in the words of the GLC's former chief strategic planner, David Eversley, it led to rising costs and static incomes. As yet this has not led to a crisis like that in New York and other American cities; the welfare burden for the low income groups is less onerous in London, and both it and other costs are cushioned by central government subsidies in a way that has not so far applied to the United States. Nevertheless the danger is present – particularly since the GLC, like other British local authorities, is almost completely dependent upon the local real estate tax, or rates, for its own income.

The GLDP therefore argued for an attempt to stabilize both population and employment – particularly through the retention of factory jobs by a system of floorspace targets. But the inquiry panel rejected the GLC's arguments, both because they doubted the desirability of keeping jobs, and because they thought the GLC lacked the powers to achieve it. One hope might be if land could be found for extensive housing schemes to provide for factory workers, especially in east London which has recorded big losses of manual jobs. But, apart from a windfall gain of land in east London's abandoned docklands – the subject of a special study in 1976, which suggested major redevelopment and economic regeneration at a cost to the public purse of over £1,100 million – the problem is that escalating land prices may price local authorities out of the market. And the outer, lower-density boroughs of Greater London do not want extensive public housing projects to house inner London overspill, for both social and political reasons.

The Strategic Plan for the South East, 1970

This is why the Strategic Plan for the South East is particularly relevant. Though the plan accepts the then GLC population target of 7 million for London in 1981 – a target the GLC themselves later had to scale down to 6.8 million, and which the GLDP inquiry panel believed should be replaced by a projection of only 6.4–6.5 million – its underlying philosophy is one of dispersal (table 2.3). The central feature of the Strategic Plan, in fact, is the rapid development of a number of major growth centres near London – five of

47

Table 2.3   Population in the South East, actual and planned, 1966–2001

	Population (thousands)			
	1966	1981	1991	2001
Greater London	7,800	7,300	7,000	7,000
Outer Metropolitan Area	5,100	6,400	7,400	8,200
London region	12,900	13,700	14,400	15,200
Outer South East region	4,000	4,900	5,700	6,400
South East region	17,000	18,700	20,100	21,600

Source: Strategic Plan for the South East, 1970.

Table 2.4   Population of the major growth centres in the South East, actual and planned, 1966–2001

	Distance from London (kilometres)	Population (thousands)		Population growth (thousands) 1966–2001
		1966	2001	
Reading-Wokingham-Aldershot-Basingstoke	56–80	500	1,200	700
South Hampshire	113–145	800	1,400	600
Milton Keynes-Northampton	145–193	300	800	500
South Essex	80–90	600	1,000	400
Crawley-Gatwick	64–97	200	500	300
5 major growth areas	–	2,400	4,900	2,500
South East region	–	17,000	21,600	4,600

Source: Strategic Plan for the South East, 1970.

Table 2.5   Employment in the South East, actual and projected, 1966–81

	Employment (thousands) 1966*	Change	
		(thousands) 1966–81	(per cent)
Greater London	4,450	−367	−8.2
Outer Metropolitan Area	2,060	+422	+20.5
London region	6,510	+55	+0.8
Outer South East region	1,709	+320	+18.7
South East region	8,219	+375	+4.6

Source: Strategic Plan for the South East, 1970.
*Corrected census figures

them, some as near as 70 kilometres (40 miles) from the centre, some up to 130 kilometres (80 miles) distant. These centres, and the smaller centres of growth which would be based on a number of towns, incorporate some of the ideas of new towns and new cities in the 1964 South East Study; they also bear a relationship to the notion of growth sectors radiating from London, separated by wide sectors of open land conserved for agriculture and recreation, as suggested in the 1967 strategy of the South East Regional Economic Planning Council (map 2.4). The major centres in the plan would be built up to sizes between half a million and one and a half million – equivalent to major English urban agglomerations like Sheffield or Tyneside – and would thus become real counter-magnets to London both as employment and service centres. They would take the lion's share of the total expected growth of the region's population in the last thirty-five years of the century: 2.5 out of 4.6 millions (map 2.4 and table 2.4). Thus the character of the London region would change; instead of an area dominated by the single built-up mass of London, it would be progressively transformed into a polycentric region.

All this would happen while Greater London's population and employment both declined (table 2.5). Thus there would be a continued overspill of people and jobs from the capital to the rings of growth around it. Many of the jobs that would move out, research reports for the plan make clear, will not be able to move far – especially the office jobs, which are expected to move out at the rate of 15–20,000 a year. This is a critical constraint on the location of the growth centres, and it will mean an open-minded application of central government controls on new office and factory floorspace, so as to encourage selective migration of employment into the Outer Metropolitan Area. But this is unlikely to find much favour either from advocates of vigorous development in areas like northern England, Wales or Scotland, or from the GLC which may want to continue to argue for retaining as many jobs as possible within its own boundaries.

In its own terms, the Strategic Plan offered a contemporary version of the same policies that animated the Abercrombie plan of 1944. Whereas Abercrombie saw the solution to London's problems in the form of new or expanded towns for around 60,000 people each, the 1970 plan saw it in terms of planned urban agglomerations for a half million and more each. These would themselves contain a whole variety of settlements, ranging from large cities through small towns to villages, all set against a background of open space, and interlinked internally by good communications. This vision may appear very modern; but it merely represents a rediscovery of the almost forgotten last chapter of Ebenezer Howard's famous 1898 tract *Garden Cities of Tomorrow*, where he advocated building new towns as part of just such a poly-nuclear Social City. Thus the plan would transform the south-east radically, from a region dominated by a single agglomeration at the centre, to one with a number of strong concentrations of people, jobs and services. Whereas London in 1970 still had almost half the population of the south-east, by 2001 it will have less than one-third. But in this process, there will be a profound resorting of both people and economic activities. In particular, London seems destined to continue losing factory jobs and more routine white-collar jobs, while adding massively to those activities which it is uniquely qualified to perform: the higher decision-making professional and managerial jobs, as well as continued growth of tourism and international business. This should guarantee continued prosperity for the London of 2000, despite a smaller population.

Reviewing the Strategic Plan

The drastic fall in birth-rate, coupled with the unexpectedly high loss of people and jobs from Greater London, and the rapid growth of new households, caused the government to update the Strategic Plan only six years after its first publication. The Review of the Strategic Plan (1976) assumes that the 1991 population of the entire south-east region – including the GLC area, the Outer Metropolitan Area and a wide zone beyond – will be 17.1 million – a sharp fall from the 19.8 million assumed in the 1970 version; the assumed population growth between 1975 and 1991 is only 174,000, against nearly 2.8 million six years earlier. But, since London's forecast population would be only 5.7 million – against 7.0 million in the earlier plan – the forecast reduction for the rest of the region would be more modest: 11.4 million against 12.8 million. In the Outer Metropolitan Area the reduction is only 700,000 – from 6.7 million to just under 6.0 million. Thus, all the five major growth zones of the 1970 plan are still assumed to be necessary – albeit on a somewhat reduced scale. The advantages of concentrating people, jobs and services in a few quite large growth centres, the 1976 authors say, are still telling – though they stress that these centres would not be unbroken masses of building, but rather clusters of settlements separated by intervening open land.

Recognizing these facts, the 1976 review called for a period of restraint in the fast-growing areas around London, in order to give London itself an opportunity to regenerate. In this, it expressed the collective views of its local authority members: the GLC and the London boroughs, desperate to stem the flow of people and jobs from the capital; the counties and districts of the region all around, concerned to slow down the pace of development that many of their own people found distasteful. The question was whether such an attitude was realistic or responsible. Clearly, the government's own response – which emerged only after long delay in 1978 – suggested that it was not. It affirmed that the growth areas of the 1970 plan would still be needed, despite the opposition that was known to exist to several of them locally; but it suggested that they might be scaled down in size. It affirmed the distinction between areas of growth and areas of restraint, but in practice somewhat reduced the distinction between the two.

In May 1979 came a change of government, and in August 1980 a clear shift in policy. A new statement from the Secretary of State for the Environment, a mere three terse pages in length, spelled out the new governmental priorities: to promote economic recovery, to restrain public expenditure, to stimulate the private sector, to sweep away obstacles to commercial enterprise, to achieve more home ownership and housebuilding for sale. It affirmed a policy that had already been developing under the previous Labour administration: that London was no longer to be regarded as a source of population and employment overspill for the areas all around. It also repeated the policy embedded in the 1970 plan and in subsequent government statements: that there shall be a clear distinction between growth areas, where development is to be concentrated, and areas of conservation, where restraint on development is to be the general rule.

The general message that emerges from this statement, however, is fairly clear: coupled with a much weaker regional policy for the declining peripheral areas of Britain, it is that development is actually to be encouraged in the growing and successful parts of the south-east. And this is perhaps the most fundamental shift in British regional planning policy since it effectively started at the end of the Second World War. Against a generally sombre background of a stagnating economy and cuts in public expenditure, the British government is backing a dash for growth in the areas that are capable of it.

This prescription does at least correspond to the facts of recent change. The Standing Conference on London and South-East Regional Planning, analysing the pattern of change during the 1970s, has found that from 1971 to 1979 nearly 40 per cent of the total population change in the south-east outside London, 156,000 out of 392,000, occurred in only four major growth areas designated in the 1970 plan. But there were very great differences as between one area and another. Seventy-three thousand – almost half the growth in the five areas, and thus 20 per cent of the region's growth – occurred in the Reading–Wokingham–Aldershot–Basingstoke area west of London. Another 47,000 – 39 per cent of the growth area total, or 12 per cent of the entire regional growth – was in the new city of Milton Keynes. Growth in the other two areas – South Hampshire and Crawley–Burgess Hill – was negligible in comparison. Significantly, the two successful growth areas were similarly located on major transportation corridors – road and rail – connecting the metropolis with the major home markets, respectively west and north-west of London. This pull towards the north and west was first noticed in the 1920s and 1930s, in the rapid growth of new industrial areas in that sector of London. Fifty years later, its major weight has merely been shifted further

51

out. The basic facts of economic geography, it seems, do not change much.

Future uncertain

Meanwhile, the problem of London's decline is nowhere near solution. The one comforting feature is that it has slowed: net out-migration, which was running at 100,000 a year during the first half of the 1970s, was down to 55,000 a year in the second half. So the 1991 population level, projected for Greater London by the government statisticians, is higher than it was at the time of the 1976 Review of the Strategic Plan: 6.3 million as against 5.7 million. But there are some ominous signs – not least the tendency for some major companies, such as Imperial Chemical Industries and Commercial Union Assurance, to announce that they are moving their headquarters operations out of central London. These trends fortify those who believe that, in the age of information technology, the big city as the centre of face-to-face contact may be an anachronism.

Meanwhile there is continuing decline in industry and in traditional goods-handling service industries. The Conservative government has taken two decisive and controversial policy steps to try to regenerate London's biggest area of industrial dereliction, the former Port of London on both banks of the Thames east of Tower Bridge. It has brought most of the area under the control of a new London Docklands Development Corporation (LDDC), loosely modelled on the successful Development Corporations that have built Britain's twenty-eight new towns. And it has designated one small area on the Isle of Dogs, in the heart of docklands, as an Enterprise Zone where industrialists will find generous financial incentives and a more relaxed planning regime. It is too early, as yet, to gauge the success of these initiatives. But from preliminary indications, it seems almost certain that the new activities coming into docklands will be very unlike the old ones that have disappeared. Heavy, manual, principally male jobs have gone; in their place will come white-collar jobs in offices and in other service occupations, many of them traditionally female. This shift, however, mirrors a general change in the nature of the London and indeed the British economy, against which it is probably useless to struggle.

But two resulting problems will not go away. They are the growing burden of an under-privileged, under-skilled, under-paid and increasingly unemployed minority, suffering multiple deprivation in London's inner city areas; and, associated with this, a possible gap between the GLC's spending burdens and the revenue needed to meet them. No single neat solution will meet these:

a bundle of policies may be needed, including more determined dispersal of low-income groups to the new towns (as Peterborough, for instance, has attempted), new sources of revenue for the GLC such as a sales tax or tourist tax or lottery; and, most controversial of all, a possible extension of the GLC's boundaries to take in a ring of growth all round.

But successive governments have rejected the idea of alternative finance, following a Royal Commission report of 1975 that found all of them to have serious flaws; and in 1983 the British government, following a series of battles with the GLC – most notably over subsidies to public transport – announced that it would soon present legislation to abolish it. Britain's experiment in metropolitan government, regarded with interest and even admiration in other countries, thus seems destined to end amidst acrimony after only twenty-one years – with real doubts, in mid-1983, about what is to take its place.

That may hold a lesson of a negative kind for other world cities. The GLC came into being in the mid-1960s because of a widespread consensus, at the time, as to the need for a strategic authority for structure planning and associated transport planning. In practice the GLC proved to have problems with the first role, because the second-level authorities – the London boroughs – had the really effective powers of implementation, and over a twenty-year period they consolidated these powers. And in large measure the GLC abdicated the second role when, in 1973, it abandoned all plans for large-scale roadbuilding in the capital. This left it merely with a general policy responsibility for the management of London Transport (LT), which led to political schism over subsidy levels and finally to tensions between the politicians and LT's senior management – compounded by the fact that the GLC's powers did not extend to British Rail's suburban commuter services. As an interim measure, the government in summer 1983 announced a new body to take over the GLC's public transport responsibilities – but with no clear indication as to how LT and BR services were to be better integrated. The GLC seems destined to disappear because it became too politicized – but without an effective regional authority, London will again be plunged into the administrative chaos of the 1950s. It seems a sad end to a noble experiment.

3 Paris

Many tourists like to claim an easy knowledge of Paris: they can pick their way from the Louvre to the Musée de l'Art Moderne, or from the night spots of the Place Pigalle to a hotel on the Left Bank; in between, if they are motorists, they may even be able to navigate the notorious one-way street system without too much trepidation. But they seldom think of the Paris they may glimpse beyond: the streets and houses and factories that make it the second largest agglomeration of Europe and the eleventh in the world. And it is doubtful whether most of them spare more than a thought for the problems of one of the most complex – and, over the last three decades, one of the fastest-growing – metropolitan complexes of the advanced industrial world.

The Parisian planners, who have to grapple with these problems every day, think of a very different Paris from that of the tourist. Their *Région Île de France* (formerly known as the *Région Parisienne*) extends to between 60 and 90 kilometres (40 and 60 miles) from Notre Dame (map 3.1). It stretches half-way to Rouen in the west – and two-thirds of the way to the Belgian frontier in the north. It consists of eight of the *départements* – the historic administrative units of France, dating from the Revolution – together totalling 12,000 square kilometres (4,800 square miles): 2.2 per cent of the land area of France. It contained, at the Census of 1982, 10.06 million people – 18.5 per cent of the national total. It contained also over 22 per cent of the economically active population; 25 per cent of major industrial establishments; 38 per cent of office workers; and 50 per cent of headquarters offices. Paris, now as in the past, is capital of perhaps the most centralized nation state in the advanced industrial world.

The innermost of these eight *départements*, Paris, is coterminous with the historic City of Paris. Its population, 2.17 million in 1982, had however been declining decade by decade ever since a peak – of 2.91 million – as long ago as 1921. Around it are wrapped three small *départements* – Hauts-de-Seine, Seine-St-Denis and Val-de-Marne – which the French call the little ring (*petite couronne*) of inner suburbs (*proche banlieue*). Four more distant *départements* – Val d'Oise, Yvelines, Essonne and Seine-et-Marne – together constitute the big ring (*grande couronne*) of more distant suburbs, and complete the remainder of the *Région Île de France* (table 3.1). If the City of Paris is roughly

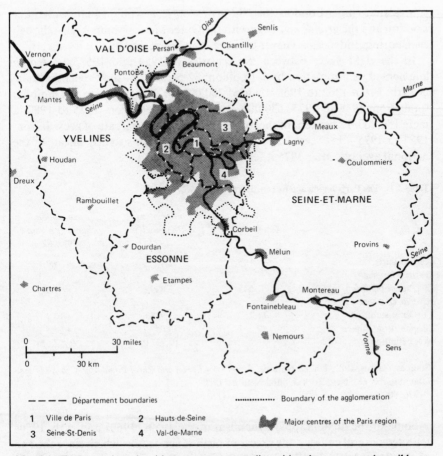

Map 3.1 *The Paris region.* As with most great metropolitan cities, there are several possible definitions of Paris. The planners' *Région Île de France* extends up to 100 kilometres (60 miles) from central Paris and embraces 12,000 square kilometres (4,800 square miles) with a 1982 population of 10.1 million. Much smaller, but still ten times the area of the historic City of Paris, is the *agglomération*. The City of Paris itself had a population of 2.2 million in 1982, and was in decline.

equivalent to inner London, then the *petite couronne* would equate with outer London and the *grande couronne* with the Outer Metropolitan Area – though such correspondence can never be more than approximate.

In the eight years between the censuses of 1954 and 1962, the region augmented its population by 1.1 million: 32 per cent of the French national growth. From 1962 to 1968 it added 780,000, or 24 per cent of the national total; from 1968 to 1975, 630,000, 22 per cent; then, from 1975 to 1982, a mere 180,000, 12 per cent of the total. Though the annual rate of growth from 1954 to 1975 – between 1 and 1.8 per cent – ran consistently ahead of the national average, after 1975 it fell significantly behind.

Table 3.1   The Paris region and its constituent parts, 1982

	Area (square km.)	Population (thousands) 1982	Population change (per cent) 1975–82
City of Paris	105	2,168.9	− 5.7
Petite couronne			
(Proche banlieue)	645	3,899.6	− 1.9
Grande couronne			
(Outer suburbs)	11,257	3,988.6	+10.7
Région Île de France	12,007	10,057.1	+ 1.8
(UN definition)		(9,907.0)	(+7.5*)

Sources: Census, 1982; United Nations, *Patterns of Urban and Rural Population Growth* (*Population Studies*, 68), New York: United Nations, 1980.
* 1970–80

Some of the demographic dynamism of the 1950s, 1960s and early 1970s reflected natural causes – the excess of births over deaths, which since the end of the Second World War has been high in France. Coming after a long period of stagnation, the rise in the birth-rate to one of the highest in western Europe was hailed in France, with some reason, as a demographic miracle – and it persisted even through the 1970s, a period of plummeting birth-rates in most advanced countries. The rate of natural increase in Paris has actually been a little higher than in France as a whole – partly because the Paris region contains a high proportion of young adults of childbearing age. Natural increase added 470,000 to the population of the region between 1975 and 1982, helping to compensate for an outward net migration of 291,500; Paris, at last, has apparently lost its magnetism for the French people. Since the 1960s, indeed, the great provincial cities of France have been exerting an even greater attraction, partly as a result of deliberate policies to build them up as 'balancing metropolises' (*métropoles d'équilibre*) as counterweights to Paris.

But this is a very recent development. Over much of the period since the

Second World War the story of Paris has been one of almost continuous growth, propelled by a rapid movement of population off the land into factories and offices. This in itself has been a matter for national self-congratulation; but the effect on an urban agglomeration already as large as Paris has been to create some very large planning problems. These problems have been examined very expertly – and imaginative and far-seeing solutions posed to them – in two official documents: the *Plan d'Aménagement et d'Organisation Générale de la Région Parisienne* (PADOG) of 1960 and the *Schéma Directeur d'Aménagement et d'Urbanisme de la Région de Paris*, a revised plan of 1965 by Monsieur Delouvrier, the *Préfet* for the region. And what is particularly interesting is that the second plan, only five years after the first, starts from different premises and reaches different conclusions. These differences will be examined in detail later in this chapter.

The Structure of Paris

First, however, how to begin to analyse this great urban complex? The 12,000 square kilometres (4,800 square miles) of the planners' Paris region contain many strangely assorted landscapes – some of them curiously un-Parisian. They range all the way from the intense bustle of the Grands Boulevards or the insanitary, close-packed tenements of the East End of Paris to the open-field landscapes of the plateaux of Brie and Beauce and the great forests of Fontainebleau and Chantilly – areas where one could wander for many hours and very nearly forget the existence of a capital of 10 million people (map 3.1).

But in fact Paris means many different things to different people. We have chosen the Paris region because it is the most liberal possible definition. But it is helpful to start by looking at other, narrower concepts of Paris.

The inner city

For the real purist, Paris is the historic City of Paris – *la Ville de Paris*. Based on the great route crossing, where the great north–south route from Flanders to the Mediterranean makes an easy passage across the Seine, in the centre of the fertile Île de France, Paris like London was a Roman creation. Like London it remained small in the Middle Ages – the first wall, built between 1180 and 1210, enclosed 273 hectares (675 acres), almost exactly the same area as the medieval City of London – but unlike London it remained tightly enclosed within its walls until the seventeenth century, and as late as 1860 – the time of Napoleon III – its urban area was surrounded by a ring of fortifications. Despite desperate attempts by the French kings to limit its growth, from the sixteenth century onwards, Paris continued to swell. By the middle of the nineteenth century it had a million people, and it was then – in 1860 – that the City of Paris received its final extension. Most people are familiar with the twenty *arrondissements* into which Paris is divided: ten of these – the 11th to the 20th – were taken in by the last extension, and form the 'peripheral' *arrondissements*. This Paris of 1860 has remained fixed since then, its limits marked by the gates in the fortifications, long since swept away – Porte des Lilas, Porte de la Villette, Porte de Clignancourt, Porte de Versailles, Porte d'Orléans, Porte d'Italie and others. The tourist knows these names well, because most of them define the outer termini of the *Métro* or underground network, which took shape in the decade after 1900.

The dominant feature of the City of Paris, its overpowering problem, is congestion – congestion of people, of jobs, of traffic, of physical equipment. The congestion of people can be demonstrated vividly in statistics. At the 1982 Census, the City of Paris numbered 2,169,000 people packed on to the 105 square kilometres (43 square miles), which include the great open spaces of the Bois de Boulogne in the west and the Bois de Vincennes in the east. Translating, that is 207 people per hectare (84 per acre) of ground, to say nothing for a moment of all the other things – roads and railways and offices and factories and warehouses and entertainments – that have to be fitted on to these same square kilometres. In comparison, the average for the equivalent area of London (inner London) in 1981 was 78 per hectare (32 per acre). The highest recorded density for a London borough – 116 per hectare (47 per acre) in Kensington and Chelsea, which contains some of the worst housing conditions in London – was lower than that for any of the twenty *arrondissements* of Paris, even the exclusive 16th in the west; it compares with a density in the 11th *arrondissement* of 397 to the hectare (161 per acre) in 1982. Of course, high density need not mean poor housing; partly it reflects a different tradition of close, in-city living in France. But as we shall see, in much of inner Paris these high densities reflect a housing problem of gargantuan proportions.

The congestion of jobs is most vividly illustrated by the central core of Paris. The Parisians have not been able to agree on what precisely constitutes the centre of their City, any more than any other city dwellers have; in Paris the problem is exceptionally difficult, because jobs and residential areas are so closely intermingled right through the inner City area, in the peripheral *arrondissements* as in the central ones. But a convenient definition is the ten 'central' *arrondissements* – the 1st to the 10th, representing roughly the built-up Paris of 1840. These form an oval area conveniently bounded by the big terminal railway stations – St Lazare in the north-west, Nord and Est in the north-east, Lyon and Austerlitz on opposite banks of the Seine in the south-east, Montparnasse in the south-west. Within this area, at the Census of 1975, 988,000 found employment: over 21 per cent of the total labour force of the Paris region, crowded on to 22 square kilometres (9 square miles) – one five-hundredth part of the total area of the region. This central concentration extends marginally into the 16th *arrondissement*, to the west, and the 17th, to the east.

Although many of the peripheral *arrondissements* also have a high density of working population, the employment pattern in the central area is distinguished by one feature, which makes for an extra planning problem: employment at the centre creates longer journeys to work than employment elsewhere. In 1975, against a resident work-force in the City of 1,145,000, a total of 1,918,000 worked there; the difference, 773,000, represents a net excess of in-commuters over out-commuters. This throws an exceptional strain on the transport system of the whole urban complex – and as we shall see the system has only very recently been adapted to the job.

This pattern of journey to work arises from the character of the jobs at the centre, and from the social composition of the people who work at them. Central Paris is the hub of *les affaires*. It contains the financial centre, around the Bourse, in the 1st, 8th and 9th *arrondissements*; the area of luxury shopping to the west of this, but partly overlapping it, in the 1st and particularly the 8th *arrondissement* (Champs Élysées, Rue Royale, Place Vendôme, Rue du Faubourg St Honoré); the centre of administration, especially around the Invalides in the 7th *arrondissement*, south of the river; and the university and its associated institutions (libraries, institutes and bookshops) south of the river in the 5th and 6th *arrondissements*. The jobs of the central area are overwhelmingly professional, managerial and clerical; the people engaged in them are those who have progressively deserted the City of Paris for homes in more or less distant suburbs. Within this area, increasingly the centre of gravity of employment has shifted westwards, towards the Grands Boulevards and the former exclusively residential area of the 16th *arrondissement* – strictly a peripheral *arrondissement* but now, due to the postwar development of international agencies such as UNESCO, functionally a part of the central area. These have helped Paris retain its role as world city, though in many respects – finance, tourism, international company headquarters, air travel – it stands second to London.

In the peripheral *arrondissements* the employment pattern throws up different problems. Particularly in the East End of the 11th, 12th, 19th and 20th *arrondissements* – the traditional home of the Paris poor – we find the home of densely-packed small industrial and commercial undertakings, packed cheek-by-jowl with the homes of the people who work in them, to the mutual discomfort of both. The figures show that here the amount of travel to work, across the boundaries of the *arrondissements*, is much less. The problem here is rather how to refurbish and replan the pattern of housing and industry. It will certainly involve the large-scale transfer of many people, and many industrial undertakings, out of the City of Paris altogether – a phenomenon already occurring on a large scale by the 1980s.

Paris, in fact, is a typical western European inner city: an area in decline. Its peak population of 2.9 million was reached as long ago as 1921. It lost 300,000 people (11.6 per cent) from 1968 to 1975 and another 124,000 (5.4 per cent) from 1975 to 1982, with particularly heavy losses in the inner *arrondissements*.

The proche banlieue *and the outer suburbs*

Beyond the gates of the City, we enter a world which the foreign tourist to Paris hardly glimpses, except on his journey by rail or from the airport, or on his ritual trip to the Flea Market just beyond the Porte de Clignancourt. In every sense this is a strange twilight world. It is administratively ambiguous, being in Paris but not of it: this is the area the French call the *banlieue*: that part of the *Région Île de France* that lies beyond the limits of the City of Paris. It includes seven of the ninety-five *départements* of France, and is administered separately from Paris by a multitude of separate communes.

As already seen, the innermost three of these *départements* – Hauts-de-Seine, Seine-St-Denis and Val-de-Marne – constitute the near suburbs (*proche banlieue*), the near-equivalent of the suburban outer London ring. Like London's suburbs, they have been developed almost continuously between the late nineteenth and the mid-twentieth centuries. After about 1880 the French bourgeoisie began to desert the densely built-up housing of the central city; between 1881 and 1911 the *banlieue* added more people than the City, and after 1921 the population of the City began to turn down. We saw that after 1951 the population of outer London reached stability and then began to decline. But the Parisian *proche banlieue* went on growing for another quarter-century: between 1962 and 1968 it added nearly 400,000 people, between 1968 and 1975 another 144,000; only after then did it follow the London pattern, losing 77,000 people from 1975 to 1982.

It could go on growing, despite a much smaller area than its London equivalent, by carrying a relatively high density of population. In 1981 the 1,235 square kilometres (500 square miles) of the London suburbs held some 4,215,000 people at an average density of 34 per hectare (14 per acre). In 1982 the Parisian inner suburbs – 645 square kilometres, 250 square miles – contained 3,900,000 people: a density of 61 per hectare (27 per acre). The density of these inner Parisian suburbs, then, is intermediate between the inner London area (78 per hectare, 32 per acre) and the London suburbs.

This reflects again a real difference in social preferences – at least until recently – as between the French and the Anglo-Saxon cultures. One-family houses are mixed with high-rise structures to an extent unimaginable in

British, German or American suburbs. As most of the *banlieue* was developed between the wars in conditions of rampant speculation, the only object was to find plots which would command a ready sale, so that large tracts of less attractive land were left undeveloped – generally those with less adequate communications. In recent years many of these have been developed by the public housing organizations known as HLM (*Habitations à loyer modéré* – dwellings at regulated rents) with large blocks of flats. Many are concentrated in the large estates, called *Grands Ensembles*, where one Parisian in fourteen now lives; the biggest, Sarcelles, was designed for 80,000 people. The *Grands Ensembles* rapidly became notorious for poor architecture, lack of social facilities and general dreariness; Sarcelles became a symbol of these qualities. In 1967, 82 per cent of those surveyed in the *Grands Ensembles* said that they would prefer to live in a single-family house rather than the apartment that a beneficient state had awarded them.

The housing pattern is heavily interspersed with industry of the newer, space-using sort, which has, however, particularly concentrated in the north-west sector, along both banks of the Seine: between the two great industrial nodes of Boulogne–Billancourt, west-south-west of Paris (the home of the giant Renault works), and the plain of St-Denis in the north. Engineering in various forms, particularly the electrical and vehicle-building branches, is the dominant industry here, as in the corresponding zone of London. This zone principally accounts for the fact that nearly three-quarters of the region's declining total of industrial jobs are outside the city: 24 per cent in the Hauts-de-Seine, another 13 per cent in the Seine-St-Denis in 1980. This type of industry has developed in the course of the present century, and stands in sharp contrast to the congested small workshop industry – light engineering, clothing, furniture, fur – of the East End of Paris.

The industrial areas are big labour magnets, drawing workers from outside. But much of the travel is relatively short-distance in character: of that part of the total work-force of the Paris region that works outside the city (2,585,000 out of 4,471,000 in 1975, or just over half), the great majority – 1,884,000 – do not commute across the boundaries of their own *départements*, but find work fairly close nearby. Many of these short-distance commuters are manual workers; in 1968, in the *proche banlieue*, manual workers travelled on average only 3.2 kilometres (2 miles) while white-collar workers – mainly bound for jobs in Paris – averaged 4.1 kilometres (2.6 miles). (For example: Boulogne–Billancourt drew heavily on the residential areas immediately to the south and south-west, within a radius of 10 to 15 kilometres or 6 to 10 miles.) Further, in a 1976 survey only 20 per cent of commuters in the City used cars, but outside 60 per cent did so. At least this movement does not throw such intolerable strains on the transport system as do the radial flows towards the centre. The real problem of the suburbs does not lie here, but rather in the poverty of the physical equipment. Haste and lack of plan were the distinguishing features of development in the suburban zone. Villages like Pantin, Aubervilliers, Boulogne, even towns like St-Denis, were swallowed up in the urban flood. They became nodes of building simply because they lay on the main roads from Paris. In consequence they frequently remained ill-adapted to their new function. Too often, today, the old villages fail to provide proper urban shopping, entertainment and social centres; the road system is basically the rural road system, engulfed by the town; the whole landscape resembles nothing so much as a vast, ill-conceived, hastily constructed emergency camp to house the labour force of Paris. As in Paris itself, so in the suburbs, a clear distinction exists between east and west: the western suburbs – Meudon, Sèvres, Chaville – were early settled and have better housing and a more coherent urban structure; but the inner suburbs of the north and east, from St-Denis through Aubervilliers and les Lilas south almost to the Bois de Vincennes, present almost the limit of urban degeneration.

After 1918 the expansion of Paris could no longer be limited to the *proche banlieue*. It spread in long tentacles along the main lines of communication, into what are now the peripheral *départements* of Seine-et-Marne to the east and (especially) Val d'Oise to the north, Yvelines to the west and Essonne to the south. In consequence French statisticians and planners have been driven to find a working definition of the urban area of Paris, which can be revised from time to time to keep pace with reality. This unit is the Parisian *agglomération*: in 1982 it was comparable in size with the Greater London Conurbation, and had a population of over 9 million. The outermost fringe of the *agglomération* — the area within the four peripheral *départements* – was the fastest-growing area of the Paris region between 1975 and 1982, as map 3.2 shows. While the City lost 131,000 people and the inner suburbs lost 77,000, the four outer *départements* gained 387,000. But here there is a distinct falling away in the degree of urbanization. The density of population in the entire area of the four outermost *départements* of the Paris region, in 1982, was only 28 per hectare (11 per acre), considerably less than that of the entire 'suburban ring' of Greater London. As one travels out from the centre, the areas of housing, often built in rigidly formal patterns around the stations, are separated by increasingly wide tracts of rural land. The uniform suburban sea of housing progressively gives way to a more distinct urban structure, with towns that were already important when they were swallowed up by Paris – l'Isle Adam, Villeneuve-St Georges, Poissy, Pontoise. Here the great problem of the planners is to control and limit growth: to guide it so that the land is used as economically as may be, with a proper balance between development and open space. This indeed has been one of the most important objects of recent planning in the Paris region.

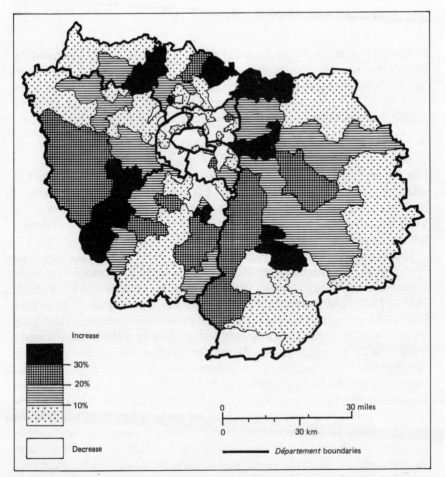

Map 3.2 *The Paris region: population changes, 1975–82.* By the late 1970s, the modified 1965 plan was having a major impact. The areas of strongest population growth include the cantons embracing the new towns of Cergy-Pontoise, Marne-la-Vallée, Evry, Melun-Sénart and St-Quentin-en-Yvelines, together with an area in the north of the region affected by the impact of the new Charles de Gaulle airport.

The central problems of the Paris region

In this rapid journey across the vast Paris region, we have touched upon the central planning problems of Paris, as they superficially appear. It is now time to sum them up, and to probe them more deeply. The problems that make the most obvious impression in Paris are traffic; housing; shortage of social capital; redevelopment versus conservation; and physical growth.

Traffic
Until recently the Parisian transport system – or, as the French delight in calling it, the transport infrastructure – has proved increasingly incapable of performing adequately the functions it is called upon to perform. Now this is being remedied – but at great expense. For this it is possible to blame a number of past mistakes.

The history of planning in Paris is bound up, more than that of any other city of the world, with the name of one man: Baron Haussmann, *Préfet* of the *département* of the Seine during the reign of the Emperor Napoleon III, from 1853 to 1870. Haussmann transformed inner Paris, tearing away the narrow lanes and alleys and replacing them by the great boulevards which today are the envy and admiration of all visitors. But in some ways Haussmann's legacy to Paris is an unfortunate one. His boulevards give a deceptive impression that Paris is a city capable of ready adaptation to the age of the universal motor car. But that is by no means so: for their great size, the boulevards are strangely inefficient carriers of great traffic volumes, because so many of them converge so often on *ronds-points* which are quite incapable of handling the resulting flows. In one respect only was Haussmann perceptive, and that by accident: he refused to widen existing streets, but built his new boulevards parallel to them (as his great north-south artery, the Boulevard de Sébastopol, next to the Rue St Martin). As a result, since 1949 the Parisian traffic planners have been able to adapt his boulevards to the most extensive one-way street system in Europe: a system which has compensated for some of the worst errors of Haussmann's road planning. The other great criticism of Haussmann's planning was that he created plenty of space for traffic to move, but none for it to park, except on the roadway itself. As, in addition, he made sure that his new boulevards were lined by lucrative commercial properties, there was every incentive for kerbside parking. In 1860, with traffic flows only one-tenth of the volume of a century later, that was perhaps an adequate solution. Today, with one of the highest car ownership rates in Europe – 3.0 million cars in the Paris region in 1977, one for every 3.3 people – it is responsible for acrimonious wrangles between the Paris police, who are trying to banish the stationary vehicle from the main arteries of their central 'blue zone', and the shopkeepers who depend on the kerbside to unload their goods and receive their customers.

One other great error was made in the planning of the pattern of Parisian circulation, and that concerns the urban railway network. It was only logical, in Paris as in other European cities, to forbid the main-line railway system to enter the central heart of the city. But if this system was to prove adequate to demands, two things were necessary; and neither happened. One was effective liaison between the terminal stations and the centre of the city. Here Haussmann failed in an essential task, because the stations are frequently sited on inadequate offshoots from the main boulevard system, and are in consequence the scenes of some of the worst traffic congestion in Paris. This particularly applies to the Gare St Lazare, which is by far the most important commuters' station, bringing in well over a quarter of a million commuters every working day. The other was that the main-line railways be relieved of pressure in the inner suburban area, by a separate network of short-distance stopping trains, such as is provided by the London underground system. This too failed to happen, because with a few exceptions the original *Métro* system was not extended beyond the gates of the municipal area. For the same reason – it was built by the City, who feared it might be taken over by the main railways – it was built on a restricted loading gauge, and could not be connected with the main system. As a result, until recently travellers bound for the *banlieue* area have had to transfer to the bus system at the *Métro* termini, throwing an increasing strain on the street system at these points at the morning and evening rush hour, and needlessly congesting the main radial highways out from the City in the zone between 5 and 8 kilometres (3 and 5 miles) from the centre.

Housing

Curiously, the second problem of Paris may also be laid, in some measure, at Haussmann's door. Haussmann destroyed quickly, without thinking too closely or too clearly where the poor of the Paris slums would go. In fact, they were merely displaced outwards; because rents were too high on the new apartment blocks that rose on the cleared sites, they went to badly built new housing in the peripheral *arrondissements* – where, today, some of the worst housing problems are concentrated. At a time of such very rapid reconstruction, the essential minimum was an adequate sanitary law; but that did not come until 1902. In the 1920s, hundreds of thousands of poorer Parisians rehoused themselves in poor shanty-type structures on suburban *lotissements*; it took years to provide them with adequate urban services.

Partly as a result of this failure, despite the advances of the last two decades the City of Paris today still suffers from a gargantuan problem of obsolescent and substandard housing. It would be wrong to pretend that this is solely the

65

problem of Paris; historically it was a problem of France, one that the 'economic miracle' under the four-year plans, from 1946 onward, began to tackle seriously only during the 1960s.

Statistics tell the tale. The Parisian housing stock, despite a huge programme of building and modernization – 378,000 new buildings between 1954 and 1975 – is nevertheless still old. Thirty-two per cent of the housing stock of the region, in 1976, dated from before 1914 and in all 53 per cent from before 1948. For the City, the proportions were 59 and 80 per cent. In 1975 55 per cent of the principal dwellings in the region consisted of only one or two rooms; for the City the figure was 59 per cent. (Households, too, were smaller in the City than elsewhere.) On average in the Paris region, in 1962 there were nearly 1.1 people to each room; by 1975 the figure had dropped only marginally, to less than 0.9. By the definitions used by the official French statisticians, 41 per cent of French households were still overcrowded in 1975, compared with 48 per cent in 1968 or 52 per cent in 1962.

Furthermore, this space is often old and poorly equipped. As late as 1962, 65 per cent of all dwellings in the entire region still lacked a bath or shower; 44 per cent an internal w.c.; 13 per cent even lacked running water. There was a notable improvement by 1975; yet even then 31 per cent still lacked a bath or shower, 22 per cent a w.c. and 11 per cent running water.

The shortage of social capital
Paralleling the lack of adequate housing has been an inadequacy in the capital equipment which must be provided, as a social obligation, by public authorities. The effects were scathingly described by M. Delouvrier in the *Livre blanc* – a 1963 survey of the needs of the region:

> The home that you only reach late in the evening because of the lack of convenient transport, the sanitary installations paralysed in summer for lack of water, the career missed or abandoned for lack of a place in a technical institute, the leisure hours wasted because of physical obstacles ...

Some of this deficiency was general, arising from the failure of the public authorities to provide in time for the explosion of population within the region: thus the water supply, which nearly failed completely in the hot summer of 1959, or the disposal of sewage – at least *half* of which was put straight into the Seine without treatment down to the mid-1960s. Another type of shortage – that of open space – is peculiarly the problem of inner Paris: the presence of the Bois de Boulogne and Bois de Vincennes hardly compensates for the chronic lack of parks within the City. But the most chronic deficiency of social capital, by the early 1960s, was experienced in the suburbs. While the suburban zone expanded mushroom-fashion, after about 1880, a strange paralysis attacked the organs of local government in the region. Some of the resulting incongruities were bizarre: thus the town hall of Argenteuil, occupying a private house bought about 1890 when the population of the commune was 10,000, then serving 90,000 people; or areas like Nanterre (90,000), Vitry-sur-Seine (78,000) or Maisons-Alfort (53,000) which completely lacked even a police station. There was a serious lack of places in secondary education in the suburbs, especially in technical branches; there was not a single university establishment in the suburbs, with the exception of the decentralized faculty of science of the Sorbonne at Orsay. Apart from a very small number built between the two wars, the suburban zone was entirely lacking in hospitals; all cases were removed to the city hospitals, which mainly date from the nineteenth century and which were chronically overloaded. On average in the early 1960s there was only one swimming bath, in the whole Paris region, for 200,000 people. The superb cultural facilities, which the visitor enjoyed, were all concentrated in the Paris he knew: beyond the tourists' regular haunts, they simply stopped. The whole of Paris outside the centre, a region housing six million Parisians, was virtually devoid of theatres, museums, cultural centres and libraries. Thus was the state of the suburbs in the early 1960s – a time when Parisian planning was transformed, with dramatic results. As will emerge, much of the impact of the planning of the 1960s and 1970s has consisted in the injection of the backlog of social capital, at long last, into the suburbs.

Redevelopment versus conservation
In the 1960s, under de Gaulle, Paris continued to demolish and redevelop on a vast scale – even after other European cities had come to stress conservation. The result is a new Paris, very different in scale and atmosphere from the old. The Boulevard Périphérique, a completely new motorway, was driven along the line of the old fortifications which mark the edge of the historic City of Paris; completed in the early 1970s, it actually involved tunnelling under the famous lakes in the Bois de Boulogne. A new one-way expressway was driven along the historic *quais* on the right bank of the Seine, and another was projected for the left bank. In the Fronts de Seine development in the 15th *arrondissement*, 2,500 new flats were provided in high tower blocks on an old factory site. In the vast Maine–Montparnasse scheme on the site of the Montparnasse station, 20,000 office jobs and 1,000 flats were provided together with shops, hotels, a congress hall and parking. A complete redevelopment was proposed for the old market site at Les Halles in the heart of the city. All these went ahead except for the Left Bank Expressway, which was abandoned after fierce protests. But the Montparnasse scheme and above all the redevelopment of Les Halles proved bitterly controversial, and by the mid-1970s it seemed unlikely that such large-scale redevelopment would ever be repeated in the historic City. In other areas, such as the historic Marais not far from Les

Halles, the state was encouraging and subsidizing a generous programme of conservation.

Physical growth

The four problems so far described all basically arise from the mistakes of the past. But they are all greatly aggravated by the continued growth of Paris and its population, which throws an increasing strain on the urban transport system and the central streets; which creates a persistent demand for new housing construction, thus competing with the vital job of renewal of the outworn structures in the centre; and which further exposes the paucity of communal equipment in the suburbs. The question is not merely one of a once-for-all onslaught on these deficiencies of social capital; it is how far we need to go on providing more such capital – and planning its provision a good deal more effectively than in the past – for a growing population. Shall Paris grow? That is the fundamental question, which has given rise to intense debate in France ever since the fact of rapid population increase became manifest.

Paris et le désert français

In 1947, a 32-year-old geographer, employed in economic planning for the Ministry of Reconstruction, published the work which was to set this debate in motion. *Paris et le désert francais*, by Jean-François Gravier, illustrated the extraordinary imbalance in the structure of the French population, which hardly has a parallel elsewhere in the world. He showed, with a wealth of telling illustration, the extraordinary concentration of French life in Paris, which had resulted from the long tradition of administrative centralization – a tradition that had passed through from the *ancien régime* through all the revolutions since 1789. He illustrated the effects on the administration itself, where affairs, which would be treated locally in any other country, are transacted through Paris; on the universities, where the Sorbonne dominates French university and cultural life to an extent almost unimaginable else-where; and in finance, where a strong tradition of provincial banking had collapsed in the nineteenth century. Gravier showed how the process of centralization had fed itself: how the railways, planned deliberately to focus on Paris in the mid-nineteenth century, tended to ignore communication between the provincial centres, and so encouraged the further concentration of commerce and industry in the one centre. Gravier demanded that this vicious circle be broken – by means of a positive policy of decentralization and a fundamental reorientation of French life, to give more effective power to the provincial centres.

Gravier's book created intense public interest in France in the techniques of positive regional planning, and since 1949 the French Government has pursued an active policy of industrial decentralization. Up to 1955 policy was limited to positive inducements to industry to set up in decentralization areas, by means of grants from special funds; after that date these were supplemented by negative restrictions on industry – and, latterly, on commerce – in Paris itself. These measures had an effect – but it was a curiously limited one. Perhaps 500,000 new jobs have been created outside Paris. But the majority of the factories have not gone any very great distance out of Paris. A ring of *départements* immediately around the region, and forming in effect an extension of it at distances up to 320 kilometres (200 miles) from Paris itself, with some big cities (Rouen, Le Havre, Amiens, Reims, Troyes, Orléans) and many small country towns, took 75 per cent of all the moves and 60–65 per cent of the decentralized jobs. Significantly, many of these were small branch operations for main plants that remained in Paris; nearly half of them, representing nearly three-quarters of the new jobs, were in mechanical or electrical engineering.

And, of course, manufacturing industry only represents a minority of all jobs in the Paris region. The important point is that Paris like London has become a city of tertiary industry. The net loss of industrial workers from the City averaged 7,000 a year from 1954 to 1962, 10,000 a year from 1962 to 1968, 19,000 a year from 1968 to 1975 and 11,000 a year from 1975 to 1982. Though service industry jobs grew – by over 8,000 a year from 1975 to 1982 – they could not compensate and the City suffered a net job loss. Further, while the decline in manufacturing was felt mainly in the east and south, the growth in tertiary employment was mainly in offices in the western Central Business District (CBD) – as well as just outside the City in La Défense, which gained 50,000 jobs, mainly in offices, from 1968 to 1975. Region-wide, from 1975 to 1980 manufacturing lost 127,000 workers, tertiary industry gained 251,000; a loss of 86,000 construction workers resulted in a net overall gain of only 38,000 jobs. The City lost 37,000, the inner suburbs 23,000: only the outer four *départements* showed a modest gain of 98,000. In fact, four-fifths of new office floorspace in this period was built in the suburbs, and 85 per cent of new tertiary employment was created there – but again, disproportionately in the west. Paris in 1980, though still less a tertiary city than London – with 67 per cent of its employment in service industries, against 73 per cent – was well on the way to becoming a white-collar metropolis.

The future of Paris: planning for growth

We have in fact already seen that, during the period of operation of this policy, from 1954 to 1982, Paris added 2.7 million to its population. However, it is very important to realize that, in terms of population, it is now unrealistic to talk of *Paris et le désert français*. Provincial France may be a desert culturally, intellectually, in social provision; but not in population. When Gravier was writing, the experience of the previous century (1851–1946) showed that the Parisian *agglomération* had in effect accounted for the entire net increase of the population of France. But in contrast, between 1954 and 1962 – as we have seen – the Paris region accounted for only 32 per cent of the increase; the proportion declined to 24 per cent in 1962–8, to 22 per cent in 1968–75 and to 12 per cent in 1975–82. In this last period, indeed, net migration was outwards. The Paris region was growing exclusively through natural increase. And in all France there were only far regions recording out-migration, none of them in the west or south. Most important, the great provincial urban *agglomérations* of the provinces are proving viable enough: their average rate of increase was slightly greater than Paris in 1954–62, and considerably greater in 1962–75. Furthermore, the decision in the Fifth Plan to designate eight of the most important (Marseilles, Lyons, Toulouse, Bordeaux, Nantes, Nancy, Strasbourg and Lille-Roubaix-Tourcoing) as 'equilibrium metropolises', or counter-magnets to Paris, has helped strengthen their growth rates in the 1970s. The question now is not whether Paris will suck the life blood from France; but rather the precise rate at which Paris is to grow, relative to the provincial cities, given that both of them seem destined to grow very fast.

The 1960 plan: PADOG
Forecasting the future population of a major metropolis like Paris is a hazardous business. There is room for doubt about the course of future national population and about the proportion that will go into the cities as a whole; but above all there is room for debate about the proportion of the urban population that will go, or should go, to Paris. The PADOG plan in 1960 worked on the basis that migration into Paris could be reduced from over 100,000 a year (the average for the late 1950s) to only 50,000 a year, to give a total increase of about 100,000 a year. Because it accepted that migration could be limited, PADOG was led to propose that a limit be put on the physical growth of the *agglomération*, as Abercrombie had proposed for London in 1944. Further, this limitation was not to be balanced, as in the London plan, by large schemes for new towns or town expansions within the wider urban region. PADOG firmly rejected new towns, on the grounds that they would

70

attract more people into the region. At most it countenanced a limited expansion of towns like Meaux, Melun, Creil, Mantes and Étampes, from 20–30,000 people to double that size plus some smaller increases elsewhere. Really big increases could be allowed only in towns well outside the Paris sphere of influence, 100 kilometres (60 miles) and more away: Rouen, Amiens, Reims, Troyes, Orléans, Le Mans. The growth of Paris itself must be accommodated within the boundaries of the *agglomération*.

These assumptions, and the resulting policies, did not go unchallenged. M. Delouvrier, in his *Livre blanc* of 1963, took as example a minimum hypothesis which was lower still than that of PADOG: that migration could be cut to 25,000 a year. Even this, he showed, would give Paris a population of 12 million by the year 2000 – an increase of nearly 50 per cent on the 1962 figure. And it would demand that the other urban *agglomérations* must more than double their populations by 2000: Lyons must reach more than 2 million, Marseilles, Lille and Nancy–Metz between 1.5 and 2 million, Bordeaux 1 million. M. Delouvrier, however, also gave a 'maximum' forecast, based on a high national rate of increase, a high rate of urbanization and a Paris which was growing as fast as the total urban population. That would give a total increase of nearly 200,000 a year – double the PADOG estimate – and a population of 16 million by 2000, double the 1962 total. The *Livre blanc* argued that the growth of Paris is merely a matter of time: be it in 2050, or 2100, the 16-million mark will be reached, and at that time the built-up area will have extended to encompass the whole Paris region. M. Delouvrier's view was reinforced by trends between 1962 and 1964: the Paris population grew by an average of 165,000 a year – three times the PADOG assumption – of which 65,000 represented natural increase, 50,000 internal migration and 50,000 repatriation from Algeria. In February 1964 M. Delouvrier calculated that, on a 'reasonable' hypothesis, the population of the Paris region would top the 12-million mark by 1985. (As we shall see, this estimate proved over-inflated.) To justify his forecast, between 1960 and 1965 the authorities granted special limits to build 25,000 houses outside the limits of the *agglomération* set by the PADOG plan, and the total population of the region topped the 9 million mark by the mid-1960s.

Against such a statistical background, the attempt of PADOG to limit the physical growth of Paris began to appear misconceived. In 1961 M. Georges Pilliet, in a powerful criticism (*L'Avenir de Paris*), claimed that the effect of PADOG policy would be to cripple the most active wealth-creating enterprises in Paris and to deny France the opportunity of becoming the capital of Europe. 'The Parisian agglomeration', he concluded, 'is thus neither too big nor is it overpopulated, it is badly-built, badly-serviced and badly-equipped'; and he argued for a plan to develop the whole of the Paris region. This theme was taken up by M. Delouvrier, who in the *Livre blanc* said flatly that

71

whatever artificial factors were blamed for the shortage of land in the Paris region – the slowness of the planning machine, the excessive areas reserved by public authorities for future use – the fundamental trouble was that not enough land was allocated for development. 'The truth', he wrote, 'is that once again the barriers of Paris are bursting. To make land available for development was not to return to the speculative anarchy of the 1920s; it was to plan effectively and to provide necessary public services in good time. That could not be done while holding the existing limits of the *agglomération*: PADOG worked on this basis, but according to the *Livre blanc* the attempt was doomed to failure.

The 1965 Schéma Directeur

This is the background to the 1965 Plan: the *Schéma Directeur d'Aménagement et d'Urbanisme de la Région de Paris* (map 3.3). Prepared by the staff of M. Delouvrier, it started from the frank recognition that Paris will expand: according to the assumptions set out at the beginning of the plan, from 9 million in 1965 to 14 million by 2000, representing a middle position between the extremes forecast by M. Delouvrier in the *Livre blanc*. This growth is likely to be accompanied by 2 million extra jobs – three-quarters in the tertiary sector; a quintupling of purchasing power; a doubling or trebling of the car fleet; and a twofold increase in dwellings. All in all, according to the calculations of the authors, these changes implied nearly a doubling of the developed area: from 1,200 to 2,300 square kilometres (460 to 850 square miles). This is the essential basis of the radical physical provisions of the 1965 plan: a basis quite contrary to the assumptions of PADOG in 1960.

The starting-point was the location of employment. This was dominated by the contrast between the over-concentration at the centre and the under-development in the suburbs. Paris then contained no intermediate level of service centre between the centre of the world city, serving the whole region and even beyond, and the purely local service centre serving at most 30,000; there was no centre of the level of major provincial cities, such as Toulouse or Strasbourg. One aim should be to create centres of this size to contain the fast-growing service sector of employment; they would include higher education, cultural facilities, sports facilities, department stores, luxury restaurants, major hotels and the centre of the prefecture. Such centres would service populations of between 300,000 and 1 million, depending on the location and the level of services provided.

The next element in the 1965 plan was the distribution of the new residential areas. This was conditioned by the need to remedy the glaring lack of living space in the region. In 1962 there were 6 million rooms in the region; to reach London or New York standards at that time, there should have been 9 million. The number of dwellings was expected to double (from 3.2 to 6 million) by 2000, the number of rooms to treble. The surface area needed for housing might well quadruple, because the evidence was that most people preferred a single-family house. At that time the effective choice was between a small and under-equipped apartment, nearer the place of work, and a bigger and better-equipped house, far from work and with poor travelling conditions. To remedy this, there would need to be a bigger range of work near the home, and faster, better travel.

Open space in the region was equally lacking. As already seen, the historic city was developed to a very high density with a corresponding lack of open space; the growth of the suburbs in a series of annular rings, with no proper planning, left an insufficiency there too. The plan sought to remedy this by reserving the Seine valley, between major urban developments on the higher ground on both sides, as a recreational zone wherever land was not used for industry. The Forest of Versailles would also be extended westwards; to the east of Paris, the fine forested land between the Seine and the Marne valleys would be left open.

The transportation element in the plan was based on the necessity to reduce travel time and fatigue. To supplement the existing structure of transportation lines in the region, which radiate from the centre like spokes of a wheel (but with a certain concentration in the Seine valley both above and below Paris), new transportation lines would be developed in accordance with the preferential east–west axis of development. These would be based on the principle that the inner *agglomération* would still depend principally on public transport, especially for the journey to work, but that in the new extensions dependence on the car would be almost complete. There was to be a completely new 260-kilometre (160-mile) system of express rail lines running both north–south and east–west, the latter fanning out to serve the new extensions to east and west; and a 900-kilometre (560-mile) network of radial and concentric motorways which would connect with more local networks of secondary and tertiary routes, serving the new centres. These in fact were inherited, like a number of other elements, from the 1960 plan.

These different elements of the plan, whether inherited or new, powerfully conditioned its urban structure, which was reached through the elimination of alternatives. As starting-point it recognized that development must take the form of major sub-regional service and employment centres, serving populations of between 300,000 and 1 million people. The plan rejected the concept of grouping these into a 'second Paris', on the ground that such a centre could not hope to compete for many years with the existing national centre. It also rejected the idea of a ring of new towns with an intervening green belt, on the English model, chiefly on the grounds that it would hinder the development programme in more distant towns 100 kilometres (60 miles) and more from Paris, such as Orléans, Chartres, Rouen and Reims (a programme retained from PADOG); additionally, it argued that the intervening green belt would tend to fill up along the radial lines of transportation into Paris, however draconian the planning powers. (And, as Delouvrier later told an interviewer, it was felt that the French were too anarchic to countenance such a solution.) The central concept of PADOG – the development of suburban nodes – was retained as part of the new plan; but it was recognized that development would be physically more difficult, and its scale more limited, than the development of new city units on land outside the existing *agglomération*.

From this analysis sprang the concept, common also to plans for other European capital cities such as Stockholm and Copenhagen, of grouping the new units along preferential axes representing main lines of transport. Throughout the history of Paris, the authors of the plan pointed out, the form of the major transportation axes has literally controlled the form of growth of the *agglomération*; in the past this has occurred spontaneously; for the future it could be planned. The radial-concentric system of transportation lines had produced the *agglomération* of today; for the future, different directions were possible. The preferred solution of the 1965 plan was to develop along a very few preferential axes. This solution, the plan argued, would alone guarantee access to open space and open-air recreation to the great majority of the people of the *agglomération*; it alone would exploit at minimum cost the new and planned investments in rail routes and motorways. It was also the only way the planners could see of rapidly decentralizing industry and other economic activities into the new towns, since it exploited the observable tendency, on the part of both people and economic activities, to move outwards along roughly radial lines.

The critical question concerned the choice of axes. In the view of the planners, more than one axis was necessary to exploit the natural tendencies towards outward radial movement. But too many axes would sacrifice the critical advantages of access of countryside and low investment costs; further, they would lead to the familiar historical process, whereby the gaps between the 'fingers of the glove' filled up with development. It was mainly for this reason that the planners finally emerged with the concept of a principal axis which was double, taking the form of two parallel lines: one, 75 kilometres (40 miles) long, north of the Seine from Eaux to west of Pontoise, the other 90 kilometres (55 miles) long, south of the Seine from Melun to Mantes. To this were attached a number of short secondary axes, designed to give some room for the natural development of the *agglomération*. The major new towns were strung out along these two axes – on the northern line at Cergy-Pontoise, Beauchamp (Vallée de Montmorency) and Marne-la-Vallée (Bry-sur-Marne/Noisy-le-Grand), on the southern axis near Mantes, at Trappes, at Evry-Corbeil and at Tigery-Lieusaint (later renamed Melun-Sénart). Later, as will be seen, Beauchamp and Mantes were dropped while two sites at Trappes were joined to make the new town of St-Quentin-en-Yvelines. The two axes, in their central sections, were tangential to the edge of the existing *agglomération* and thus can incorporate many of the ideas for new nodes in the existing Parisian *banlieue* - a central concept of the 1960 Paris plan, here retained (map 3.3).

Polycentric Paris

This in fact was the most revolutionary notion of the 1960 plan: to revertebrate the suburbs (the word was Gravier's) by establishing gigantic new nodes of employment, social equipment and housing at a few selected points in the suburban zone. To choose such areas was a delicate task, because they needed considerable land and also good transport facilities. This was a little easier in Paris than (say) in London, because of the characteristic we described earlier - the chaotic pattern of Parisian suburban development, which had left many open or half-developed spaces.

PADOG finally lighted on a number of major nodes, and the 1965 plan retained them. The first and most dramatic is the zone known as La Défense - a 690-hectare (1,700-acre) site, then largely undeveloped, only 4 kilometres (2.5 miles) west of the Arc de Triomphe, and immediately west of the exclusive inner suburb of Neuilly, on the direct continuation of the line of the Champs Elysées. For decades the central heart of Paris has been drifting westwards - a trend partly associated with the rise of new types of 'central area function', such as headquarters offices, advertising and public relations, business consultancies and institutes. (The trend is parallel to the one which has changed the West End of London, during this century, from a residential into an office zone.) The 1960 plan recognized this trend, but sought to guide it. Already a pioneer undertaking - the *Centre National des Industries et des Techniques* - had settled at La Défense. There was already a plan which grouped offices, shops, showrooms, public buildings and homes around it. To provide for the increased traffic flows, the area would be served by the new west–east express *Métro* and by an ambitious system of new roads, culminating in a complex multi-level system of junctions at the heart of the development. Largely complete by the early 1980s, but in the course of extension, La Défense promises to be one of the most exciting pieces of twentieth-century central area development of any city of the world - though it was already being criticized by a younger generation of architects and planners for monolithic soullessness. It has 20,000 residents, 100,000 workers; it is in the course of doubling its office content from 800,000 to 1.5 million square metres (8.6–16.1 million square feet), and has a huge exhibition complex, a regional shopping centre and public transport interchange. The general development extends westwards to take in the vast 'Paris No. 10' University

75

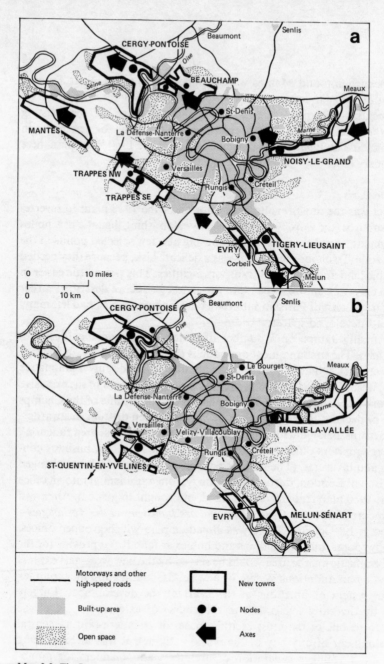

Map 3.3 *The Paris region: the 1965 plan and the 1969 amendments.* (a) The original 1965 plan provides for eight large new towns disposed along two axes, north and south of the Seine. (b) The amended 1969 plan retains the axial arrangement but reduces the eight new towns to five.

at Nanterre – scene of some of the main events in the May 1968 revolutionary disturbances.

The second great node lies west of Paris – and south of La Défense. Immediately east of Versailles lies the plateau zone of Velizy-Villacoublay, then occupied by a military aerodrome. This was badly sited, especially in relation to Orly; its removal released a considerable space for housing and for new central area activities.

The third node is in some ways the most important for the suburban zone itself. It represents a gigantic effort to renew the most impoverished and desolate sector of the whole inner suburban zone – the industrialized sector of St-Denis, Aubervilliers and Bobigny. On the outer edge of this zone lies the former second airport of Paris – Le Bourget – which had become inadequate with the arrival of bigger planes. In 1973 it was replaced by the new Charles de Gaulle airport further north, at Roissy-en-France, which is now the first Paris airport. This is a position peripheral to the main *agglomération* – a position which will hopefully permit supersonic operation without intolerable discomfort to the neighbouring population. The existing airport was being redeveloped during the 1970s as a service and residential node, a node exceptionally well-served by rail facilities and by the *Autoroute du Nord*. This central focus will be ringed by major new housing developments in the northern suburbs.

Lastly, in the south-east the 1965 plan borrows from PADOG the idea of a major zone of redevelopment of growth based on Rungis – the new location for the famous wholesale food markets of Les Halles, moved here in 1969 – and the adjacent centre of Créteil. Together with Versailles-Velizy-Villacoublay, this node relates closely to the southern development axis of the 1965 plan – just as St Denis-Bobigny-Le Bourget are incorporated into the northern axis.

These and other nodes have witnessed an extraordinary expansion of both private and public services during the 1970s. There are eight major commercial centres in the suburbs. Ten new hospitals were built between 1962 and 1977 and nine others completely rebuilt. The University of Paris has been divided into separate campuses, some of them – Nanterre and St Denis – in the suburbs.

Implementing the plan

Combining as it did many of the more ambitious elements of the 1960 plan – the new suburban nodes, the radial and circumferential motorways and the regional express *Métro* – together with the eight completely new towns, the

1965 plan amounts to a formidable programme of investment, one of the most heroic of any major urban area in the world. Only in a country like France, with one of the highest rates of growth of GNP of any advanced industrial country during the 1960s and 1970s, would it be possible to contemplate such a scale of investment at the same time as a vigorous programme of development was being carried through in the other regions of France – particularly in and around the eight *métropoles d'équilibre*.

Throughout the 1970s, work continued on the construction of the new towns and of the suburban nodes. La Défense, the biggest central area redevelopment in Europe and probably in the world, was being extended in the early 1980s; to the south of Paris, and close to the decentralized Les Halles at Rungis, Créteil had been developed as a regional centre for 100,000 people, complete with university, teaching hospital and office centre. But by then, even while it was being implemented, the 1965 plan had suffered major modification.

In 1969 there was already a drastic reassessment. The new towns were cut from eight to five; two were eliminated (Beauchamp, Mantes), two combined into one (two at Trappes); their overall target was slashed from 4.5 million to only 1.7 million and their individual targets were similarly cut by 50 per cent or more (table 3.2). The reason was the new and drastically revised forecast of regional population growth, down from an eventual 14–16 million (1969) to only 12 million (1979). But in fact the new towns failed to meet even these reduced targets: during the Sixth Plan (1971–5) only 115,000 dwellings, 47 per cent of target, and 41 per cent of planned jobs, were achieved. The jobs failed to materialize for a number of reasons: the state's financial incentives, which encouraged movement out of the region altogether; the general decline in manufacturing activity; a surplus of office space; and the continuing attraction of the centre for many offices.

But there were political factors too. The new towns were created by a cumbrous form of co-operation between two separate bodies: one technical, resembling British new town Development Corporations, the EPA (Établissement Publique d'Aménagement), one political, SCA (Syndicat Communitaire d'Aménagement); clashes between these two led to delays and some financial crises. The new towns did better in the second half of the 1970s: indeed, from 1975 to 1982 they accounted for no less than 94 per cent of the net population growth of the region (table 3.2).

One feature of the French operations, however, might well be envied by planners in other countries – including Britain. Land values are frozen in areas scheduled for major development, and the profits from assembly and resale of the land are retained by the public bodies responsible for the planning operation. Though private enterprise is represented on these bodies in a minority role, it is expected to win its profits from development contracts –

Table 3.2 The Paris new towns, targets and reality, 1965-82

	Original target population (thousands) 1965		Revised target population (thousands) 1969	Actual population (thousands) 1982
Beauchamp	300–500		abandoned	—
Cergy-Pontoise	700–1,000	Cergy-Pontoise	330	116
Evry	300–500	Evry	500	50
Mantes	300–400		abandoned	—
Noisy-le-Grand	700–1,000	Marne-la-Vallée	300	47
Tigery-Lieusaint	400–600	Melun-Sénart	300	114
Trappes NW	300–400 ⎱	St-Quentin-en-Yvelines	300	150
Trappes SE	400–600 ⎰			
Total	4,500		1,730	477
% Paris region growth	90 (1965–2000)		28 (1971–5)	94 (1977–82)

Sources: J.M. Rubenstein, *The French New Towns*, Baltimore, 1978; Census, 1982.

not from financial speculation in land. Thus, with the aid of financial guarantees from the state, the French system ensures that land values created by community action revert to the benefit of the community as a whole.

Reviewing the 1965 plan

A decade after the historic 1965 plan it was already clear that some basic assumptions must be modified. The general slackening in growth, so typical of big cities in advanced countries, had occurred here too. Population growth in the Paris region from 1968 to 1975 was down to 1.4 per cent a year against 2 per cent between 1954 and 1962; net migration was now outward to provincial France, though still inward from abroad; and there was marked outward movement within the region, with a declining city and a fast-growing outer ring. Employment growth was less than had been expected, mainly due to a big fall in manufacturing; in the city this had been compensated by increases in tertiary jobs, but in the eastern inner suburbs there was an actual problem of declining job opportunities. Though there had been a prodigious effort to modernize housing, the result had been social polarization, since

79

little public housing had been provided in the City or inner suburbs. The new towns had taken off, with between 60,000 and 70,000 new homes in five years and one-fifth of the new factory floorspace in the region; but progress had been slower than planned, due to the scale and complexity of the whole operation (table 3.2).

Yet overall the 1965 plan, truly audacious in its plan to restructure Paris within thirty-five years, was working. The need now was to readapt it to projections of slower growth: 12.5–13 million by 2000 if trends continued, or 12 million if restriction was successful, against an expected 14 million a decade earlier. But employment would grow, by between 500,000 and 800,000, needing major new construction of offices and factory floorspace.

Faced with this evidence, the authors of the 1975 *Schéma Directeur* – produced by the Prefecture for the Paris region together with the Institut d'Aménagement – reassert the fundamental principles of the 1965 plan. Paris is to grow into a polycentric city along the two main axes; major poles of growth, both within the existing urban fabric and in the new town centres, are to be planned for maximum diversity; open space is to be defined and protected, especially by so-called *Fronts Ruraux* which will limit urban growth; the transportation system is to be planned deliberately so as to tie together the elements of the future multi-centred region.

It is in details, therefore, that changes occur. In the City of Paris, the objectives now are to maintain the residential function for all groups of the population, and to stabilize employment – especially industrial employment in the east. In the inner suburbs, the aims are to maintain and improve existing built structures, to improve local environment, and to develop the service and employment 'poles' at places like Vélizy, Rungis, Créteil, Rosny, Bobigny and la Défense. These, and the new towns farther out, will be tied together by the A86, a new orbital motorway through the suburbs, about 10 kilometres (6 miles) further out from the centre than the already complete Boulevard Périphérique; important parts of this system were already in place by the early 1980s (map 3.4).

The RER

The Express Rapid Transit Network (*Réseau Express Regional* or RER) is being developed in stages (map 3.5). Line A, a new east–west connection through the centre of Paris, links the new town of Marne-la-Vallée with Châtelet–les Halles and La Défense; during the early 1980s it will connect over SNCF tracks with Cergy-Pontoise. Line B links the existing Ligne de Sceaux from the southern suburbs to Châtelet–les Halles and the Gare du Nord and Charles de Gaulle Airport. Line C links two existing suburban lines of SNCF, from the south-east into the Gare d'Austerlitz and from the south-west into the Gare d'Orsay, via the left bank of the Seine; it serves St-Quentin-en-Yvelines and

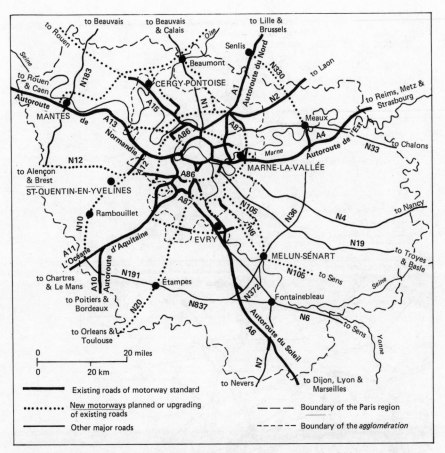

Map 3.4 *The Paris region: highway plans.* The 1965 plan contained an ambitious programme for new radial highways connecting to a Boulevard Périphérique encircling the historic City of Paris (the circular highway in the centre of the map). This network was complete by the early 1980s, but another element – two outer circumferential highways, the A86 and A87 linking the suburban nodes and the new towns – still existed only in fragments.

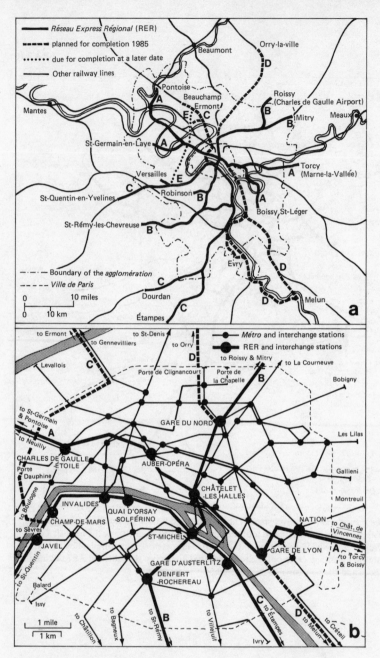

Map 3.5 *The Paris region: Mass Transit proposals.* (a) The new Regional
Express Network, an express rail system linking the new towns and the new
airport to each other and to central Paris, was in an advanced stage of
development in the mid-1980s. (b) *Métro* extensions, outside the limits of the
City of Paris, are linking some of the major suburban nodes to the centre of
Paris.

82

a branch will traverse the northern suburbs. Later in the 1980s, Line D will bring in the south-eastern new towns of Evry and Melun-Sénart, connecting them via a reconstructed Gare de Lyon and a new link to Chatelet-les Halles, the Gare du Nord and the northern suburbs. Finally Line E, a late addition to the network, will be the first to bypass the historic centre of Paris: it will run tangentially from St-Quentin-en-Yvelines and Versailles, via La Défense, to the north-western suburbs. The system thus links French Rail (SNCF) and Paris Transport (RATP) trains, on old tracks and on new, via new tunnels under central Paris to give rapid access to the suburban nodes and the new towns, bringing them within 50–70 kilometres (30–45 miles) of the centre. Thus it will do for Paris what the underground extensions did for London in the 1930s and for Stockholm in the 1950s and 1960s – but on a huge scale.

An important new notion developed in the 1975 plan is that of a *rocade*: a new line of route embodying a motorway and a public transport line using its own tracks. Such a notion will permit rapid access both by road and by public transport from one new town to another, generally via one or more of the restructured 'poles' of the suburbs. Some of the new orbital public transport lines can use existing pieces of infrastructure, including the rail 'Ceinture' already developed in the nineteenth century which is being incorporated into RER Line C. Finally, there will be particular stress on convenient interchange between one part of the public system and another, and also with the motorway system – generally at the 'poles'.

In the late 1970s and 1980s, the priority public works have been shaping the new structure of Paris. While the City itself will be largely maintained in a state of balance, with little new employment and an emphasis on physical conservation, the eastern and southern parts of the City will see renewal. In the inner suburbs the new poles, and the connecting *rocades*, will at last provide the structure that was always lacking. And from there growth will be channelled out along the new transportation lines towards the new towns. It will be one of the most awe-inspiring programmes of urban restructuring in the world.

The new towns
The central element in the plan, now as in 1965, is of course the new towns. And here the verdict must be that their progress, though less spectacular than imagined in the heady mid-1960s, has nevertheless been impressive. Their target populations have been cut, and might even so not be achieved; housing completions, and new jobs, have fallen behind plans. Nevertheless, by 1982 the five new towns together housed 477,000 people – about 150,000 of them new residents – and had grown by 170,000 in only seven years since 1975, of which 130,000 represented net in-migration. During this period, indeed, it

appears that their growth was almost equal to the entire net population increase in the region.

The Parisian new towns had some other things in their favour. They did seem to have achieved a reasonable social balance, at least in comparison with the one-class *Grands Ensembles* that preceded them, by making many houses available for sale. Though they had created too few new jobs, their record in that field was better than the *Grands Ensembles*. They had produced strong shopping centres serving wide sub-regions around them. They had proved a reasonable bargain because of their low land costs (only 10 to 20 per cent of the average for outer suburban sites) which are frozen under a special procedure, the ZAD (*Zone d'Aménagement Différé*) scheme. Their inhabitants, polled in surveys, are generally well-satisfied. But they cannot be said to have achieved one of the principal dreams of the authors of the 1965 plan: to make them major centres of higher-level services, equal to the leading provincial cities of France. Despite generous investment in cultural infrastructure, that was clearly some way from realization.

In particular, the five towns have had rather unequal fortunes. Cergy-Pontoise, 32 kilometres (20 miles) north-west of central Paris, had an early start at the end of the 1960s. It already is the Prefecture of the new *département* of Val d'Oise and has a major shopping centre with big surrounding office developments; it is planned to be the seat of a new university. In 1982 it had achieved a population of 116,000 – 26,000 of them new residents – against its target of 330,000. The other new town to start construction in the late 1960s, Evry, occupies a similar position on the opposite south-east side of Paris; it, too, is the seat of administration for a new *département*, Essonne. By 1982 it had nearly 50,000 people, a major shopping centre, and a big concentration of private offices – though some had been slow to let. Its near neighbour to the east, Melun-Sénart, was a late starter and the most distant from Paris (45 kilometres, 28 miles); in the early 1980s it appeared to be the most problematic of the new towns, with least new development to be seen on the ground.

In contrast St-Quentin-en-Yvelines, 30 kilometres (19 miles) south-west of Paris, was thriving: it already had 150,000 people, 85 per cent in privately-owned houses and apartments; it also had 40,000 jobs, a large part of them in tertiary industries. It has clearly benefited from its good location at the end of a branch of the *Autoroute de l'Ouest* and on a good rail line which was in course of being linked to the RER. And it, too, is the seat of a prefecture: that of Yvelines.

Perhaps the most ambitious new town in conception, Marne-la-Vallée, is an elongated linear city stretching for 20 kilometres (12 miles) from west to east, on the first RER line east of the city. The plan, unveiled in 1970, provides for a population of 300,000 living in a series of urban villages next to unrivalled recreational facilities. Served by the *Autoroute de l'Est*, a vital artery of the

Common Market linking France with Germany, the new city will have its major commercial and cultural centre at the western end closest to Paris itself, at Noissy-le-Grand. The planners see it as a counter-magnet, reversing the long-continued trend of business and other service industries to move west-wards from the centre of Paris. Somewhat reinforcing this traditional trend, Marne-la-Vallée had a slow start, but accelerated after completion of the RER link from central Paris in the mid-1970s; though in 1982 it was still the smallest of the five new towns, with only 47,000 people, its rate of new in-migration had been second only to St-Quentin-en-Yvelines.

Verdict on the Parisian experience

In many respects, Paris provides a useful comparison – and a contrast – with London. In all Europe, they are the two greatest concentrations of people around a single centre of population and employment. In important respects, they are rivals for many of the important international functions which are developing so rapidly in western Europe. They are the truest world cities of a continent which boasts many examples of the genre. Both enjoy unique advantages, and yet suffer unusual social costs, from the concentration of people and their activities. In both, continued dynamism and growth led to alarm on the part of many thoughtful people, resulting in attempts at con-tainment and decentralization of industry to the provinces.

Yet there the similarities end. Paris has been a much more dynamic city than London, in terms of both population growth and economic growth, since the Second World War – above all in the 1960s, when London began to show signs of stagnation. After a brief attempt to restrain this growth, the planners of the Paris region have wholeheartedly accepted it, and have pro-duced a plan for vigorous expansion. True, as we saw, the London region, too, has its plan for growth; but it is significant that it is based on the creation of counter-magnets to the capital on the traditional model of the new towns policy, while the so-called new towns of the Paris region are seen as arms of the city itself. The new motorways and the regional express *Métro*, themselves symbolic of the worship of technology in the new France, are deliberately designed to bind the new towns and the old Paris, creating of them a single *agglomération* both physically and functionally.

During the 1960s, in fact, the Parisians found that they could not limit the growth of their city – perhaps because finally they lacked the will to do so. This is not necessarily to say that their planning is ineffectual. In many respects – in its capacity to carry through bold schemes at speed, and in its determination to seize community-based land values for the benefit of the public - it is more effective than the British system, and among the more successful in the world. Though Frenchmen and others may have their reservations about the architectural and human quality of some of the results, few would doubt that they are - even on a world scale of comparison - impressive.

The problem, still unresolved and almost certainly worsening in the 1980s, is that of imbalance within the Parisian region, between east and west. As in London, so in Paris, the west was traditionally the seat of the court, of the aristocracy, of conspicuous consumption. During the nineteenth and twentieth centuries, it became the seat first of luxury shopping, then - as was also true of London - of offices. The east and south in contrast were the homes of the working class and of small-scale industry - though both cities had an anomalous industrial enclave in their north-west sectors. During the 1960s and 1970s, population and employment have decentralized out of the congested inner city - but at the same time, manufacturing jobs have been disappearing while tertiary employment has inexorably grown. The problem is that this employment has contracted in the east and expanded in the west. Cergy-Pontoise and St-Quentin-en-Yvelines have been the main beneficiaries; Marne-la-Vallée has had to struggle to prosper, but - aided by the early presence of the RER - has probably succeeded; a question mark still hangs over the future of Evry and, above all, Melun-Sénart. Thus, perhaps unexpectedly, in Paris as in London, traditional patterns of location reassert themselves within the new geography of the city region.

4 Randstad Holland

From the Aéroport Charles de Gaulle, 15 kilometres (9 miles) north of Paris, to the Luchthaven Schiphol, in the polders 16 kilometres (10 miles) south-west of Amsterdam's Muntplein, it is 400 kilometres (250 miles) as the crow flies and an hour's journey by jet. As the aircraft loses height and comes through the cloud cover which so often covers this part of Europe, the traveller's first glimpse may well be of water: he sees the complex distributaries of the great Rhine and Maas rivers, and the great harbour basins, mixed with oil refineries, chemical plants and warehouses, which mark the port of Rotterdam – first port of the world in the tonnage it carries. Rotterdam's heart, devastated by German bombardment in 1940 and magnificently rebuilt after 1945, lies below. The city spreads far to the west, on the northern side of the New Waterway, Rotterdam's main outlet to the sea: it has swallowed up former towns like the fishermen's centre of Vlaardingen and Schiedam, the birthplace of Dutch gin, which now appear ringed by suburbs. And as he looks west towards the North Sea, the air traveller will realize that Rotterdam – city of 579,000 people in 1980 – is only part of a much larger whole. Along the great motorway that runs straight as a die across the polders to the north-west, an infinitesimal gap appears to separate the suburbs of Rotterdam from those of the old pottery town of Delft. Farther away towards the North Sea, along the same ribbon of road, an even smaller gap separates Delft from the vast urban spread of the Hague along the coastal sand-dunes. To the north of that, just inland from the coast, appear the towns of Leiden and Haarlem; north of Haarlem, right on the coast, industrial haze marks the steel town of IJmuiden. As the plane loses height rapidly, the city of Amsterdam, with its 717,000 people (in 1980), appears behind the runways and terminal buildings of Schiphol. To the right, on the higher forested ground behind the polder edge, are the suburbs which extend outwards from Amsterdam towards the radio and television masts of Hilversum, and then again southwards along the ridge of high ground to the city of Utrecht with its quarter of a million people.

Schiphol airport, in fact, lies in the centre of one of the most extraordinary urban regions of the world. All around is the polder landscape of the provinces of North and South Holland, which has always dominated the nation of which it forms a part: so much indeed that English-speaking people habitually confuse the two, and say Holland when they mean the Netherlands. Beyond the polders, just as in a landscape by Ruysdael, are the houses and spires of the nearest town. It is only from the air, or from the map, that you can appreciate the real change that has come over Holland in the three centuries since Ruysdael – indeed in the century since 1860. The cities, which Ruysdael and Vermeer and de Hooch painted, are recognizable today. But, as in their day, the cities have prospered; and they have spread far beyond the limits which they knew. Today the cities and towns of Holland have grown so close together that they form, in an important sense, one city, though a city of a particular form. The Dutch call it Randstad Holland: the Ring City. It has the shape of a great horseshoe, pointing with its open end towards the south-east: a horseshoe over 50 kilometres (30 miles) in length, some 50 kilometres (30 miles) also at its maximum width, and altogether, if some supernatural blacksmith were to straighten it out on his anvil, some 180 kilometres (110 miles) in length. It runs from Dordrecht, south-east of Rotterdam, through Rotterdam and along the north side of the New Waterway to the Hook of Holland on the coast; turns there through a right angle to the Hague on the coast, taking in Delft within the angle; runs in a belt, some 16 kilometres (10 miles) wide, along the coast, to incorporate the considerable towns of Leiden and Haarlem, as well as the many small seaside resorts and the steel centre of IJmuiden; turns thence, north of Haarlem, through another right angle to run inland to Amsterdam; runs from there across the high ground to Hilversum, out of the provinces of Holland to Utrecht, and even beyond there to the river Lek (map 4.1). This complex, in 1980, had two cities – Amsterdam and Rotterdam – of between half and one million people; two – Utrecht and the Hague – of between one quarter and one half million; and two – Haarlem and Leiden – of between 100,000 and 200,000. These are city populations; the agglomerations around them are much bigger. Together with three smaller cities – Delft, Dordrecht and Hilversum – they form the urban horseshoe, or ring: nearly 29 per cent of the population of the Netherlands, living on just over 5 per cent of its area. (These calculations, for the end of the 1970s, come from the Dutch geographer van Ginkel.) This urban ring encloses the green heart, or central area, of the Randstad, which can be subdivided into a rural core and a number of fringe areas subject to the suburban outgrowth of the urban ring. Finally – according to the terminology adopted by van Ginkel – the Randstad also includes an outer area, on the far side of the urban ring, which looks outwards towards the rest of the country, and which also tends to be subject to intense suburban growth pressures (table 4.1 and map 4.2). The total population of the entire Randstad, as thus defined by van Ginkel, was 6,018,100 at the beginning of 1981: 42.4 per cent of the national population, crowded on to only 16.7 per cent of its land area. After London,

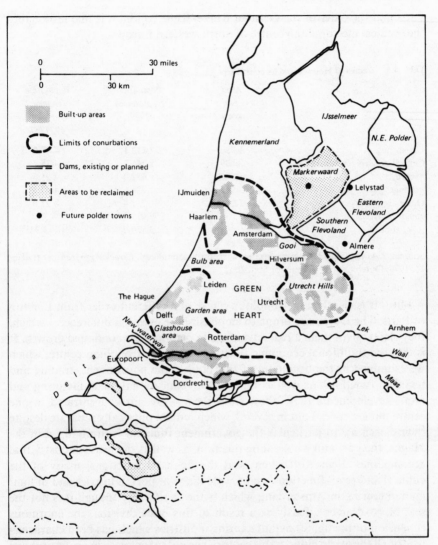

Map 4.1 *Randstad Holland.* The complex urban agglomeration of the Randstad (Ring City) takes the form of a horseshoe open to the south-east. It contains three major conurbations, grouped around the cities of Amsterdam, the Hague, Rotterdam and Utrecht. The planners aim to preserve the agricultural heart of the Randstad and the gaps between its cities. It will grow outwards into regions like the polders, north Kennemerland and the delta region.

Paris and the cities of the German Rhine–Ruhr region, it is unquestionably the greatest metropolitan centre of north-western Europe.

Table 4.1 Randstad Holland and its constituent parts, 1981

	Area (square km.)	Population (thousands) 1981	Population change (per cent) 1971–81
Urban ring	1,736	3,912.1	− 7.0
Central area (green heart)	2,609	1,346.7	+ 35.4
core	1,680	622.0	+ 25.4
fringe	929	724.6	+ 45.4
Outer area	1,293	759.4	+ 22.0
Randstad Holland	*5,638*	*6,018.1*	*+ 3.3*
(UN definition)		*3,850.0*	*− 3.3*

Sources: J. A. van Ginkel, 'Suburbanisatie en recente woonmilieus', *Utrechte geografische studies*, 16, 1979; Dutch Central Bureau for Statistics.

But this is clearly a metropolitan centre of a different order from London or Paris. The Dutch are prone to emphasize the essential difference – which, they claim, gives them a real advantage in planning for continued growth. It is that the traditional economic functions of the metropolitan centre, which we examined in the beginning of this book – the government, trading and financial functions, as well as the cultural, educational, manufacturing and retail developments that follow from them – are not concentrated in one centre but are spread out in several, which remain physically separate despite their closeness. In particular the government function is firmly fixed in the Hague; the port and wholesaling function, as well as the heavy industry that accompanies it, in Rotterdam; and the financial functions, many of the cultural and retail functions, and a wide range of port industries and of light manufacturing in Amsterdam, which is the capital city though it is not the seat of government. Partly as a result of this basic division, the enormous expansion of the lighter manufacturing industries which has been character-istic of all the world cities in this century has not taken place in an amorphous ring round one city, but has gone to a great extent into towns quite separate from the three big cities though within easy reach of them. Prominent among these are Leiden, Haarlem and the area known as Het Gooi around Hilver-sum. Thus the cities still remain physically distinct – and distinct, too, in important elements of economic structure. Each remains separated from the next by a buffer zone of open land. And, in the centre of the horseshoe, there is still a vast tract of open rural land – a feature that led the British planner Gerald Burke to christen the Randstad 'Greenheart Metropolis'.

The Randstad in history

The cities of the Randstad are nearly all medieval foundations; the Hague is the great exception, for it was only a castle up to the sixteenth century. And in 1584, when the Netherlands won its independence from Spain, it was the most heavily urbanized country in Europe, with half the population living in cities. Yet even in the seventeenth century – the 'Golden Century' when the Dutch conquered the seas, dominated the trade of Europe and contributed powerfully to the development of western art and science – the cities remained small. As late as 1795, only Amsterdam had more than 200,000 people; no other city had even 60,000. And it was only at this time that the Hague – third town in size, and the centre of the government – attained city status; for two centuries the jealousy of the provinces had kept it 'the biggest village in Europe'.

The figures show, in fact, that the real rise of the Dutch cities dates from the revolution in trade and industry of the nineteenth century. In 1825 came the first Dutch steamship; in 1839, between Amsterdam and Haarlem, the first Dutch railway line. But the most significant changes of those years occurred outside the Netherlands: through the medium of the customs union or *Zollverein*, German unity was being effectively achieved. Finally, in 1871, the German empire became a reality and the Ruhr began its mushroom growth into the greatest industrial area of Europe; with it, the Rhine became western Europe's major commercial artery. But the mouth of the Rhine was the Netherlands' prize; as Germany rose to industrial might, the Netherlands rose with it to commercial power. Rotterdam benefited the most: aided by the construction of the sea canal known as the New Waterway in 1872 and its improvement in 1885, the city's population rose more than fourfold between 1850 and 1913. Amsterdam profited less: despite the North Sea Canal, a ship canal cut through to IJmuiden on the coast in 1876, it lost its position as first port of the Netherlands to Rotterdam about 1900 and its population rose only about two and a half times between the mid-nineteenth century and the outbreak of the First World War. The Hague benefited from an unprecedented growth of the functions of the central government, and its population multiplied over four times between 1850 and 1914.

This growth continued between the wars; but since 1945 it has accelerated, aided by the highest natural rate of increase of any western European population, and by the marked increase of trade within western Europe and between western Europe and the rest of the world. The progress of the cities is plotted in table 4.2. But the whole period since 1918 has seen the rapid acceleration of a process which was already starting, in the region south-east of Amsterdam known as Het Gooi, in the 1870s: the spread of the suburbs.

Table 4.2   The growth of the Randstad cities, 1650–1980

			Population (thousands)			
	c.1650	*c.1795*	*1850*	*1900*	*1947*	*1980*
Amsterdam	115	201	225	510	804	717
Rotterdam	30	58	112	368	646	579
The Hague	17	41	65	236	533	457
Leiden	45	31	36	54	87	103
Haarlem	39	21	26	65	157	225
Utrecht	22	32	49	104	185	482

Sources: Tertius Chandler and Gerald Fox, *3000 Years of Urban Growth*, New York, 1974; International Urban Research, *The World's Metropolitan Areas*, Berkeley and Los Angeles, 1959; Statistical Yearbook of the Netherlands, 1981.

Though they built their seventeenth-century houses fairly closely, the Dutch have always had a very English (or un-French) preference for the single-family house with its own garden. With rising living standards and the improvement of urban transport after about 1900, the result was rapid growth of low-density suburban housing around all the Randstad cities, involving many annexations of surrounding territory by the municipalities. Rotterdam extended itself on no less than eleven occasions in the century between 1860 and 1960, the Hague on five occasions. The suburbs grew especially rapidly in the attractive sandy areas outside the low-lying polders, like Het Gooi, in the wooded hills north and south of Utrecht, and in the sand-dune country along the coast. Haarlem, one of the most attractive examples of large-scale seventeenth-century town building, grew partly as a dormitory suburb for Amsterdam 20 kilometres (12 miles) away, though it also developed some light industries of its own.

The physical expression of this growth can be seen in map 4.2. In 1850 the towns of the Randstad, though close together by the standards of many areas of Europe, were still separate entities. By 1980 they had spread towards each other, to form the almost continuous urban ring of the Randstad; and the problem of future growth had become acute.

Factors in future growth

Basic forces – of demographic and industrial growth – have been at work in the Randstad since 1870, and especially since 1945. They are not likely to diminish in the remaining years of the twentieth century; indeed, if anything they are likely to strengthen.

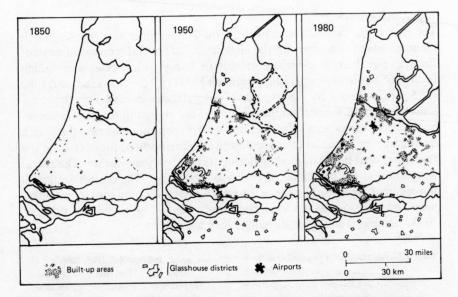

Map 4.2 *Growth of the Randstad.* In 1850 the cities of the western Netherlands had little sign of forming an incipient urban agglomeration. But, beginning about 1870 in Het Gooi region near Hilversum (see map 4.1), rapid suburbanization set in. Today urban activities compete for land with traditional intensive agriculture which is expanding in acreage. The dilemma can be resolved only by diverting the growth of the Randstad into new channels.

Population growth

The first is the population growth in the Netherlands as a whole. Dutch planners have to reckon with the highest rate of natural increase in western Europe. But, here as elsewhere in western Europe, birth-rates were falling from 1965 onwards – very rapidly between 1970 (18.3 per thousand) and 1980 (12.5 per thousand). By 1980 the rate of natural increase was 4.5 per thousand – slightly behind France though still one of the highest in Europe. In consequence, like the experts of most other west European countries, the Dutch demographers have had to revise downwards their official projections of the future national population after raising them a few years earlier. The actual population at the beginning of 1980 was 14,091,014. The central Statistical Bureau, making some allowance for possible net migration into the country, projected in 1975 that the total might only rise to 15.6 million by the year 2000 – compared to the 19–21 million forecast in 1965.

Table 4.3 Distribution of population in the Netherlands, actual and forecast, 1965-2000

	Actual population (thousands) 1965	Forecast population (thousands) 1965 for c.2000		Actual population (thousands) 1975	Forecast population (thousands) 1975 for c.2000	Actual population (thousands) 1980
		with continued 1960s trend	with greater dispersal			
North	1,300	2,250	3,000	1,490	1,770	1,560
East	2,200	4,000	4,250	2,600	3,310	2,710
West	5,700	8,500		6,170	6,340	6,290
			12,000			
South	2,600	4,750		2,990	3,810	3,120
South-West	300	500	750	330	370	350
The Netherlands	12,100	20,000	20,000	13,600	15,610	14,090

Sources: Second and Third Reports on Physical Planning in the Netherlands, 1966 and 1976; *Statistical Yearbook of the Netherlands, 1981.*

The second and critical question is how this increase will be distributed region by region. Until 1960 the three urbanized western provinces of the Netherlands – North Holland, South Holland and Utrecht – had been gaining population rapidly, due both to natural increase and to migration from the rest of the country. It had been the planners' aim to balance in- and out-migration, in other words to reduce net migration to zero. In fact by the 1960s the current had been reversed: the west was actually losing population, by migration, to the rest of the Netherlands. A 1965 forecast was that, if the prevailing trends continued, population in the west might rise from 5.7 million in 1965 to 8.5 million in 2000, or by 2.8 million over thirty-five years; but a policy of increased dispersal could reduce this somewhat. In either event, the west would have a declining share of the population of the country. In the event, this proved only too true: by the 1970s the Randstad was losing population to the south of the country through migration, and this was expected to continue. So the radically revised 1975 forecast gave the west only 6.34 million by the year 2000 – a mere 200,000 increase over 1975 (table 4.3).

The changing industrial structure
Yet the result, because of a fall in household size and increased demands for space per person in and around the house, could still mean a large increase in the total urban area – and this at a time when the Dutch government are concerned to save space and reduce demands for mobility. It is altogether too much to hope for a greater degree of decentralization, because of continuing trends in the economy of the Netherlands and of Europe. In the first place, like other EEC countries, the Netherlands is experiencing a pronounced shift of labour out of agriculture and into manufacturing and services. In 1947, 19.8 per cent of the economically active population were in agriculture; by 1971 this was reduced to 7.2 per cent and by the early 1980s it was less than 6 per cent. Secondly, and associated with the first tendency, the Netherlands in the 1960s and 1970s showed a rate of growth that was rapid even by contemporary western European standards. Thirdly, an important part of this industry is tied physically to the Randstad because it depends on the processing of imported bulky low-value goods, and so must be located on deep navigable water. The leading examples of such industry are oil-refining and the associated petrochemical industry, which is particularly concentrated on the New Waterway below Rotterdam, and the iron and steel industry, which is located in the great integrated plant at the entry of the North Sea Canal into the sea at IJmuiden. True, the prospects for these industries are not as rosy in the 1980s as they were in the expansionist years of the 1960s. Oil-refining and its derivatives should however grow, as oil progressively replaces coal as an energy source and as a raw material for chemicals. And where coal continues to be used, as in iron and steel manufacture, it is found cheaper to import it from low-cost producers in North America than to use European coal; while of course the ore has long been imported from Sweden or Spain. So the tendency in iron and steel manufacture has been to favour the coastal sites, as on the south Wales coast in Britain, at Bremen in Federal Germany and here at IJmuiden. Of course all the deep-water industries are capital-intensive in character: they use a relatively small labour force to produce a large volume of output. But they create a great deal of employment in ancillary and service trades, a large part of which must be close to the areas where the basic industries are located. The main growth zone for the tidewater

95

industries will continue to be the New Waterway below Rotterdam, which has had a powerful impetus from the completion of the great Europoort complex opposite the Hook of Holland; but Amsterdam and the North Sea Canal are also improving their capacity for bulk handling of goods.

Other industries, it is true, are not tied to the west, and the statistical trends of the 1960s and 1970s show that they are decentralizing out of the western part of the country. These are the labour-intensive manufacturing industries with a relatively high proportion of value added in manufacture; they can bear high transport costs for materials and products, but because labour costs are a large part of total costs they are particularly sensitive to wage competition from the capital-intensive industries in the west. These industries have been particularly attracted, since 1945, to the province of North Brabant in the south-east Netherlands, where a strong Catholic majority produces a high natural increase of population. Between 1950 and 1980 North Brabant's increase in population and labour force was consistently about 50 per cent higher than the national average; it now rivals South Holland, traditional industrial province of the Netherlands, in numbers of workers. Eindhoven, symbol of this development, has grown with the Philips electrical complex from a mere village in 1890 to a city of over 194,000 people in 1980. Elsewhere, in Limburg in the south and in Groningen to the north, chemical industries have developed, and the discovery of natural gas off the coast in Groningen province is undoubtedly giving another powerful impetus to development in the north: development even, perhaps, of capital-intensive tidewater industry. But meanwhile much of the lighter industry still remains in the west, where it is apt to decentralize into unsuitable locations: as for instance the electronics industry around Hilversum, which has led to large-scale building since 1930 in the agricultural and recreational zone of Het Gooi.

Perhaps the critical question concerns the service industries. Clearly many of them perform a purely local function for a population working in factory industry. But some are much more than local in character. Outstanding among these is government service, which is important not only for its direct effect on employment but also for the fact that the presence of government is apt to attract other semi-official public organizations. Of the 437,000 administrative workers in the Netherlands in 1971, no less than 53,000 were in the Hague. In another 'industry', which is expanding rapidly in every advanced country – higher education – the concentration in the west is as marked; for out of six universities in the Netherlands in 1960, only two were outside the west. Clearly direct government action could help to alleviate this state of affairs; and in 1960 the important report on physical planning in the Netherlands recommended that a policy of government and university decentralization should be actively pursued. By 1980, seven out of thirteen universities were outside the west.

Problems of the Randstad

Regionally, then, the Netherlands is faced with a dilemma of long standing, which some other European countries have only begun to experience more recently. Whatever is done to promote decentralization out of the west, there is bound to be a rapid growth of population in the western provinces themselves, if only because of the natural increase of an already numerous population. But this growth raises acute problems of competition for scarce land. It is a commonplace that the Netherlands is the most densely populated country in western Europe: with over 419 people per square kilometre (1,085 per square mile) in 1981, it stands ahead of England and Wales. By the year 2000, if the population reaches 15.6 million, the figure could be 460 to the square kilometre (1,200 to the square mile). The concentration was even more marked in the west, where already in 1981 the density was over 917 to the square kilometre (2,375 to the square mile).

And in the west, in the coming decades, there are four dominant types of land use, all of which will be making heavy demands for space. The first is agriculture. There is here a prosperous, intensive and efficient market-gardening industry, much of it under glass, with a very heavy capital investment on each hectare. It produces 40 per cent of the Netherlands' total crop of garden products. But between 1935 and 1970, in the three western provinces which contain the Randstad, agricultural land use fell by nearly 12 per cent, and by the end of the 1970s more than 20 per cent of the total area was built up. The second competitor is heavy industry and port installations. In 1958 it was estimated that the port of Rotterdam alone might increase its land needs by 6,625 hectares (14,820 acres) in all between then and 2000. A third and most obvious need is for housing. The average number of people per dwelling tends to fall, because of smaller families. A report of 1966 suggested that a rise in population of 2.8 million between 1965 and 2000 might mean a need for one million or more extra dwellings, which at the prevailing densities in the urban areas of the western Netherlands (taking into account all necessary services) might mean the appropriation of 57,000-77,000 hectares (140,000-190,000 acres) from agriculture down to 1980: an area greater than that of East Flevoland, which the Dutch reclaimed from the former Zuiderzee in the late 1950s, without taking account of the need for dwellings created by urban-renewal schemes in the congested inner cities which inevitably displaced some people. In fact, in the period 1960-79 alone, the three western provinces lost some 60,300 hectares (149,000 acres) – or nearly 12 per cent – of their agricultural land; the prediction had proved on target. A fourth need is recreation. The west is already chronically short of adequate open space with public access, and the shortage will be aggravated by three factors: the fact that the relatively short coastline has to serve the needs not only of much of the interior of the Netherlands but also of areas as far inland as the Ruhr; the increasing population in the whole hinterland, including the areas across the German frontier; and the rapid increase in mobility, following the spread of the motor car, coupled with the limited capacity of the North Sea beaches.

Most serious of all is the need for housing land. Inevitably, it is being felt most acutely outside the limits of the existing cities and towns. Within the period 1950–80, the fastest-growing populations of the Netherlands, both in the west and elsewhere, were those of the suburban zones outside the municipalities. (Indeed, the largest cities began to lose people by migration from the 1950s, and by the 1970s they were in rapid absolute decline: between 1970 and 1980 Amsterdam, Rotterdam and the Hague together lost 353,000 people.) In the west the areas of growth are concentrated in areas peripheral to the Randstad itself: they include the island of Voorne, south-west of Rotterdam; the northern Kennemerland, north of the North Sea Canal between IJmuiden and Alkmaar; the polders in the agricultural centre of the Randstad, adjacent to Amsterdam; and the southern fringe of the area known as the Veluwe, east of Utrecht, between Wageningen and Arnhem. A curious incidental result is that population in the urban ring of the Randstad has been falling, while in the green heart it has been growing rapidly (table 4.1). During the whole period 1960–78, according to the calculations of van Ginkel, the nine Randstad cities lost 14.1 per cent of their aggregate population (422,000) and the four biggest ones lost 17.7 per cent (435,000), while the green heart or central area gained 428,000 or 60.8 per cent (compare map 4.3). By 1978 the population density in the central area or green heart had risen to 461 per square kilometre (1,194 per square mile); and, during the period 1974–7, more than half the net increase in the central area represented net in-migration.

Here lies the real threat. It is not only that the growth of the suburbs will cause the cities of the Randstad to coalesce along the line of the 'horseshoe', so that the Netherlands will have a continuous linear city 180 kilometres (110 miles) long; even more, it is that the agricultural heart of the 'horseshoe' will fill up, so that the Randstad will lose its unique character among the world cities and become merely another vast urban sprawl – a Dutch Los Angeles. The threat is most serious in two places: one in the north of the Randstad, where a continuous town is in process of development along the line of the North Sea Canal, connecting Amsterdam, Zaanstreek, IJmuiden and Haarlem; and in the south-west, where the cities of Rotterdam, Delft, the Hague and Leiden could easily coalesce into a miniature Randstad, only about 24 kilometres (15 miles) across, the centre of which could then fill up. But there are other areas where the problem is more insidious, as in the east at Utrecht, where the city is tending to spread both north and south into attractive hilly country that is important for both agriculture and recreation.

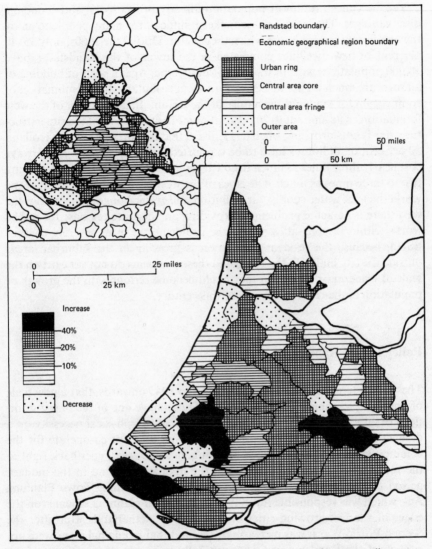

Map 4.3 *Randstad Holland: population changes, 1971–81.* As in most other metropolitan regions of the world, the central cities of the Randstad are declining, while big increases occur in the suburban areas outside them. Especially disturbing are the rapid increases in the core area (green heart) of the Randstad (see inset). These add urgency to the plans for diverting growth further outwards into such areas as the delta and the polders.

99

Yet the concentration of population already brings social and economic disadvantages. The lack of space makes it difficult for many people to enjoy the one-family type of house which they prefer. During the 1960s, only 35–40 per cent of new dwellings completed in the towns of the Randstad (above 50,000 population) were of the single-family type. Again, costs of building of all sorts are much higher in the west – a fact attributable to a combination of competition for land and the nature of the terrain. In a large part of the west foundation costs amount to 20 per cent or more of the costs of the superstructure; this is not surprising when it is realized that in North and South Holland 80 per cent of all houses have to be supported on concrete piles. Motorways cost nearly three times as much to construct in the west as in the east; housing two to three times as much. The cities of the west have problems, familiar the world over, of water supply, air pollution and traffic congestion. Within the west there is an acute problem of providing an adequate tax base for public works within the big cities, where the problems are most severely concentrated, because the resident population is growing in the suburban areas outside the city limits. In the Randstad these problems do not yet exist on the scale of London or Paris. But they could become serious with the growth of population in the remaining years of this century.

Policy for the Randstad

These considerations made it apparent, from 1945 onwards, that a new scale of regional planning was necessary. The Dutch have one of the oldest traditions of city planning in Europe, which arose out of physical necessity: in a difficult environment, it was early realized that all must co-operate for the common good. The idea of town planning, in some cases, goes back right to the foundation of the Dutch cities in the middle ages; and in the modern period it expressed itself as early as 1901 in a far-reaching Town Planning Act, which was responsible for many notable town-planning schemes on the edges of the fast-growing cities of the western Netherlands. But after the Second World War it was increasingly realized that municipal plans were not enough: if the Randstad was not eventually to envelop a great part of the western Netherlands, its growth must be planned as a whole, both in its relation to the development of the whole country and in its internal structure. Starting in 1949, with an official report on The Distribution of Population in the Netherlands, a whole series of official studies have analysed the trends of population growth, examined the problems which result, set out the planning choices and evolved a coherent set of policies for the Randstad. The most important are The West of the Netherlands and the other Provinces (1956), a joint study by the economic and the physical planners; The Development of the Western Netherlands (1958), a study by a special working party, which outlined a set of policies for the Randstad; the First Report on Physical Planning in the Netherlands (1960), a statement of general policies by the government Physical Planning Service, which set out the planners' objectives for the Randstad in relation to the regional development of the rest of the Netherlands; the Second Report on Physical Planning in the Netherlands (1966), which updated the analysis and policy recommendations of the earlier report, and the Third Report on Physical Planning in the Netherlands, in three parts: the Orientation Report of 1974, the Urbanization Report of 1976 and the Report on Rural Areas of 1977. These documents make up a coherent whole; for in the Netherlands official policies, evolved in the course of careful analysis and exhaustive discussion, command a wide measure of agreement and are not lightly modified. Yet there has been radical modification – in the Third Report. And this reflects a fundamental shift in the background to the Dutch planning process between the mid-1960s and today.

The 1958 study and First (1960) Report

A basic element of policy, first set out in the 1958 study, is the development of the peripheral regions of the Netherlands, outside the west. A number of cities here, and especially in the north, are to be expanded to over 100,000 and even over 200,000 people, so as to serve as adequate growth points for regional development. Cities of this size, the Dutch planners argue, are necessary for the performance of the specialized functions of business, entertainment, professional life, culture and education. The programme includes old towns and regional capitals with development potential, like Groningen, Arnhem, Nijmegen and Breda, as well as some developing industrial towns like Enschede and Tilburg.

Nevertheless, it is clear that the Randstad will remain, and that it (and even more so the areas adjacent to it) will continue to grow. So certain principles of growth must be maintained.

The first of these is to preserve the historic cities of the urban ring, as separate and distinct points of concentration. Because of the danger that some cities may soon coalesce, the 1958 study first suggested the establishment of buffer zones, at least 4 kilometres (2.5 miles) wide, between all of them. This may well be difficult, as the 1960 report recognizes, because often local municipal extension plans make inroads into the buffer zones, not so much for extension of the built-up area as for city-fringe land uses like parks, sewage beds and swimming pools. Amsterdam grew eastwards towards the Gooi during the early 1970s with a new town for 100,000 at Bijlermeer; while Rotterdam grew westwards towards Delft.

The second policy line consists in the preservation of the agricultural heart

101

of the Randstad 'horseshoe'. An absolute priority will be given to agriculture in certain areas where it is of distinctive character and where it makes a particularly intensive and important contribution to national production – the glasshouse industry of South Holland, particularly south of the Hague; the bulbfields between Leiden and Haarlem and the intensive garden cultivation round the villages of Aalsmeer and Boskoop, east of Haarlem and Leiden. Any growth of population that does occur in this central area will be concentrated into a few existing historic towns, such as Gouda, Alphen and Woerden, and into the development of a new town next to the village of Zoetermeer, necessary to house the overspill from the Hague agglomeration.

The third and perhaps most revolutionary proposal, first contained in the 1958 study, concerns the growth of the Randstad. If it is not to expand laterally, by coalescence within the urban ring, or inwards, into the agricultural heartland, it can only grow outwards. Short of unplanned sprawl, two possibilities suggest themselves here. One is the establishment of a green belt, on the London model, separating the Randstad from an outer ring of towns and cities, old and new, surrounding it. The other, which the 1958 study chose in preference to the idea of the green belt, is expansion along the main transport routes – road, rail and water – in radial lines extending outwards from the Randstad. These zones of growth would themselves be separated by wedges of open land which could continue the agricultural buffer zones of the Randstad.

Four possibilities offer themselves for this sort of linear expansion: northwards, north-eastwards, eastwards and south-westwards. The first and third of these are the more conventional. To the north, development can be guided into a series of existing towns within the area known as Kennemerland, north of the North Sea Canal and the IJmuiden steel works, as far as the old cheese town of Alkmaar and a little beyond. With the completion of Bijlermeer in the mid-1970s, Amsterdam's next major development was to the north-west, in Purmerend. To the east, the Randstad must not be allowed to spill out beyond Utrecht into the fine forest and heath country of the Utrecht hills. Here, a positive policy of decentralization must guide growth into the small towns on the far eastern side of these hills, lying in the Gelderse Valley south of Amersfoort. This valley has already demonstrated its capacity to take light industry, and it may eventually form a continuous industrial zone from Amersfoort south to Arnhem and so nearly to the German frontier (maps 4.1 and 4.5). In the early 1970s it was proposed to concentrate growth in this area around the small town of Leusden.

The revolutionary proposals are the other two; for in them the Dutch have sought to relieve the problems of the Randstad by developing outwards on to new land (map 4.4). To the north-east, the drainage of the Zuiderzee polders reached a critical stage in 1968, when the dike enclosing the South Flevoland polder was completed and the polder itself began to become dry land. For this substantially changed the geography of the Netherlands: a substantial area of new land existed next to one of the most heavily populated parts of the Randstad joining it with the main agricultural northern region. Almost immediately the Dutch opened a new highway – Rijksweg (National Highway) 6 – across this polder and the adjacent East Flevoland polder, which was drained in 1955-7. By 1969, via a bridge on to the older North East Polder, it had joined the national capital, Amsterdam, direct to the major city of the northern Netherlands, Groningen, reducing journey time between the two by as much as an hour. There will also be a rail link, to be completed by 1988.

This new motorway will serve the new capital of the new southern polders – Lelystad, named after Cornelius Lely, the nineteenth-century engineer who conceived the whole Zuiderzee drainage scheme, which lies on the north-west corner of the East Flevoland polder. Lelystad is already less than an hour's journey from Amsterdam; it stands near the mouth of a new stretch of water, the Oostvaardersdiep, which will bring 2,000-ton ships from Amsterdam and the North Sea. So Lelystad, and the land along the route to Amsterdam, are uniquely fitted to relieve the population pressure in the capital and its suburbs. Though most of the new polders will be reserved for agriculture and recreation, this Amsterdam – Lelystad strip will be urbanized: the main concentrations will be at the western end of the South Flevoland polder, next to Amsterdam, and around Lelystad near the junction of the East and South Flevoland polders.

Later, in the late 1980s, it is planned to drain the last Zuiderzee polder: Markerwaard, north of South Flevoland, and separated from it by the Oostvaardersdiep. The plan was still controversial throughout the 1970s, though by 1981 agreement seemed likely on a smaller reclamation scheme than originally planned. The southern strip of the new polder, with direct access to Lelystad, will also be available for urban growth; although, with falling population projections, it was being suggested that this would more logically provide a site for Amsterdam's new airport, the idea was apparently buried for good by 1981.

In 1964 Lelystad was still little more than a collection of temporary buildings along a dike; it received its first people in 1967, and by 1980 had close on 40,000 towards an eventual target of 100,000. Its major problem was still communications: some 40 per cent of its employed population commuted to Amsterdam, and the direct 45-minute rail link to Amsterdam was not scheduled to open until 1988. At the south-west corner of the South Flevoland polder, next to the new bridge to the mainland of the Gooi and thus the nearest polder site to Amsterdam, the new town of Almere received its first

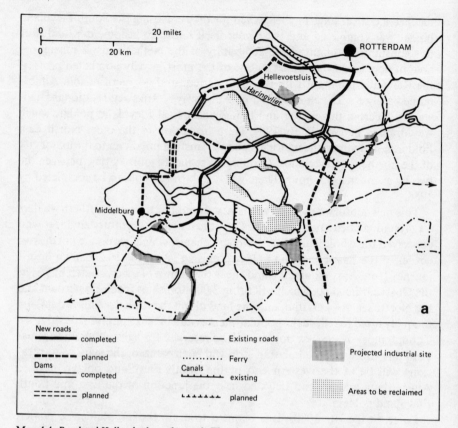

Map 4.4 *Randstad Holland: planned growth*. The planners' strategy is to divert growth outwards. (a) Southwards: reclamation of the delta region will allow a new town at Hellevoetsluis on the Haringvliet. (b) North and north-eastwards: development can take place parallel to the coast in north Kennemerland, and in parts of the polders, which will become an extensior of the Amsterdam conurbation, especially around the new towns of Lelystad, 'polder capital', and Almere.

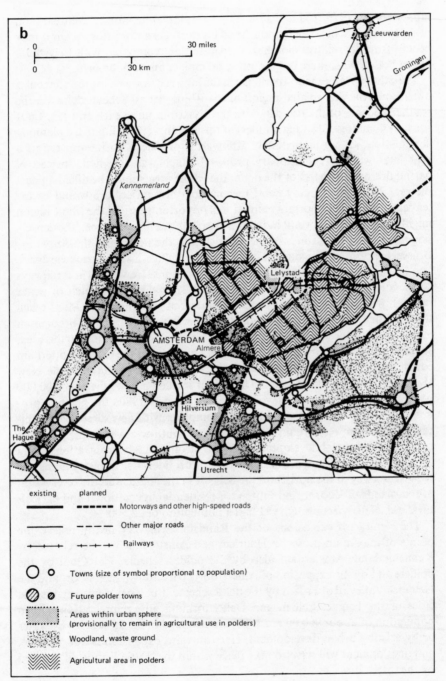

b

0 _____ 30 miles

0 _____ 30 km

Leeuwarden

Groningen

Kennemerland

Lelystad

AMSTERDAM
Almere

Hilversum

The
Hague

Utrecht

existing	planned	
▬▬▬	▬ ▬ ▬	Motorways and other high-speed roads
─────	─ ─ ─	Other major roads
+─+─+	+─+─+	Railways

○ ○ Towns (size of symbol proportional to population)

⬤ ⬤ Future polder towns

▓▓▓ Areas within urban sphere
(provisionally to remain in agricultural use in polders)

░░░ Woodland, waste ground

〰〰〰 Agricultural area in polders

105

inhabitants in 1976, and had 12,000 by 1981; it planned for an eventual total of up to 250,000 in six neighbourhood clusters. As a dormitory town it may benefit from its relative closeness to Amsterdam compared with Lelystad – but in both towns, there is a big stress on indigenous employment.

The other development – perhaps, in the long run, an even more spectacular one – concerns the isolated region of the Rhine–Maas–Scheldt delta, on the southern border of the Randstad. In the disastrous flood early in 1953, 1,601 square kilometres (618 square miles) of this region were inundated; a planning commission, set up immediately afterwards, produced an interim report a year later with a revolutionary proposal which was accepted. Instead of partial drainage of parts of the delta, the whole area should be diked against the sea. There were many good reasons for this: agriculture would be extended, there were important recreational opportunities, and the whole region might become an important industrial area, lying as it did between the densely populated industrial zones of the Randstad to the north and the Antwerp–Brussels region to the south. The key to the delta's historic backwardness, and to its future development, was communications. New roads and railways could connect Rotterdam direct with the Haringvliet, the stretch of water through which over half the combined waters of the Rhine and Maas reach the sea; then almost undeveloped, this waterway could rapidly become an extension of the great port of Rotterdam. The 1958 study, taking up this idea, suggested that a major part of the overspill problem of the city of Rotterdam could be met by development on the island of Voorne, between the New Waterway and the Haringvliet. This might include a new town for 200,000 people at the village of Hellevoetsluis. By the early 1980s the gigantic programme of public works was virtually complete, with new direct communication lines from Rotterdam southwards and south-westwards; the plans for urban and industrial development foresaw strong axial concentrations along the northern, eastern and southern edges, with tidewater industry along the New Waterway in the north and the Scheldt in the south, and the reservation of the islands of Voorne and Putten for residential, recreational and agricultural use. Hellevoetsluis by 1981 had a population of 22,500.

These outward extensions of the Randstad will very neatly relieve the points of maximum pressure: Haarlem and Amsterdam will be relieved by Kennemerland, Amsterdam also by the polder scheme, Het Gooi by the polders and by the expansion of Amersfoort, Utrecht by Amersfoort and the Gelderse Valley, Rotterdam by the delta scheme. But a problem remains: the cities of the Hague, Leiden and Delft, forming an agglomeration with a population of about 900,000 in 1980, are hemmed in on three sides by water or by existing urban development. Here outward expansion is not possible, and development will have to take place within the 'Little Randstad' formed by the three cities.

The Second (1966) Report

Policy for the Randstad, then, is based on two suppositions: one, that net migration into the west can be reduced roughly to zero; two, that the growth of the Randstad itself can be channelled into certain areas and out of certain other areas. The question is whether these suppositions can be made real. This depends on the effectiveness of government policy, both at central and at local level.

These outgrowths make it all the more necessary to protect carefully the intervening rural land. So the Second Report on Physical Planning in the Netherlands, published in 1966, called for an extension of protection policies from the green heart of the Randstad to other belts of open land outside the Randstad proper, but likely to be affected by its planned outward spread; they included the open land along the Rhine waterway, the heart of the delta region and the wooded Peel region around Breda and Tilburg. At the same time, the report stressed, the buffer zones which separated the Randstad cities had to be carefully preserved; to this end, the government offered subsidies to local authorities to buy up threatened land.

The Second Report went much further, though; in some detail, albeit diagrammatically, it sketched out a planned structure for the urban areas of the Netherlands around the year 2000. This structure is based on the principle of concentrated deconcentration: strong concentrations of people, homes, services and jobs at the city regional scale are internally decentralized into a variety of grouped sub-units of different sizes. Map 4.5 shows four of these basic building blocks, ranging from a village unit of 5,000 people (unit A) with intermediate units of 15,000 (B) and 60,000 (C) to a city of 250,000 (D). Such a structure, the report claims, has a number of advantages. First, it is almost inevitable because of the constraints on further development; people are showing that they prefer a more dispersed form of living than in the past, but unlimited dispersion would be impossible in a country as densely populated as the Netherlands is likely to be by 2000. Secondly, the scheme provides for a variety of different styles of living to suit different tastes, ranging from the city to the village but with a major emphasis on small scale units at fairly low residential densities, which many people appear to want. Thirdly, it provides fairly short work journeys to major concentrations and employment. And fourthly, it provides good levels of services, either locally or via good transport to higher order centres nearby.

The broad regional policy must be the responsibility of the central government in the Hague. Here the critical question is whether to rely on positive measures of attraction and inducement in the underdeveloped areas of the north and the east; or whether restrictive measures are not also needed in the west. The government remains convinced that the problem of the Randstad is not serious enough to merit restrictions on industrial location like those

107

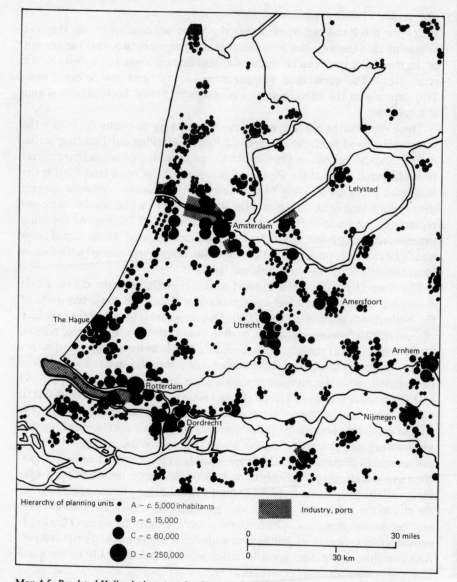

Map 4.5 *Randstad Holland: the principle of concentrated deconcentration*. The Second Report on Physical Planning (1966) suggested local groupings of differently-sized settlements to give a choice of residential life styles within limited commuting range. Unfortunately, in practice decentralization proved more explosive.

adopted in the London region since 1945 and in the Paris region since 1955. They prefer to use the possibility of restrictions, in the words of the 1956 study, 'as a stick behind the door' in case gentler measures fail. And they rely on government aid to the unfortunate regions of the Netherlands, together with the direction of public investment: the decision, in the late 1950s, to drain the South Flevoland polder before Markerwaard, was taken deliberately with the idea of improving access to the problem region of the northern Netherlands. The experience of the 1960s and 1970s, with the net migration flow *out of* the west, seems to justify government policy.

The planned growth of the Randstad itself, on the other hand, involves close co-operation among different levels of government – national, provincial or regional, and local. And difficult problems of conflict of interest inevitably arise. The philosophy of the Netherlands government, as expressed in the Planning Law of 1962, is to give the maximum possible planning power to the municipalities. Under the 1962 Act, regional plans, showing broad land uses, will still be made by planning offices of the provincial government, and broad national lines of planning policy will be laid down in the Hague. But only the municipal plans will be legally binding, though the provincial authorities' regional plans may restrict building where 'extra-municipal' forces are involved. Yet the regional plans have clearly a critical role to play in guiding the growth of the Randstad, as the government recognized when they asked for plans for certain critical areas to be prepared as a matter of priority; they include northern Kennemerland, where it is critical to provide for a rapid growth of population north of IJmuiden and the North Sea Canal, and the Utrecht Hills, where it is necessary to protect the area as an agricultural and recreational zone for the benefit of the people of the Randstad. The test will be whether the municipal plans follow reasonably faithfully the guiding lines laid down in national and regional plans. And here there is room for doubt. The municipalities of the Netherlands are small, as were the planning authorities in England until the 1947 Act gave power to bigger authorities. In 1980 no less than 246 out of 994 municipalities had less than 5,000 people each. All municipalities, regardless of size, have equal powers – though there is a requirement for provincial government approval and even for national intervention should serious disagreement arise. The danger will be that many will see only their own problems in isolation, and will be tempted to allow urban expansion where it should not occur, or to prohibit it where it should be encouraged. And it is doubtful whether they can pursue an active land policy, as is already practised by the larger municipalities, so as to prevent speculation in development land.

The problems here are intimately bound up with the existing structure of local government in the Netherlands, which – as so often the world over – is failing to keep pace with the rapid growth of urban populations. Thus in

109

Amsterdam it was agreed that there should be a large-scale extension out from the south-east corner of the city, but building – and hence the renewal programme in the inner city – was held up while it was determined whether the city boundaries should be extended, or whether a completely new municipality should be created out of the small authorities at present governing the area. (Finally, in the late 1960s and early 1970s, the new town of Bijlermeer was built outside the city boundaries.) Many smaller towns, both within the agricultural heart of the Randstad and outside it, are finding difficulty in getting boundary extensions, and this is preventing them from performing their proper function of taking overspill population from the bigger cities. The government, in their 1960 report, frankly said that boundary reform must be speeded up. They stressed also the need for inter-municipal co-operation and even perhaps eventually for super-municipal authorities.

The truth is that many important jobs in the growing Randstad cannot be performed adequately by the existing authorities. Two important cases are the protection of the buffer zones, and the provision of urban transport over wide suburban areas. In the first case, the government recognize that the sums involved are beyond the purses of local authorities, and that the government in the Hague must provide them. The same goes for much of the investment that will be necessary to provide adequate planned recreation areas, such as the proposed park running through the heart of the Randstad between Amsterdam and Rotterdam. With transport, the steady growth in commuting from suburbs beyond city limits has caused the Dutch planners to look with favour at the idea of a super-municipal authority on the model of London Transport.

By the 1970s, in fact, it was embarrassingly evident that the government's broad regional planning objectives were endangered by weakness in local implementation. The green heart of the Randstad was in danger of being progressively built over; during the 1960s, it had actually experienced higher rates of population growth than the nation as a whole, as the pressures for low density living proved too strong for the local municipalities' planning controls. The late Professor Steigenga, one of the most distinguished Dutch urban planners, was writing in 1972 that the urban areas of the Randstad were in danger of turning inside out on the American model, thus making of the Randstad a vast, highly dispersed, non-hierarchical structure: the very antithesis of what the official government planners had proposed in their Second Report on Physical Planning.

The Third (1974–7) Report

By the early 1970s, it was plain in the Netherlands – as elsewhere in western Europe – that the policies of the mid-1960s were in important respects no longer relevant. On the one hand, certain basic assumptions had ceased to apply. Thus the Randstad was no longer expected to grow rapidly; there was strong out-migration from it to the south and east, and its cities were losing people; contrary to expectations, long-distance commuting was on the increase as people travelled from their new homes in the south and east to jobs in the Randstad; car ownership had risen fivefold during the 1960s; there had been an evident failure to apply the policies of concentrated deconcentration at the local level, and the green heart of the Randstad had been massively invaded. Yet, on the other hand, both the energy crisis and the new strength of ecological arguments suggested a planning policy that moved in a different direction: towards conservation of energy and land, protection of the natural environment, reduction of the need for mobility and greater concern to reduce social inequality.

Thus the Third Report on Physical Planning, published in 1974-7, was forced into a quite drastic reappraisal of the policies of the 1960s. One major casualty was the idea of large-scale planned movement from the Randstad; developments like decentralization of government offices from the Hague, the new report suggested, had taken this quite far enough. Instead, the first aim should be to encourage a good urban structure within the Randstad itself, and at its edges. To that end, the green heart should be resolutely protected, as should the buffer zones that separate the Randstad cities and thus give access to the more open country of the northern, eastern and southern Netherlands. First mentioned in the 1960 report, the buffer zones by 1976 had acquired a new function: to act as recreational zones for the neighbouring Randstad cities. Yet at the same time, planners must recognize that there was a basic uncertainty about many basic variables: the rate and nature of economic growth, the locational preferences of industrialists and homeowners, the future role of the city. So planning had to be based on flexibility.

Tentatively, the Third Report looked at alternative models of development. One concentrated development in certain areas at a rather high density (54 dwellings to the hectare, 22 to the acre, net), with most travel by foot, bicycle and bus; most of the housing would be near city centres; there would be an emphasis on rehabilitation, and large amounts of open space; planning would be based on small city regions with short travel distances. This might prove a good alternative where it was still feasible; but in the Randstad, generally, it was not.

A second alternative spread the population more widely over the western Netherlands, with net densities around 36 dwellings to the hectare (14 to the acre), and travel times to work of up to 25 or 30 minutes by public transport. Some new residential areas would be developed in attractive residential zones; the existing residential function in urban areas would be preserved. A third alternative would closely resemble this, but with higher densities (54 to the hectare, 22 to the acre; even higher in the cities), concentrated near urban

111

centres, and with a great deal of rehabilitation. The Third Report tentatively suggests that in the Randstad these two alternatives may be the most appropriate: the higher-density variant in and around the largest cities, the lower-density variant elsewhere.

The last alternative followed the trends of recent years. New residential areas would be built at low densities; there would be widespread renewal in the towns; open space norms would not be very stringently applied; there would be widespread commuting by car over distances up to 35 kilometres (20 miles); in consequence the largest cities would have to adopt drastic measures to control traffic. The government planners clearly considered that this alternative, if continued, would place intolerable strain on city centres and would threaten to destroy both the green heart of the Randstad and its external buffer zones.

So finally the stress was on a city region solution, with growth centres close to the bigger cities to provide homes and some local services within easy daily reach. Many of these would be on the outer edges of the main north and south wings of the Randstad. Each of these centres should be under the control of a single municipality, with a single development agency; to that end, transfers of territory might be necessary. The government would supply subsidies for land purchase, infrastructure development and other essential purposes. Within the cities the emphasis would be on selective renewal or rehabilitation to improve the quality of the housing stock, but undertaken so as not to threaten the existing lower-income inhabitants; the main emphasis would be on preserving the human activities and the unique character of the city. Densities would be up to 80-100 dwellings to the net residential hectare (32-40 to the acre) in the largest cities, 40-60 (16-24) elsewhere; commuting distances would be kept below 35 to 40 minutes by the development of new public transport links, including railways and light railways.

The main emphasis of the 1970s, therefore, was not outward from the Randstad but inward (map 4.6). The cities were to be protected from decay; their centres were to be encouraged; new residential areas were to be provided close to jobs, both in the older inner urban areas and in new districts within easy reach. Therefore, the cities and the areas around them were to be planned as integral city-regional wholes. To provide for new households and improve living standards, 195,000 extra homes would be needed in the Randstad between 1980 and 2000; the report suggested that, while some would be provided in more distant growth towns, the great majority should be provided in so-called growth centres close to the cities of the north and south wings of the Randstad. By 1980, four growth towns had been designated to house 562,000 people (by 1990) outside the Randstad: Breda, Helmond, Groningen and Zwolle. In addition the Dutch planners had designated thirteen growth centres for a total 1990 population of 864,000. These were partly within – or

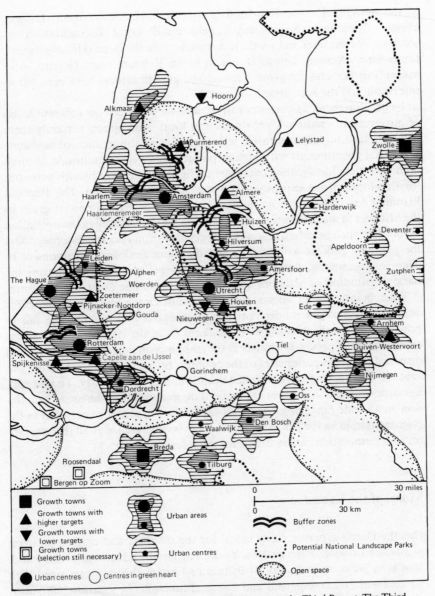

Map 4.6 *Randstad Holland: principles of urban development in the Third Report.* The Third Report on Physical Planning (1974–7) suggests that provision must be made for continued decentralization from the Randstad cities, particularly by growth centres on the outsides of the two urbanized 'wings'. Buffer zones will separate the major cities within the wings.

113

at the margin of – the Randstad (Purmerend, Haarlemeremeer, Huizen, Houten, Nieuwegen, Spijkenisse, Capelle aan de IJssel (Barendrecht-Smit-schoek), Zoetermeer) and partly just outside it: in the delta (Hellevoetsluis), the polders (Almere, Lelystad) and in north Kennemerland (Hoorn, Alk-maar). Further sites for growth towns and growth centres have been left in reserve should the need arise.

To develop these, agreements will be necessary between the different levels of government – national, provincial and local. And almost certainly there will be a need for administrative reform, including the creation of new-style provincial governments with greater powers vis-à-vis the multitude of small municipalities. Lastly, the government will need to be ready with subsidies for development on expensive land and for urban renewal. The Physical Planning Act will have to be reformed, with better defined powers given to the Minister to make directives; amendments will be required in the legislation on matters such as urban renewal, soil conservation and water supply. And the planning process will need to become more flexible and responsive to changing conditions, with broad structure plans (*Streekplannen*) showing the basic distribution of activities and land uses in outline diagrammatic form.

Thus, in important respects, the evolution of Dutch planning in the 1970s and 1980s follows a model that earlier emerged in London. The fall in population growth, coupled with the flight from the cities, forces a radical reorientation of policy. No longer is the emphasis on longer-distance regional dispersal to the far peripheries of the country. Instead, the concern is to try to save the great cities from continued decline and eventual decay. To that end, resources and physical plans are focused on maintaining a balanced popula-tion and a wide range of jobs and services close to the city's heart. But in the Netherlands, as in the London region, there is no evidence at all that govern-ment determination can by itself turn the tide.

Moral of the Randstad

Has the Dutch experience any moral for the planners and citizens of urban giants like London, Paris or New York? The unique advantage of the Rand-stad is its *polycentric* quality. If Britain or France also had developed their government and commercial and financial functions in separate but nearby cities, they would suffer less intractable problems today; but history decided otherwise. Yet it must be remembered that history is always on the move. The central areas of London and Paris have seen profound changes since 1900, both in form and function; they will see more yet, and it is not beyond the ability of government to make these changes radical ones. If only a part

114

of the British or French government machine was decentralized to a site within an hour's journey of the capital, there seems little doubt that a certain re-orientation of the London or Paris regions would result; they could eventually become, to a limited extent, more like the Randstad in form.

The Netherlands offer another moral, especially for the British, who have led Europe in many aspects of physical planning. The British early grasped the problem of metropolitan growth, and their answer was the green belt. But the green belt is admirably adapted to a city with a static population; as we have already seen in London, with a rapidly-growing population it creates many problems and is subject to serious pressures. Coming later to the problem, and faced with the necessity to plan for growth, the Dutch have rejected the belt in favour of the linear extension and the green wedge: a solution which allows unlimited extension along the transport lines, where much of the existing development has taken place, while keeping all the advantages of open country between those lines. There seems little doubt that, for most of the still growing world cities of the present time, the Dutch solution is the right model.

The principal of concentrated deconcentration, too, demonstrates the hard-headed realism of Dutch city regional planning. It accepts the social trend towards greater dispersal of the population in search of space and more tranquil living conditions, but attempts to balance this by good accessibility to nearby urban jobs and services. It promises maximum choice of living environments, of job opportunities, and of services of all kinds. It is a model well worth study by other nations.

One final word of doubt must enter in: it concerns implementation. Paper plans may be admired, but the final test must be whether they can be made to work on the ground. Up to now, Dutch urban planning has been stronger at the high conceptual level than at the mundane level of effective enforcement. It would be a pity indeed if such essentially realistic, flexible plans were finally frustrated by failures at the local government level. But that, in the 1980s, is too clearly the danger.

5 Moscow

London, Paris, the Randstad: all these great metropolitan regions belong to the world which, for lack of a more accurate and meaningful title, we call the capitalist world. The socio-economic historian might well conclude that, in some way, they were a product of the evolution of capitalism. As chapter 1 has already argued, that view would not take account of the fundamental causes of modern urban growth. For the communist world has its giant metropolitan cities too; and no better example exists than the city which (despite Peking's insistent rival claims) may fairly be called the world city of communism. The city of Moscow, in 1980, had a population of over 8 million; and it was the centre of a great urban complex containing satellite cities and towns, which altogether numbered well over 9 million people. Thus, after London and Paris, Moscow is the greatest urban complex of continental Europe.

Growth and spread: Moscow and *sputniki*

This fact may surprise western observers. But more surprising is Moscow's growth. The city's population was 360,000 in 1860, the year befor Tsar Alexander II abolished serfdom, and 1.7 million in 1917, the year of the October revolution; by 1935, helped by the transfer of capital functions from Leningrad, it had risen to 3.66 million. At this point the authorities acted. The Central Committee of the Communist Party of the USSR had, in 1931, already declared itself against the further growth of big cities and from 1932 the policy was to restrict further industrial growth in Moscow and Leningrad. In the 1935 General Plan of Reconstruction for the City of Moscow, limitation of the city's growth was made into a central planning objective, perhaps for the first time in city planning history anywhere. The future population target was to be 5 million, which the city would reach eventually by natural increase alone; net immigration was to be cut to zero.

Even by the 1939 Census, despite close attempts to limit migration into Moscow for work, the city's population had reached 4,132,000 – 80 per cent of the ultimate planning limit. The war undoubtedly brought some relief, as many people and activities were evacuated eastwards; yet by the first postwar census of the Soviet Union, in 1959, Moscow's population had risen to 5,046,000 – a figure already above the ultimate 1935 limit. Nor was this any longer a meaningful figure; for on 18 August 1960 a decree more than doubled the area of the city, to incorporate the suburban areas which had grown up outside the former limits. Thus, by a stroke of the pen, nearly one million people were added to the city's population; and it became quite clear that the 'ultimate' target figure of 1935 had long been passed. By the 1979 Census the population of the extended city had reached 8,011,000, having added nearly one million in the nine years since the previous count – a rate comparable with the faster-growing western European capitals in their peak growth during the 1950s and 1960s, but by the 1970s a memory of the past there. Though much of the increase in Moscow may well represent natural increase of the city's own population, in most years there has been a balance of in-migration which has made Moscow a city of young, working-age people. By the start of 1981 the estimate was 8,203,000.

However, even this extended city of Moscow is only part of a much larger urban whole (map 5.1). The Soviet geographer Davidovich, as long ago as 1961, made a careful estimate of the population of the Soviet satellite cities (*goroda-sputniki*), defined as: 'those cities, towns and villages that develop around a large central city and are related to it by common features in the life of the population – commuting to places of employment and for cultural and other service purposes (the second order satellites)'. These satellites, some fifteen in number, had a population of nearly 2 million in 1979 as against only 1.2 million twenty years earlier. They should not be regarded as planned satellites like the London or Paris new towns – though some of the more recent among them have this character. The older ones were developed immediately after the 1935 plan, as part of the limitation of the city's growth. Many are one-industry towns specializing in a single branch of engineering.

Some *sputniki* are considerable towns in their own right: for instance My-tishchi (139,000 in 1979) and Lyubertsy (160,000), which are part of the green belt ring, and Podolsk (202,000), Elektrostal (139,000) and Noginsk (119,000) outside it. They are grouped along the main railway lines, and some even merge together, especially along the earliest electrified lines. The nearest of them – towns within 35 kilometres (20 miles) from the centre, and only 50–55 minutes' travelling time away – are, many of them, big commuter towns: Odintsovo, Balaskikha, Pushkino. They send 600,000 commuters into Moscow every working day. But, by the late 1960s, the commuting ring had broadened to take in towns like Serpukhov, Mozhaisk and Kashira – up to 100 kilometres (60 miles) distant and up to 2 hours' travelling time away. In fact, by 1980 it could be said that the satellite ring was spreading so as to

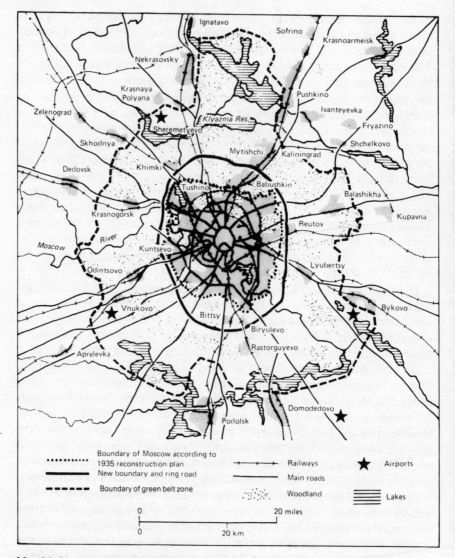

Map 5.1 *Moscow: city and region.* Moscow's city limits were extended in 1960 up to the ring motorway, then under construction. The population of this extended city is now over 8 million. But outside this, in the green belt zone, 16 kilometres (10 miles) wide, and beyond, the satellite towns (*goroda-sputniki*), with close commuting and other ties to the city, brought the total regional population to nearly 10 million.

become coterminous with the Moscow administrative region (*oblast*); this, together with the city, had a 1979 Census population of 14,371,000, representing an increase of no less than 3,400,000 since 1970. About one-quarter of this growth had occurred in the *sputniki* themselves (Table 5.1).

Table 5.1 The Moscow region and its constituent parts, 1979

	Area (square km.)	Population (thousands) 1979	Population change (per cent) 1970-9
Moscow City	886	8,011	+13.5
Satellites	7,120	1,987	+20.8
City plus satellites	*8,000*	*9,998*	*+14.8*
Outer ring	39,000	4,372	+ 5.9
Moscow city and			
oblast	*47,000*	*14,371*	*+12.0*
(UN definition)		(7,757)	(+9.2)

Sources: Census, 1979; United Nations, *Patterns of Urban and Rural Population Growth* (*Population Studies*, 68), New York: United Nations, 1980.

Moscow's future

Official Soviet policy is still to restrain city growth – Moscow's in particular. But that limitation does not extend to the surrounding suburban ring, where extensions of existing towns, and the development of new *sputniki*, are seen as ways of channelling city growth outside the city limits. Soviet planners do not see the continued growth of the capital region as somehow perilous to the nation's economic and social health, as British or French planners might. Metropolitan congestion, which obsesses west European planners, is a barely comprehensible idea in a country as big as the Soviet Union; the aim is rather to channel more people and resources into the still underdeveloped areas outside the western, European part of the Soviet Union. This aim has been pursued with some success: from 1959 to 1970 over 60 per cent, and from 1970 to 1979 over 67 per cent, of growth took place in the south-west (the Soviet Union's 'Sunbelt') and the east. This partly reflects migration, partly a much higher rate of natural increase in the Asiatic USSR.

But broad regional analysis omits what is perhaps the most significant feature of Soviet population growth: the growth of the cities. In 1939, 32 per cent of the Soviet Union, 60.4 million, was classed as urban; in 1959, 48 per cent, 99.8 million; in 1970, 56 per cent, 136.0 million. During the 1970s the biggest cities grew fastest, absolutely and relatively; by 1979 there were eighteen 'million cities' in the Soviet Union.

The changing economic base

Some three-fifths of the total increase in urban population, between 1939 and 1959, represented migrants from the countryside; after 1959 natural increase and migration were more evenly balanced. This great shift out of agriculture is common to all peasant or ex-peasant countries, in both eastern and western Europe; it has contributed to the growth of Paris and the Randstad and in the USSR, as elsewhere, it is still continuing. (In 1981, 20 per cent of the total labour force was still in agriculture and forestry: a high proportion by western standards.) This shift will benefit all other sectors, including manufacturing and construction, but above all the service industries like education and public health, or trade, public catering and supply. Here today there is a sharp divergence between American and Soviet employment patterns: the United States employs close on 70 per cent of its labour force in the tertiary sector, the Soviet Union (in 1981) 41 per cent. The Soviet planners claim that the American figures represent a waste of labour resources, but they are providing for a rapid increase in their own figures; for the service system is on their own admission still inadequate. In 1976, it was stated that about half of total employment in Moscow was in the 'non-productive' sector; 1980 figures suggested that more than 50 per cent of Moscow's total employment was in services.

In the capitalist west observers are all too aware of the fact that many service trades tend to be disproportionately concentrated in the metropolitan cities. It is difficult to discover how far this is also true of the Soviet Union; but there are some pointers. One concerns the administrative machine. Up to 1957 the vast Soviet planning apparatus was highly centralized in Moscow. Then, a fundamental reversal took place: major economic planning went to the economic planning regions, originally sixteen in number but then increased to eighteen. Of course many of these regions are concentrated in the Moscow area and the areas around it, especially to the south; for this central region contains almost one-fifth of the population of the USSR and more than one-quarter of its industry. But the net effect has been to take many administrative planning decisions out of Moscow, and to put them in the provincial cities.

In other activities within the service sector, possibilities for decentralization may be more limited. Moscow remains the main transport focus of Soviet Russia, with eleven main radiating railways and two major airports – Vnukovo and Sheremetyevo (which supplanted Vnukovo as the international airport in 1960), supplemented since March 1964 by a new airport, one of the world's biggest, at Domodedovo. Moscow is the centre of all forms of entertainment, from the Moscow Arts Theatre and the Bolshoi Ballet to the great new all-Union television station at Ostankino, which was started in August 1963 and completed in 1967. This station not only provides the central technical link between the existing television networks in the USSR; it contains also a large administrative building, to house all the editorial offices of the USSR central television system. Moscow is also the unquestioned centre of the USSR's developing tourist trade, with an ambitious programme of hotel construction, including one 6,000-guest hotel – the Rossya, Europe's biggest – completed in 1967. The USSR's very extensive range of higher educational institutions also shows a pronounced clustering in Moscow – especially the higher research institutions. Here are found the USSR Academy of Sciences with its many specialized sections, the Lenin Library (largest in the USSR and in the world), the Moscow University with 40,000 students, more than fifty specialized institutes of higher education, three hundred scientific research institutes, and the Lenin Museum. Altogether, scientific workers numbered 233,000 in 1971, one-quarter of the total for the USSR. There were also 600,000 students in higher education. The problem is that, although industry could develop technologically with an actual reduction in the labour force, the chief problem in controlling Moscow's growth lies with the research institutions, design organizations and bureaux.

In factory industry Moscow's attractive power is less sure, though the Moscow region still accounts for 20 per cent of the total industrial output of the USSR. The traditional industry of the Moscow region, textiles, has been somewhat displaced since the October revolution by the engineering group of industries – the most characteristic growth industry of modern metropolitan cities the world over. By 1970 over 55 per cent of total manufacturing employment was in the engineering and metal processing group. These industries have shown the largest increases in volume of production of all industrial groups in the USSR since 1917. Especially during their period of rapid growth under the early Five-Year Plans, skilled labour proved to be the limiting factor in their development; and, in so far as this labour existed, it was concentrated in the Moscow region. So, critical decisions were taken to set up plants here; the existence of the plants created complexes of component suppliers (thirty-four factories in the Moscow area produce components for the Gorki motor-car plant, 600 kilometres, 400 miles away), and the complexes cannot now easily be shifted. Besides vehicle and vehicle component manufacture, which are still disproportionately concentrated in the Moscow–Gorki region, other important Moscow industries include machine tools, precision instruments like watches and calculating machines, and consumer goods like refrigerators and sewing machines. Of these, machine tools employed most workers in 1970, though instrument-making had grown fastest in the previous decade – indicating the increasingly science-based character of Moscow industry.

Admittedly, industrial expansion has occurred rapidly east of the Urals. By 1960, for instance, well over one-third of all Soviet machinery was produced there. But it appears that a great deal of this activity represents the production of heavy goods which incorporate local raw material and which may be uneconomic to send over long distances – construction equipment, power station equipment, mining and chemical plant. The same goes for other types of industry. Current Soviet plans for the development of the eastern regions – eastern Siberia for instance – visualize them chiefly, for a long time ahead, as producers of cheap fuel and power and of products incorporating that fuel and power: steel, ferro-alloys and synthetic chemicals. Official plans, developed during the 1960s and confirmed in 1971, provided for two hundred industrial enterprises – those orientated towards raw materials and transport – to move out. But high-technology engineering with a big research component, including electronics, will stay in the Moscow region, especially in the satellites – and this, since the 1950s, has been the fast-growing sector. And it will be a long time before eastern Siberia takes over traditional Muscovite staples like printing and publishing. In any event, the centralized planning system has meant that it is easier to achieve targets through power and influence exerted at the centre; hence managers, aided by Ministry officials, resist pressures to move out.

During the 1960s and 1970s, Soviet industrial economists sought increasingly to analyse locational problems in a rigorous way, using quantitative models. But underneath, the realities of the system mean that location is often a matter, not of rationalities, but of political power and influence. Undoubtedly many features of Soviet economy and society contribute to this: the tremendous premium put until recently on production at the expense of almost any other consideration; the division of responsibility for many aspects of urban construction between different ministries and authorities, frequently with contradictory interests; and the relative weakness of the city planning organizations themselves.

Planning within the Moscow region

Within the Moscow region, planning is the responsibility of a special organization: the Institute of the General Plan (GLAV APU MOSKVA). In west European or North American terms, the Institute is a regional planning organization. It is concerned with the broad problems of employment, population, housing, communications, open space and the green belt, and the planning of satellite towns within the Moscow region. It works through plans on a scale of 1:10,000 which are monitored by a state planning agency GOSGRAJDANSTROI (the Committee of State for Civil Construction and Architecture); after approval the plans are handed over for detailed development to a building organization, MOSSTROI, organized in thirteen sections covering various sectors of the city. The Institute uses varied skills: it employs economists, geographers, demographers, engineers and architects.

The housing drive
The broad objectives of planning are clear. Within the city limits as extended in 1960 – that is within the belt motorway, which was opened in 1962 and which completely encircles the city at a radius of about 18 kilometres (11 miles) from the centre – the intention (not realized in the event) has been to stabilize population, and the emphasis is on a rehousing programme of awe-inspiring scale, and speed of execution. It is clear that during the Stalinist period, despite the ambitious schemes outlined in the 1935 Moscow plan, housing took a low priority behind military needs and the development of industry. As a result, after the Second World War the USSR suffered from an acute deficiency of urban housing: Maurice F. Parkins has estimated that on average there were 4.02 persons to each habitable room in 1950. But in 1956 the Twentieth Congress of the Communist Party of the Soviet Union decreed an end to the housing shortage within twenty years – thereby marking, perhaps, the first significant shift in emphasis towards consumer goods in Soviet planning. Overall, throughout the whole period 1956–70, housing production was remarkably even at around 2.3 million dwellings per year, of an average size of 42–42.5 square metres (452–7 square feet), making the USSR the world's most prolific housebuilder. In Moscow alone the plan was to complete 2.2 million apartments between 1961 and 1980, by which time every family would have its own dwelling. In fact this was not quite achieved; but between 1971 and 1981 734,000 new dwellings with 37 million square metres of floorspace were finished – an increase in dwellings of 39 per cent. And by 1981 no less than 85 per cent of apartments had been finished since 1956 – virtually all of them in the outer part of the city.

This extraordinary rate of progress was largely made possible by the development of industrialized building techniques using factory-built parts, assembled on site. As recently as 1957 one-third of the total floorspace of urban housing consisted of individually built homes. But, private housing was condemned as wasteful of land; it was said to take three to five times as much land to house an equivalent number of people compared with four- or five-storey flats, with a consequent steep rise in servicing costs. In August 1962, therefore, the Central Committee of the Communist Party of the USSR and the Council of Ministers adopted a resolution which aimed at replacing

123

the construction of individual housing, progressively, by multi-storey co-operative buildings. This applied to all towns and cities – beginning with the biggest cities where the problem of space was most acute. The co-operatives would be financed by a mixture of contributions from their members and state loans. In 1973 11 per cent of total Moscow housing completions were in the co-operative sector. By then, however, public apartment construction was the norm.

The aim of Soviet housing policy was to eliminate the worst aspects of the housing shortage by 1970; by then, all families in overcrowded and substandard housing were rehoused. In order to fulfil the first stage of the programme, however, standards of space were deliberately cut to the minimum in 1958, so as to reduce the costs of construction per dwelling by up to 30 per cent and thus make possible an increase within the budget of nearly one-third in the number of dwellings built. This necessarily meant flats, during the 1959–65 planning period, with small halls, combined bathroom and lavatory, and some rooms reached only through other rooms. Space norms in Moscow in 1970 averaged three rooms totalling 60 square metres (646 square feet) for a family of four; actual averages were much lower, less than 10 square metres (108 square feet) per person. It is now planned to raise norms rapidly, to reach one room per person (22 square metres, or 240 square feet) by 1990; this is especially important for housing the bigger families, for whom the standard designs seem to provide rather inadequately at present.

The overriding need for economy has also produced an extraordinary degree of standardization in the design and layout of the big new housing developments like the south-western district of Moscow. More than 50 per cent of state housing in the early 1960s, rising to between 70 and 75 per cent by the end of the seven-year planning period in 1965, consisted of four- and five-storey flats without lifts, which were said to be most economical.

By the early 1970s the emphasis shifted. By then the main emphasis was moving from construction of new housing areas on the Moscow outskirts, to urban renewal of older housing areas nearer the centre; and this was taking the form of high-rise blocks (fifteen storeys), rising from podia with shops and services, and leaving 80 per cent of the ground space open. In other sections, massive prefabricated blocks up to thirty storeys were planned with underground vehicle circulation and servicing. By 1981 56 per cent of the housing stock, as against only 31 per cent in 1971, consisted of structures of nine or more floors. Ironically, this trend towards construction of architectural megastructures was occurring just at the point when in western countries – such as Britain and the United States – architectural ideas were moving in the opposite direction.

The residential areas: failure in planning

Detailed planning of Soviet residential areas is based on the fundamental concept of the 'micro-district' (*mikrorayon*). The Russian word *rayon* means a 'district'; it is also used to indicate an administrative district, roughly of the same order as a borough in British or American practice. The city of Moscow has twenty-nine such *rayons*; the new town of Zelenograd, actually well outside the city limits proper, makes a thirtieth. (Because of this the word *mikrorayon* is sometimes translated, misleading, as 'microborough'.) These areas are ideally between 30 and 50 hectares (75 and 125 acres) in size, housing between 5 and 15 thousand people, together with necessary community services like public restaurants, nurseries, kindergartens, club rooms, public workshops, a library, a swimming pool and a park. The service radius of a micro-district is normally not more than 300–400 metres (1,000–1,300 feet). Because most necessary everyday services can be found there, the city centre then has to provide merely specialized services – a department store, a cinema, a hotel, a car rental centre, higher grade schools and specialized cultural facilities. Clearly the essential idea of the micro-district is the same as that of the 'neighbourhood' in western planning practice: it is that of a unit of life based on local shopping and public services. But by the 1970s, it was recognized that people would demand higher-level services over a wider area.

The point about public services may be more important for Soviet planners than for western ones. Soviet ideology has traditionally stressed that after the transition to communism there will be less role for the family. Children will be brought up communally from an early age; and most meals will be taken, not round the family table, but in a communal dining room. In practice, however, it is clear that Soviet architects and planners have provided traditional family apartments. Nevertheless, Soviet planning philosophy is internally quite consistent: collective dwellings, public rather than private open space, public transport.

Though the concept of the micro-district has remained basic to Soviet ideas of planning since the 1930s, its physical expression has recently changed. The micro-district of the mid-1950s was still typically built in the form of blocks arranged round a closed rectangular courtyard, a type of planning all too familiar from many western housing schemes of pre-1939 vintage. In the USSR, combined with standardized building types and the pseudo-classicist architectural excesses inherited from the Stalin period, it produced an effect of crushing monotony and oppressiveness in some of Moscow's biggest housing projects, notably the enormous development on the Lenin Hills in south-west Moscow, which was being severely criticized in the Moscow press by 1960. Here, despite the hilly nature of the relief, the same rigid geometrical layout was followed everywhere, with only the most minor concessions to the nature of the terrain. Instead of being placed in separate buildings, the shops were put in the ground floors of the residential blocks, so that goods loading often had to take place via the central courtyards, and columns and service ducts within the shops got in the way of staff and customers. It was mistakes like these that led to the new emphasis from the late 1960s on 'three dimensional' planning of massive integrated structures in which servicing functions were buried underground.

Traffic planning

The story of Soviet urban traffic planning is a curiously mixed one: a story of gigantic achievement and of equally colossal failure to seize opportunities. Ever since the 1935 plan, a major concern of Moscow's planners has been the recasting of the transport net. Moscow in 1935 had a typically continental European street plan, composed of straight radial roads, formal squares and ring boulevards. But many of the streets were narrow by twentieth-century standards. The 1935 plan therefore provided a scheme of street widenings and of new arteries which rivalled Haussmann's grandiose projects in nineteenth-century Paris. Though execution of the schemes was delayed by the war, it is evident that during most of Stalin's lifetime they took a much higher priority than more banal programmes like the provision of housing. The central area of Moscow is surrounded by a ring boulevard – the Sadovoye Ring – which was widened so that it rivals in scale many of the great *Ringstrassen* of Hapsburg or Prussian capitals. It was lined by commercial and residential blocks. The radial streets which cut through the older (pre-1917) areas of housing, immediately outside the Sadovoye Ring, were similarly widened: the most notable was Gorki Street, which was transformed over a forty-year period from 1917 to 1958. Then, as an integral part of the suburban extension of Moscow in the postwar period, a number of the existing radial highways were developed as extensions of the inner street improvements. In this way Gorki Street was continued to the north-west by an improvement of the Leningrad Highway, partly renamed Leningrad Avenue, between 1945 and 1960. To the south-west a completely new radial road, the Lenin Avenue, was developed in similar fashion across the Lenin Hills to serve as the central artery of the great south-western housing development (map 5.2).

Like Haussmann's planning, these developments were fundamentally monumental in their conception. There was little or no apparent understanding of the character of traffic, or of the needs of people who were to live or work or shop in such close proximity to the great radial traffic flows to and from the city. Despite the great width of the streets – over 100 metres (300 feet) from pavement to pavement – many intersections are simple signal-controlled crossroads, and there are delays at some of them. In the residential areas the new avenues are lined by residential blocks which are thus exposed to the

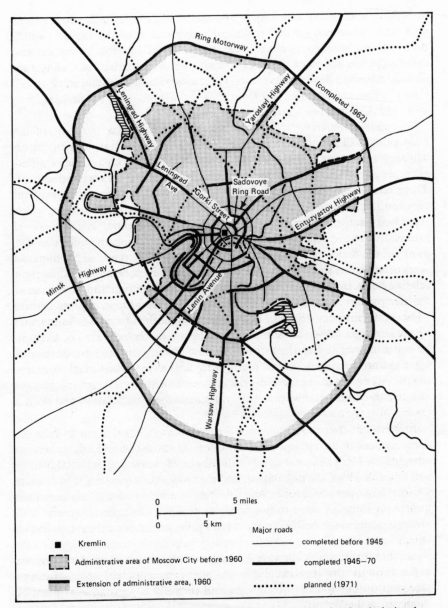

Labels within map: Ring Motorway, Leningrad Highway, Yaroslavl Highway, (completed 1962), Leningrad Ave, *Gorki Street*, Sadovoye Ring Road, Entuzyastov Highway, Minsk Highway, Lenin Avenue, Warsaw Highway

0   5 miles
0   5 km

Major roads

■ Kremlin
▨ Adminstrative area of Moscow City before 1960
▨ Extension of administrative area, 1960

——————— completed before 1945
━━━━━━ completed 1945–70
•••••••• planned (1971)

Map 5.2 *Moscow: road planning.* From 1935 until the late 1950s, with a break only during the Second World War, the Moscow authorities carried through a prodigious programme of road improvements, widening the old streets to create a network of broad arterial boulevards. But traffic engineering was often sacrificed to monumental effect, and the main effort in the 1960s and 1970s was to improve traffic flow by building two-level intersections. A start has been made on a middle ring road connecting the main railway stations and industrial areas.

maximum noise, dust and fumes. The monumental approach betrays itself also here in the exaggerated scale and heavy design of the façades, which derives from the mistakes made in the design for the Moscow University and other public buildings of the early 1950s. Although 'excesses' in architecture were condemned by a resolution of 1955, following the resolution of an all-Union architects' congress in 1954, they continued to persist in designs up to 1960 and perhaps even later.

The shift in planning style after 1960 was towards free planning of the residential blocks themselves around their service cores and their open spaces. Through traffic was segregated on express arteries, with separation of different types of traffic at different levels, and with no direct frontage development. These roads separated the residential districts, and ran through open land between them; the housing areas were reached by distributor roads, which separated each micro-district from the next. In the inner areas two-level intersections have been built at the most important points of traffic conflict, as along the Sadovoye Ring and at Red Square. New roads like Leningrad Avenue are being similarly improved. There is a new concern about the right relation between land use and traffic generation: press criticism is directed at the narrow streets and the lack of parking spaces around the big central Moscow department stores, or at the bad siting of the Dynamo Stadium next to the Leningrad Avenue. Some of these mistakes, though, are not likely to be corrected easily. For the future, Moscow traffic planners have developed some extraordinarily advanced ideas, with deep level traffic tunnels connecting the city centre to the main district centres, linked to underground garages and to sub-surface highways which will relieve the existing rings and radials (map 5.3b)

It is evident that in recent years Soviet planners have begun to face the consequences of an automobile revolution. If so, they are doing so well in advance. In 1969, the total number of cars in Moscow was only 100,000, or one for each 730 of the population; this rose to 930,000 (one in 83) by the late 1970s. The Soviet idea of a 'reasonable' future proportion was one car to ten to fifteen people, or three to five families. This is a low ratio compared with western projections; originally the Soviet planners claimed that it would be adequate because they planned to introduce popular motoring, not by private ownership but through the very extensive development of car-hire schemes and taxi pools. But then came a major policy reversal, with the decision to speed up production of private cars and to build a gigantic Fiat plant at Togliatti on the Volga.

For the great majority of journeys, especially work journeys but including many leisure-time journeys, Soviet thinking is still in terms of generous investment in a cheap and efficient public transport system. Most observers seem to agree that, at present, the Moscow city transport system justifies the claims made for it. By the standards of most western cities, investment in the Moscow Metro system for instance is prodigious. By 1981, 184 kilometres were complete; it was proposed to increase this to 350 kilometres by the mid-1980s and then to build a second system of similar proportions, linked to the first at key interchanges (map 5.3).

The Metro is fundamentally a city service; it provides a system that is very frequent (every eighty seconds at peak hours), very capacious (70,000 passengers an hour in one direction at the peak) and very cheap (maximum fare 4p). These low fixed flat-rate fares have, however, meant increasing losses for the whole public transport system. And the system extends only some 18 kilometres (11 miles) from the centre, within the city limits. Beyond this, for the wider zone of the green belt and the satellites there are commuter services from the main-line terminal stations, which have been completely electrified and which are serious contenders for the title of the world's best commuter service. One such service, between Yaroslavl station and Mytishchi (18 kilometres, 11 miles), runs for all but ninety minutes of a twenty-four hour day, with an on-peak service of twenty-two or twenty-three trains per hour and an off-peak service of fifteen per hour. Of course, 'on-peak' and 'off-peak' are relative terms in the Soviet Union: because of frequent shift working and staggered hours, even during daytime off-peak hours about one-half of the seats are occupied at the Moscow end of the trip. These lines carry very heavy commuter flows – 500,000 in-commuters into Moscow – and commuting times are long, averaging one hour each way. Plans provide for extra tracks to give express services, cutting typical journey times to forty minutes; there will be twenty-two direct interchanges with the Metro system in the outer parts of the city. Latterly the idea has been mooted of linking Metro lines, in the suburbs, with surface railway stations, so as to provide direct and easy interchange in the inner suburbs.

Green belt and satellites
The great housing areas of the Moscow suburbs are all found within the belt motorway, 106 kilometres (66 miles) long, which was opened in 1962 and which rings the city at a radius of about 18 kilometres (11 miles) from the centre. This is the city boundary against the Moscow district (*oblast*); it forms the inner boundary of the green belt, which was first proposed in the 1935 plan as a ring 10 kilometres (6 miles) wide, surrounding the city. Since 1960 work has proceeded rapidly to develop this belt into a readily accessible recreation area for the city, a project warmly urged in his day by Mr Khrushchev. The particular concern of the Soviet planners in this zone is that continued pressure for the construction of individual summer *dachas* would eat rapidly into the available green land. It has been calculated that, if every Muscovite received land to build a *dacha*, the result would mean building

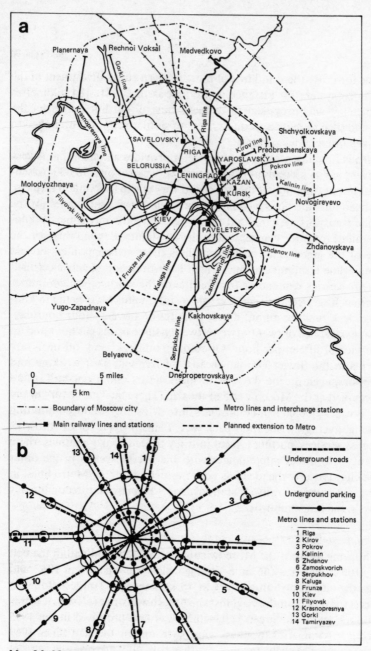

a

Planernaya Rechnoi Voksal Medvedkovo

Gorki line
Krasnopresnya line
Riga line

SAVELOVSKY RIGA
BELORUSSIA Kirov line Preobrazhenskaya
Shchyolkovskaya
YAROSLAVSKY
LENINGRAD Pokrov line
Molodyozhnaya KAZAN Kalinin line
Filyovsk line KURSK
Novogireyevo
KIEV PAVELETSKY
Zamoskvorich line Zhdanovskaya
Frunze line Zhdanov line
Kaluga line

Yugo-Zapadnaya
Serpukhov line Kakhovskaya

Belyaevo

0 ____ 5 miles
0 ____ 5 km
Dnepropetrovskaya

— · — · — Boundary of Moscow city   ●——● Metro lines and interchange stations
+—+—■ Main railway lines and stations   - - - - - Planned extension to Metro

b

13 14 1
2
12
3
11
4
10
5
9
8 7 6

- - - - - Underground roads

◯ ⌒ Underground parking

●——● Metro lines and stations

1 Riga
2 Kirov
3 Pokrov
4 Kalinin
5 Zhdanov
6 Zamoskvorich
7 Serpukhov
8 Kaluga
9 Frunze
10 Kiev
11 Filyovsk
12 Krasnopresnya
13 Gorki
14 Tamiryazev

Map 5.3 *Moscow: metro, railways and underground roads.* (a) The Metro system will be rapidly extended to 350 kilometres (220 miles) by the mid-1980s, while the suburban railways will be upgraded by express tracks and connected to the Metro at new interchanges in the outer parts of the city; a new outer circle Metro line is also projected near the city limits. (b) Plans for 2000 include a new underground road net connecting the new peripheral district centres with the inner ring road (Sadovoye Ring).

130

over an area four times that of the present city. Current policy, therefore, is to prohibit further *dacha* construction in the green belt, but instead to develop a variety of public accommodation, ranging from hotels through hostels to simple camps, with public restaurants as well as kitchens for families who want to cook their own food. Also available will be a wide range of services – kindergartens, athletic grounds, boat and yacht cruises, dance halls and parking lots. In keeping with the Soviet emphasis, the areas will be connected by frequent public transport services from central Moscow; there will be Metro extensions, special high-speed electric trains, and even express boats. In one such centre, the Klyazma Reservoir north of Moscow, the first hotel opened in summer 1963, and was immediately followed by two others. A hutted summer camp, nearby, costs only one-quarter as much to live in as the hotel. Eventually all the developments at this centre will hold up to 200,000 visitors a day. In 1975 it was estimated that 2 million people – 28 per cent of the population – regularly left the city on summer weekends, 70 per cent of them travelling to within 30 kilometres (18 miles) of the city limits; the great majority of course depended on public transport, which gave very unequal access to different parts of the green belt ring.

But the future of the green belt is still a matter of concern. In 1962 Moscow's chief architect, M. Posokhin, was still having to demand that construction must be strictly controlled, and prohibited on undeveloped land; and that the existing satellite towns within the belt, which send 400,000 commuters a day into central Moscow, must be reconstructed so as to introduce more work opportunities. In particular, the many old houses in these towns could be reconstructed to house research and design organizations. Evidently, then, office decentralization is not merely a concern of the western world.

These *goroda-sputniki* do not lie only within the green belt zone; most of them are beyond its outer edge. The term, as the Russians use it, is ambiguous. Most of the satellites are not planned: they grew up first in the pre-revolutionary period, as part of the nineteenth-century industrial development of the wider Moscow region, but then expanded prodigiously after 1917, particularly as a result of the growth of the engineering industries. A few were consciously created by the Soviets themselves as part of the policy of relieving the pressure of industry and population within the city itself. These include Elektrostal, Khimki and Krasnogorsk. Most interesting of all is the new planned satellite town of Zelenograd, 29 kilometres (18 miles) north-west of Moscow on the main railway line to Kalinin and Leningrad, and just beyond the main international airport of Sheremetyevo, which was started in 1960. The basic idea here is the same as that behind London's new towns, in the immediate post-1945 period: industry and population are being developed together in a self-contained community. The industries that have come here are high-technology ones like electronics, radio and precision engineering;

131

they have close links with the city itself, so they cannot be moved far, but it is undesirable to leave them to grow within the congested city.

Zelenograd is planned in micro-districts which in concept closely resemble the neighbourhoods of the older British new towns. Each is based on a school which provides the basic eight years of Soviet education: other, more special-ized education is provided on a whole-town basis. The green spaces between the blocks open out into the garden of the micro-district, which in turn merges with the forest outside the town. Schools and kindergartens and nurseries are at the forest edge, farthest from the road. The housing is of various types to suit the needs of different family groups. The net residential density of population in the residential areas is 200 people on each hectare (80 people on each acre), more than double the 'higher densities' which were being recommended for British new towns in the early 1960s.

Zelenograd was originally planned with a target population of 65,000; by 1979 the total had already reached 130,000 and was growing at 10,000 a year. The new target was 200,000, with the possibility of creating a polycentric Social City on the lines that Ebenezer Howard suggested in his pioneer work on garden cities.

Moscow 2000: the 1971 and 1973 plans

Despite a fundamental difference of philosophy, Moscow's planners face many of the same problems and uncertainties as their western counterparts. They are unsure about future population growth, including both natural increase (which is among the lowest in the world) and migration to the Moscow region; about the type of economic growth, in particular the develop-ment of the service sector in which the Soviet Union still lags; about conflicts between economic growth and environmental protection; about the balance between wholesale urban renewal and conservation of the city's historic fabric.

Most of all, they are concerned for the future form and internal coherence of their vast urban region. Soviet urban planning dogma has always accepted the radial-concentric form of development – though the green belt itself, a borrowing from British planning principles of the 1930s, disturbs the princi-ple. Continuing growth of population and employment, albeit more slowly than in other parts of the Soviet Union, means that increasing numbers of Muscovites must find homes outside the city limits – a majority, in fact, by the year 2000. So the future organization of this growth is a matter for intense debate.

Within the city limits, the problem is easier: the inner ring and parts of the middle ring were declining in population, and the future intention was first to stabilize population at around 7.5–8.0 million, then to allow slow decline. Here, therefore, the main emphasis is on restructuring. The 1971 General Plan for the Development of Moscow, approved by the Central Committee of the Communist Party and the Council of Ministers, aims to create in Moscow the Model Communist City, as Brezhnev put it to the Twenty-Fourth Party Congress in the same year. It starts from the position that decentralization from the city centre will continue. Progressively, the city will be developed in a polycentric way: the city centre will be balanced by seven peripheral centres, each serving a sector of the city with between 600,000 and 1,200,000 people, which are in turn subdivided into districts of 200,000–400,000 people, each with between five and ten subdistricts of 30–70,000.

The central area population will shrink through redevelopment, from its present 600,000 people to between 250,000 and 300,000; employment will also shrink drastically. Some 455,000 will be employed in other centres, the biggest with between 40,000 and 110,000 workers. The aim is to balance residence and employment in each major sector. Thus, these centres will provide the higher order services, which at present are unduly concentrated in the city centre – and this will permit the evolution of the service sector of the Moscow economy while conserving much of the historic centre's urban fabric. The centres themselves will be located astride major transportation junctions, where the suburban commuter railways make direct connections with the city Metro system; in future, they will be directly linked to a deep-level highway system which will provide direct access to the city centre. There will be five new radial Metro lines and a great circle (outer) line linking the major metropolitan centres and some smaller centres. The Metro will be expanded to 350 kilometres (220 miles) in total length; plans were also being made in 1971 for trebling the number of private cars in the city, to 1.5 million by 1980, though the probable actual figure by that date was little more than one million. Around the centres, the city sectors will be demarcated by green belts and wedges, which will follow natural lines – especially the Moscow river and its tributaries – to penetrate directly into the heart of the city (map 5.4)

Following as it did the big battle between the city and the central planning ministries, the 1971 plan is a compromise whereby the city's population will be allowed to rise on the condition that, sometime in the future, it falls again. Otherwise the plan is fairly orthodox and follows the broad lines already laid down in 1935: the city will be developed as the basis of functionally segregated land uses and self-contained, socially-balanced residential zones linked by good public transport. What is conspicuously missing, from the 1971 as from the 1935 plan, is any sense of revolutionary zeal for the reconstruction of society, such as had characterized Soviet planning in the 1920s.

But it is in the zone beyond the city limits – in the belt of satellite towns,

133

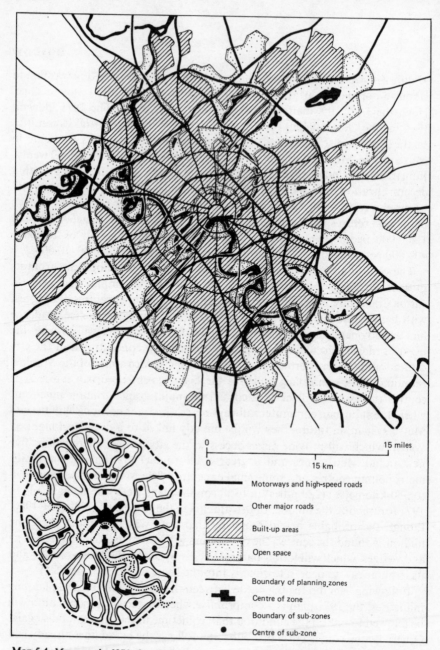

Map 5.4 *Moscow: the 1971 plan.* The city is to be restructured through the development of seven major district centres at major transport interchanges in the outer parts of the city, dividing the entire city into sectors separated by green wedges which will penetrate (especially along river valleys) into the heart of the city.

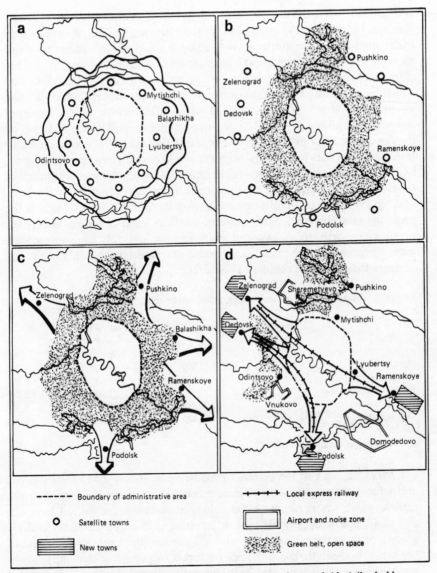

Map 5.5 *Moscow: 1973 Regional Plan alternatives*. (a) Concentric growth (the 'oil splash' principle) invades the green belt. (b) Green belt and satellites, following the 1944 London plan. (c) Axial development along major transportation corridors. (d) Major growth centres along the preferred corridors, at distances more than 50 kilometres (30 miles) from the centre.

135

and beyond – that the major future choices lie. Consequently, the 1971 city plan was followed in 1973 by a plan for the entire region. This considers four major alternatives for future growth (map 5.5 a–d). One would consist of more or less spontaneous growth in the form of concentric rings around the city, which would lead to erosion of the green belt (map 5.5a). A second would be based on preservation of the green belt plus the creation of satellite towns within about 50 kilometres (30 miles) of the centre, on the model of Abercrombie's 1944 plan for London (map 5.5b). A third would be based on the development of preferential axes outside the green belt, based on major transportation lines (map 5.5c). A fourth would develop large growth centres, housing 400,000 or 500,000 people, at distances over 50 kilometres (30 miles) from the centre (map 5.5d); this last, which has clear affinities to the Paris plan of 1965 and to the Strategic Plan for the South East of 1970, is the preferred solution. Particularly good possibilities for such centres exist in the north-west, north, south-east and south sectors; and only four or five such major centres would be needed to house the expected growth in this ring down to the end of the century (Table 5.2).

Table 5.2   Population of the Moscow region, actual and forecast, 1973–2000

		Population (thousands)	
	1973	1985–90	2000
Moscow City	7,400	7,500	6,500
Green belt ring	1,700	1,800	1,800
Internal (satellite) zone	2,000	2,900	3,800
External zone	2,300	3,300	4,500
Moscow region	*13,400*	*15,500*	*16,600*

Source: Moscow Regional Plan, 1973.

Farther out still, in the external zone between 70 and 100 kilometres (40 and 60 miles) from the centre, even more rapid growth is planned as the medium-sized towns receive 1,000 industrial plants, decentralized from the city itself. But here a flexible type of planning suffices, based on the orderly growth of these towns; for open land will predominate well after the end of the century. Nevertheless, the preferred axes of growth – especially north-westwards (towards Klin and Volokolamsk), southwards (towards Serpoukov and Toula) and to the south-east (towards Kolomina and Riazan) – are planned to receive a substantial share of the growth. Elsewhere, the existence of reservoirs, airports and other open land will limit the possibilities of growth – and thus the application of radial-concentric dogma.

The regional plan thus presupposed – as plans had in the past – a limit on Moscow's growth and a strong decentralization of people and activities

European counterparts, with some significant differences in social life. What seems certain, even if the Soviets do limit net immigration into the cities of European Russia, is that natural increase of urban population alone will lead to the further development of great and complex city regions, each embracing a central city, a green belt and a system of satellite towns bound by a variety of social, economic and cultural ties to the central city. Such giant urban areas are already a feature of Soviet life, as of life in the industrialized west; planners, of whatever political persuasion, are having to come to terms with the fact.

6 New York

Among the great urban agglomerations of the world, New York in 1980 still narrowly led Tokyo for first place in size of population. Its unique interest does not stem from that alone, but also from the fact that it is American; the question – will American cities set trends for the rest of the world? – has recently taken on new and ominous implications. But the size is the most immediately recognizable feature. The United States Census of 1980 recognizes a *New York–Newark–New Jersey City Standard Consolidated Statistical Area* – a union of no less than nine contiguous Standard Metropolitan Statistical Areas, which are the units used to define comparable functional urban areas in the United States. This Consolidated Area embraces eighteen counties in the States of New York, New Jersey and Connecticut, with an area of 12,551 square kilometres (4,846 square miles) and a 1980 population of 16,120,023. An even bigger area for analysing socio-economic trends and problems is the *Tri-State New York Metropolitan Region*, devised as long ago as 1922 by the Regional Plan Association of New York – a private organization which in the 1980s was the only body, official or unofficial, taking a serious and continued look at the planning problems of the New York region as a whole. Its area stretches on average up to 160 kilometres (100 miles) from Times Square, conventional centre of the region; it embraces 33,483

Table 6.1   The New York region: definitions and constituent parts, 1980

	Area (square km.)	Population (thousands) 1980	Population change (per cent) 1970–80
New York City	777	7,071.0	−10.4
Rest of New York–Newark– Jersey City SCSA	11,774	9,049.0	+ 8.5
New York–Newark–Jersey City SCSA	*12,551*	*16,120.0*	*− 0.3*
Remainder of RPA region	23,302	3,069.5	−14.0
RPA region	*33,483*	*19,189.5*	*− 2.8*
(UN definition)		(20,383.0)	+10.5

Sources: Census, 1980; United Nations, *Patterns of Urban and Rural Population Growth* (*Population Studies*, 68), New York: United Nations, 1980.

140

square kilometres (12,928 square miles) in thirty-one counties (three of which are in the State of Connecticut) and had a 1980 Census population of 19,189,507. Both these definitions of the extended New York region suffered net population loss between 1970 and 1980 – the first decade in which this had occurred (table 6.1 and map 6.1).

A problem tour

Most of the problems of this vast region stem, paradoxically, from rapid economic and social advance. They spring from the increasingly complex nature of the United States economy, which causes large and rapid shifts in the composition of the labour force; from the high living standards which this economy guarantees for the great majority of Americans; from the social strains set up by the continuing existence of an undereducated, underskilled, underpaid and underprivileged minority, which is a particularly acute problem in New York; from the failure of local administration to evolve in line with the rapidly changing social and economic structure of the region. These problems will most readily emerge from a bird's eye view of the entire region, working outwards from centre to periphery.

Manhattan: congestion at the centre

Of the world's great metropolitan cities, two alone are distinguished by being centred upon an island. They are New York and Hong Kong, and both these cities draw an extraordinary combination of advantages and disadvantages from the fact. It was no accident that both became great world ports – New York the world's greatest. The southern tip of Manhattan Island between the Hudson and the East rivers – the area first occupied by the Dutch in 1615 – was bounded on two sides by open water, offering unsurpassed facilities for loading and unloading ships. Logically, warehousing and wholesale trade gathered in this tiny triangular area; with equal logic, risk-bearing finance developed in the same place to serve the shipping men; and even before the revolution of 1776, New York's 'Downtown' was established. Today, some 400,000 workers still congregate, every working day, in just over one square kilometre (three-fifths of a square mile) of skyscrapers which cluster between the cavernous streets of the Wall Street area. Some wholesalers still remain in this colony; but those requiring space, for the storage of bulky goods, have been forced out by steadily rising rents, and Wall Street is dominated above all by banking and by certain types of insurance.

Up to about 1880, finance and wholesaling were the most characteristic activities of any commercial metropolis. But then, rapidly, American cities

141

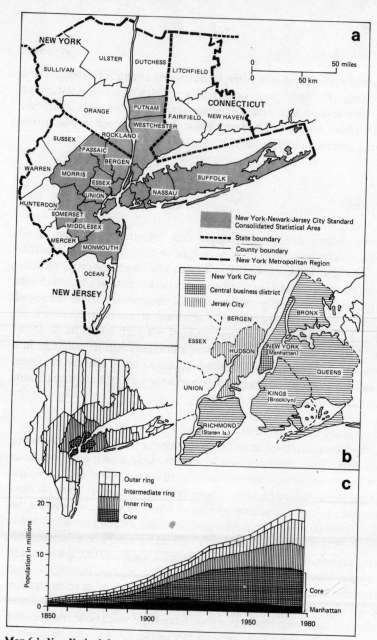

Map 6.1 *New York: definition of a metropolis.* (a) The urban region of New York far exceeds the City, with its five boroughs having a 1980 population of 7,071,030. The Standard Consolidated Statistical Area had 16,120,023 people in 1980; the larger New York Metropolitan Region, defined by the Regional Plan Association, had thirty-one counties and a population of 19,189,507. (b) The CBD of this vast area, covering only 23 square kilometres (9 square miles) of Manhattan Island, had one-quarter of its total employment. (c) But residential population has been decentralizing from the core counties to the intermediate and outer ring of the region, and by the 1970s the massive losses in the inner areas were producing a general regional decline.

were transformed by the 'bureaucratic revolution' which has already been described in chapter 1 of this book. About 1880, railroads and financial trusts began to set up offices in New York. They chose not to locate in the Downtown financial district or in the densely populated and highly industrialized area to the north of it – the so-called 'loft district' between Chambers and Houston streets, which between 1880 and 1910 became the leading reception area for immigrants from southern and eastern Europe. Instead they built their new offices in what was then the luxury residential quarter of 'Midtown' Manhattan, north of 34th Street. (Similarly in London offices colonized the West End; and in Paris the Grands Boulevards and the Champs Elysées.) Other types of office – especially the head offices of the big new industrial combines – followed suit. In the twentieth century they were followed by a host of non-profit making organizations like trade unions, research institutes and professional bodies, as well as government which extended its operations enormously. Around them, a host of special services progressively developed to minister to them – real estate experts, advertising, taxation experts, engineers, designers, draughtsmen and operational research consultants. Many of these professions changed from small-scale ancillary factory activities into large-scale, full-time office jobs. Other activities shifted relatively. Some insurance head offices began to find Midtown Manhattan a more attractive site than congested Downtown. The growth of business was so great that by the 1950s the banks also were beginning to set up second offices to tap the Midtown trade.

Other types of central employment have seen a similarly rapid growth, though yet others have been displaced in the competition for land. Midtown had been traditionally the home of luxury specialized shopping. As a mass market developed, the specialized shops steadily broadened their market; after 1880, the new department stores settled in the same area to tap the available shoppers. An important segment of manufacturing industry, working rapidly to unpredictable orders, had also to locate on Manhattan: thus the women's fashion industry, in the Garment Centre on the lower middle West Side, and various types of specialized printing.

In the middle 1980s, Manhattan's Central Business District (CBD) runs up from the Battery in the south to a conventional boundary along 61st Street – that is about two-fifths of the way up the island and just above the southern end of Central Park (map 6.1b). Since 1900 it has shown a strong tendency to migrate steadily northwards. The big department stores have shifted progressively from the northern edge of the financial district to 34th Street; the specialized luxury shops have moved north of 42nd Street; since the Second World War the new industrial headquarters offices – Seagram, Lever, Pepsi-Cola – have been built in Park Avenue between 46th and 59th Streets. There were signs in the early 1960s that the CBD might spread further north – signs like

143

the establishment of the Lincoln Centre for the Performing Arts, in the middle 60s of the West Side. But by the early 1970s the main movement seemed to be westward and southward. The City Plan Commission had encouraged the redevelopment of the western part of the Midtown district, between 40th and 57th Street and west of the Avenue of the Americas; the first stage involved new office space plus redevelopment of the live theatres for which this district is renowned, while a second stage will create a combination of offices, homes, an exhibition centre and a new ocean liner terminal on the Hudson River, with extensive pedestrian ways. A key to this development is the planned 48th Street crosstown subway, which will bring new accessibility to this part of Manhattan Island. But down at the island's southern tip, even more dramatic developments were taking place in the early 1970s, following publication of the City's Lower Manhattan Plan. This involves extensive decking over the peripheral highways which surround the island's lower end, coupled with extension of the land area into the rivers by landfilling. The spectacular Port of New York Authority's World Trade Centre, with its twin 110-storey towers – the highest in the world, with a total office space of over 650,000 square metres (7 million square feet) – was a first stage in this development, completed in 1973; the excavation for the centre has been used as landfill for the even bigger development in front of it, the Battery Park City which is creating 1,400 square metres (15,000 square feet) of new office space and 15,000 apartments on reclaimed land. Notable in these developments is the careful integration with public transportation. The World Trade Center, for instance, is served by three subways and by the Cross-Hudson tubes from the New Jersey shore, which terminate underneath it.

Meanwhile, the 24 square kilometres (9 square miles) of Manhattan Island south of 61st Street – an area equivalent in size to Kennedy International Airport – had on an average 1976 weekday an estimated working population of 1,845,000 – a drop of 410,000 since the peak year of 1969; this was one-quarter of all the employees of the New York Region as defined by the Regional Plan Association. (A mere 3 per cent of the region's population, in contrast, lived here.) Of the total, close on half were office workers. And just under one-half of the region's office employment was found in the CBD. Here too were 76 per cent of the live theatres, 26 per cent of the department store floorspace, 25 per cent of employment in manufacturing and warehousing, and 14 per cent of the region's college enrolment.

This concentration of workpeople – the second greatest in the world, since it was overtaken by Tokyo in the early 1970s – can be explained only by the extraordinary economic advantages which individual activities derive from location at the centre. The heart of Wall Street or Midtown is the small minority of the whole work-force – variously estimated at one in ten, or in twenty, or in fifty, or in a hundred – who make decisions; the business and

professional élite. Many of them are in the national headquarters offices that make up over 45 per cent of total CBD office employment. The executive's job essentially consists of taking rapid, informed decisions on a wide variety of new, unpredictable, non-standard problems. To do this, he must achieve quick person-to-person contact with a large number of other decision-takers, whether in his own business or outside it; he must be able to command also a wide range of specialized expertise. It is therefore almost impossible to conceive of the executive functions being shifted far from their present home. Technological developments, like teleprinters and closed-circuit television, will make some difference; but they are unlikely to provide an adequate substitute for person-to-person contact. True, a very large majority of the labour force cannot be classed as 'executive' and so are not tied to Manhattan; but for a variety of reasons most of them remain there. Too many of them are preparing and processing information which may be needed, at short call, by the executives. Too many more are being supervised in their routine work by the same executive. Though they do not constitute the élite, many of them have their special skills; and their employees find that these skills are available in greater variety here than elsewhere, because of the highly centralized transport system. Originally created in response to the existing centralization of jobs, this system has now become an important factor working for further centralization.

So the growth of Manhattan's office jobs showed little sign of slackening until the end of the 1960s (map 6.2). Between 1959 and 1965, office jobs in office buildings – about nine in ten of all office jobs – rose from 760,000 to 804,000, or nearly 1 per cent per year. But during this period CBD factory jobs fell by 50,000 while other jobs – in warehousing and retailing, for instance – rose; total CBD employment remained almost static, as it had since 1930, while in the rest of the region employment rapidly rose. But because office space standards are rising, these increases bring a much bigger increase in floor-space. Between 1950 and 1970, total CBD floorspace rose from 12 to 21 million square metres (128 to 226 million square feet), an increase of 77 per cent.

In the late 1960s, the Regional Plan Association produced a detailed projection of employment in the New York region. They then expected total employment to rise from 7.7 million in the mid-1960s to 13.2 million in 2000 – a growth of 71 per cent. This represented a marginal fall in the region's share of total United States employment, from 11 to 10 per cent. Whereas commodity production – basically manufacturing – was expected to employ a static total of the region's workers, other employment would nearly double: from 5.5 million (72 per cent of the total) to 10.9 million (83 per cent of the total). While blue-collar jobs would barely grow, white-collar jobs would double, rising from 54 per cent to 64 per cent of the work-force; office jobs would rise from 29 per cent to 37 per cent of the regional work-force.

145

The critical question was how this employment would distribute itself within the region. The Regional Plan Association believed that many of the new office jobs would need the unique advantages the Manhattan CBD offered – above all the top jobs in headquarters offices, which would form an increasing share of the total. Total CBD jobs might rise from 2.0 million to around 2.2–2.3 million between 1967 and 2000. There would be an increase in office jobs from 0.8 million to about 1.3 million, with headquarters jobs rising from 46 to 54 per cent of this total; factory jobs might halve, to 0.3 million, while a range of other jobs might employ about 0.7 million. Space to accommodate the extra CBD office jobs would be no problem, since the decline in manufacturing would release more than enough land; though the Regional Plan Association suggested grouping the new space above subway and other rail connections for greater efficiency of movement, with pedestrian and shopping space at below ground level linked directly to the subway access. The real problem was that the increase of about half a million CBD office jobs would be accompanied by steady dispersal of the region's resident work-force, coupled with lack of appropriate white-collar job skills among the remaining inner city population. All in all, the Regional Plan Association expected the number of CBD office commuters almost to double during this period, from 780,000 to 1,310,000, with an even bigger proportionate increase (220,000 to 570,000) in long distance commuters from outside New York City – a daunting prospect, when it is realized that already in 1960 the CBD took in a total of over 1.6 million commuters each workday. But it would still leave the great bulk of the new jobs – an expected 5 million, of which one half would be office jobs and one-third in purpose built offices – to be housed outside Manhattan's CBD.

Reality failed to live up to these optimistic expectations. Total employment in the region fell by 375,000, nearly 5 per cent, from 1970 to 1976. This was made up of a loss of 542,000 (nearly 15 per cent) in New York City – 400,000 in the CBD alone – and a compensating gain of 167,000 in the rest of the region (map 6.2). Since the regional labour force grew, by about 176,000, unemployment was on the rise: it more than doubled, to 10 per cent, and in Manhattan and Brooklyn – where the labour force was declining but employment was falling even faster – it was 12.5 per cent. The region, totally contrary to all the projections of the 1960s, was in economic decline; and that decline was concentrated in its very heart.

Map 6.2 *New York region: employment changes, 1970–6.* (a) Employment was still highly concentrated at the region's core, on Manhattan, in 1976, but here – and in the surrounding boroughs of New York City – heavy losses were occurring; gains at the periphery failed to compensate, so that total regional employment declined. (b) Manufacturing showed big job losses in the core and inner ring, while service employment gained almost everywhere except in the Manhattan core.

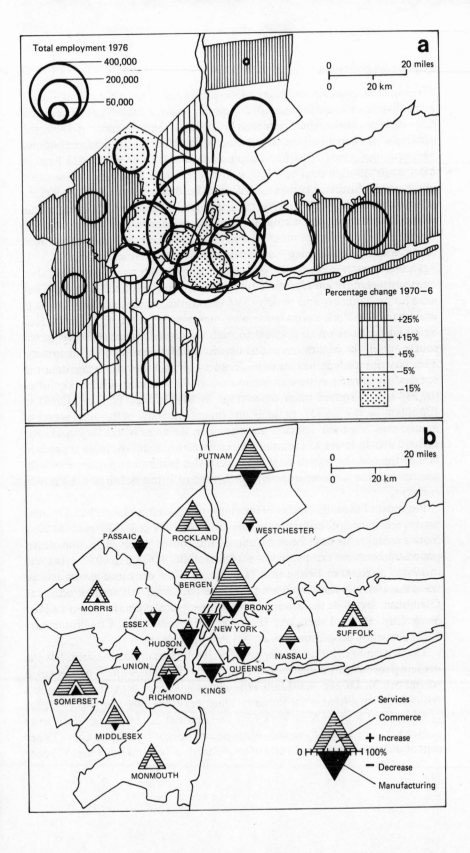

a

Total employment 1976

400,000
200,000
50,000

0   20 miles
0   20 km

Percentage change 1970–6

+25%
+15%
+5%
−5%
−15%

b

PUTNAM

0   20 miles
0   20 km

ROCKLAND

WESTCHESTER

PASSAIC

BERGEN

MORRIS

BRONX

ESSEX

NEW YORK

HUDSON

SUFFOLK

UNION

NASSAU

RICHMOND

QUEENS

SOMERSET

KINGS

MIDDLESEX

MONMOUTH

Services
Commerce
+ Increase
0 ├┼┼┼┼┼┤ 100%
− Decrease
Manufacturing

Harlem, West Side, Bronx: black belt and grey belt

Immediately outside the congested core lies another New York. The actual City of New York, which achieved its present size and form in 1898, still accounts for almost half the population of the whole Standard Consolidated Metropolitan Area: 7,071,030 people in 1980. Of these, 1,427,533 lived in Manhattan, though relatively few of them are on the expensive blocks south of Chambers Street or between 23rd and 61st Streets; another 2,230,936 are in Brooklyn across the East River; a further 1,169,115 are north of Manhattan in the Bronx. Here, but above all in northern Manhattan, in the adjacent south Bronx and parts of inner Brooklyn, are concentrated some of the most intractable problems facing New York – or any other American city.

These areas were mainly developed during the great wave of late nineteenth-century immigration from eastern and southern Europe. They were built up quickly and poorly to an extraordinarily high density: in 1900, when half New York's population was foreign-born, parts of the Lower East Side had densities up to 250,000 to each square kilometre (640,000 to the square mile), the highest recorded density of population in world history. They have lost population for some decades now, but they still retain densities unusual by current American standards: 24,030 on each square kilometre (62,238 to the square mile) on average in Manhattan; 12,342 (31,968) in Brooklyn; 10,949 (28,357) in the Bronx (map 6.3). Some of the older waves of immigrants, and their descendants, remain in the areas which they colonized before 1910. In lower Manhattan, Delancey Street is still the main thorough-fare of the historic Jewish East Side; west of it is the Italian quarter; south-west of it is the Chinese quarter; north-west of it the Polish and Ukranian enclaves.

But most of the older waves of immigrants have left, to be replaced by new waves. Since the anti-immigration legislation of 1921 and 1924, most of New York's immigrants have been citizens of the United States. The 'non-white' population of New York City was 60,000 in 1900, 776,000 in 1950, 1,141,000 in 1960, 1,846,000 in 1970 and 2,777,000 in 1980. Even more recent, dating from the 1940s, is the flow from the congested island of Puerto Rico in the Caribbean. By 1980 there were 1,406,000 people of Spanish origin in New York City. In total, between 1970 and 1980 New York City lost nearly 1,775,000 white people and gained 931,000 non-whites.

The Jewish and Italian immigrants of 1900, in many cases, soon left the densely packed central ghettoes; the blacks and Hispanics find it harder to do so (map 6.3). Of the 4,391,000 non-whites – 23 per cent of the region's population – recorded in the Regional Plan area at the 1980 Census, 2,777,000 or 64 per cent were in New York City and another 228,000 (5 per cent) were in Newark. The bulk of the non-white population of New York City (39 per cent of the city's population) and of the Spanish-origin (mainly Puerto Rican) population (20 per cent of the total) concentrate in Harlem at the northern tip of Manhattan, in the Bedford-Stuyvesant area of Brooklyn and in the South Bronx. By 1980 the Bronx, with 52.6 per cent of its population non-white, for the first time led both Brooklyn (44.0 per cent) and Manhattan (41.1 per cent).

The black population of New York records a lower average income, a small percentage of owner-occupancy, a higher degree of overcrowding and a higher tendency to occupy old buildings than the population at large (map 6.3). In 1969, 19 per cent of non-white families in the city – as against 16 per cent of the white – were below official poverty levels, though the white/non-white differential in average income narrowed during the decade, partly because more non-whites have gone into white-collar jobs. It is thus no coincidence that New York City recorded 64 per cent of the region's non-white population and also 59 per cent – 1,165,000 – of those living on incomes below the official poverty line. In Harlem the red brick houses, built mostly to accommodate white middle-class citizens who left after 1890, have become one of the most concentrated areas of black population on the North American continent. Between 110th Street on the south and 155th Street on the north, between 8th Avenue on the west and the East and Harlem rivers to the east, live some quarter of a million blacks. Here are found all the signs of extreme poverty and physical degradation: the pawnbroker's shops, the horrifying advertisements for rodent and pest exterminators in every druggist's window, the aimless unemployed teenagers on the street corners. And, since 1940, the position of the blacks has relatively deteriorated. New waves of blacks and Puerto Ricans have arrived so quickly – attracted both by better employment prospects, and by much more generous welfare payments than in their areas of origin – that the city's housing stock has been overwhelmed. Urban renewal, carried through under the 1949 Housing Act, has exacerbated the problem since it has been carried out by private developers on a commercial basis, with only limited procedures for public housing of low-income families. Typical ghetto schools have a fifth grade average reading score, over 1½ years behind white schools. Out of a hundred children entering ghetto schools, fifty-five will drop out before completing high school and only thirteen will graduate with the academic diploma (as against forty-five in a middle income neighbourhood) which is a prerequisite for a job with reasonable prospects; while three-quarters of New York city jobs are in the white-collar or skilled craftsman categories, only 16 per cent of ghetto unemployed (in 1966) had these skills. And ghetto unemployment is well above average levels for the city – especially for teenagers, where it may reach 30 per cent and more. In the ghetto, too, are found a large part of the estimated 100,000 heroin addicts in the city – half the national total, and the greatest single factor in the crime rate.

149

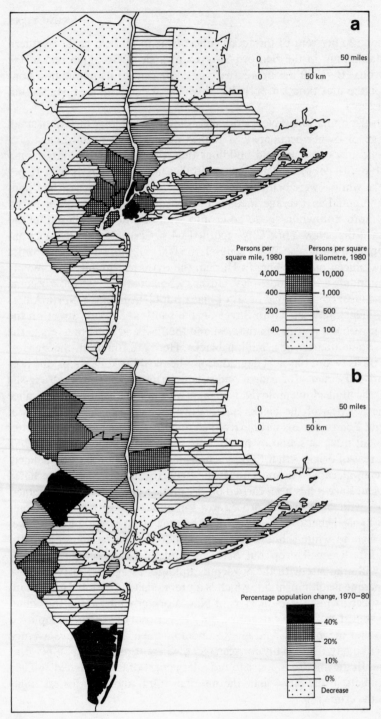

a

0   50 miles
0   50 km

Persons per   Persons per square
square mile, 1980   kilometre, 1980

4,000 — 10,000

400 — 1,000

200 — 500

40 — 100

b

0   50 miles
0   50 km

Percentage population change, 1970–80

40%

20%

10%

0%

Decrease

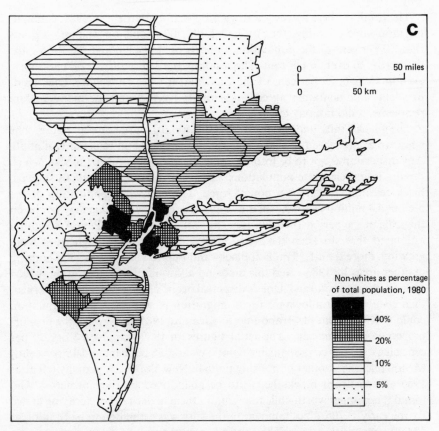

Non-whites as percentage
of total population, 1980

40%

20%

10%

5%

0   50 miles

0   50 km

C

Map 6.3 *New York region: population indices, 1980.* (a) Population density per square
kilometre: this rises to more than 10,000 per square kilometre (25,000 per square mile) at the
core, falling to less than 100 per square kilometre (250 per square mile) at the periphery. Much
of the region consists of low-density suburbs at between 100 and 500 per square kilometre
(250–1,250 per square mile). (b) Population change, 1970–80; there were big losses in the
boroughs of New York City (except Richmond), the older New Jersey cities, and the inner
suburbs. The biggest gains were at the periphery, at least 80 kilometres (50 miles) and mainly at
least 130 kilometres (80 miles) from Times Square. (c) Non-white percentage of total
population: this proportion rises to more than 40 per cent in Manhattan, Brooklyn, the Bronx
and Essex County (Newark), New Jersey, but then drops sharply to less than 10 per cent in
most suburban counties.

The result of these forces is a staggering welfare burden. In 1981, eliminating all double-counting, the city had 1,392,000 people on welfare - no less than 20 per cent of the population; in parts of Brooklyn and the Bronx, the figure rose to over 30 per cent. The resulting burden to the City is enormous: even in 1975-6, 29 per cent of the City budget went on welfare. One major problem, commentators agreed, was the 'poverty trap': for many welfare recipients, it did not pay to work.

The blacks thus find themselves under almost impossible pressure. The white areas are closed to them, and give way slowly and reluctantly if at all. Any dispersion is apt to be into the immediately neighbouring blocks, which rapidly lose their white populations. As incidents during the 1960s showed, black resentment can be a potent force. The non-white population of the region, 4.4 million in 1980, will grow, even though the increase may not be on the scale of the period 1940-80. Even in 1968, the Regional Plan Association estimated that, to keep the New York City and Newark ghettoes from growing, more than 1.25 million blacks and Puerto Ricans must find housing in other areas by 1985 - and this made no allowance for in-migration, which seems certain to continue. Unless dispersal occurred, the Association warned, then even without allowance for in-migration New York City's population could be 43 per cent black and Puerto Rican by 1985; in Newark the proportion could be 90 per cent. (The actual figures for 1980 were: New York, 25 per cent black, 20 per cent Spanish origin; Newark, 58 per cent and 19 per cent.) Meanwhile, the number of housing units in New York City actually fell after 1965 as apartment blocks began to be abandoned by their owners - who found it no longer worthwhile to maintain them in decayed or decaying areas. By the early 1970s, abandonment in the City was estimated to be running at 50,000 apartments a year. The causes were not easy to unravel, but one was undoubtedly rent control: a relic of the Second World War Federal legislation, maintained here long after its disappearance from the rest of the United States. When the City took over administration of the scheme in 1962, almost by definition it found rent increases impossible because of the political power of the tenants - who comprise 80 per cent of households, against less than 40 per cent in the United States as a whole. At last, in 1971 a State law provided for decontrol of tenancies, and in 1972 the City introduced a system allowing rents to rise nearer to market levels. Nor did public agencies step into the breach; in fact, Federal housing programmes virtually halted at the end of the 1960s, as construction costs exceeded budget limits.

One important basis for postulating a marked shift is the character of the areas just outside the black ghettoes. Here, in the Bronx and in outer Brooklyn and inner Queens, and in Hudson County on the New Jersey shore, are the grey areas of the New York region. They are the interwar suburbs: the creation of the subway and tube age. The New York subway opened its first line in 1904. By the mid-1920s it was throwing out long tentacles into the developing fringes of the city, 8 to 16 kilometres (5 to 10 miles) from the centre, and it was carrying 4 million passengers a day. Similarly, the deep-level tubes under the Hudson opened up the New Jersey shore. Then, America was far from being the land of the universal automobile. In the mid-1920s, one family in two in the United States owned a car. For work and for play, the most important consideration was access to the subway stations. So these areas (which Europeans would call suburbs, but which Americans do not), were built densely by later American standards: houses at 25 or 30 to the hectare (10 or 12 to the acre), houses mixed with apartments at up to 125 dwellings per hectare (50 dwellings per acre). They were built and occupied quickly, for between 1910 and 1930 the population of the Metropolitan Region rose by 4,000,000. The people who settled here were America's new middle class, many of them the first-generation children of the Jewish and Italian immigrants of 1900, who were marrying and having children in the middle 1920s. By the 1960s, these people were already old; their children had grown up, married and moved away, and areas like the Bronx lost population after 1950. These older inhabitants were already dying or moving away from New York. And their houses do not prove fully acceptable to young people forming new families in the 1970s and 1980s: they are small, with small gardens, with insufficient space for the two cars which many Americans are coming to regard as the essential standard, and because they were too quickly and speculatively built they often look tawdry, neglected and unattractive. The cheap building materials, the undeveloped weed-grown lots, the overhead railway tracks, the garish advertisements along the main avenues and the surrealist patterns of overhead cables make these areas singularly dispiriting and uninviting in comparison with most European counterparts; some of the neglected suburbs of northern Paris provide perhaps the closest parallel. From these areas the commuter travels by subway, which gives a cheap but slow and uncomfortable journey to Manhattan.

The result, in the 1980s, is a big stock of available housing, fifty or sixty years old and semi-obsolescent by modern middle-class American standards, in a wide belt between 8 and 25 kilometres (5 and 15 miles) from Times Square. True, not every American family can afford the newest and best: five-sixths of Americans never earn sufficient income to buy a new house. But in this period, there will be relatively few families to take up the offer of rather cheap, slightly substandard housing; for these are the years when the poor crop of depression babies is passing into the housing market. Here is a paradox: for the statistics show that many Americans, and in particular many New Yorkers, are inadequately housed. The problem is that these people tend to be poor, unskilled, poorly educated – and black. What seems likely is that large tracts of the grey areas will pass to the blacks. Already by 1980, nearly 53 per cent of the population of the Bronx was black – a proportion greater than that of Manhattan and Brooklyn; in Queens nearly 30 per cent was black, and even suburban Westchester County recorded nearly 16 per cent. Yet it seems doubtful whether the dispersal process can satisfy the pent-up demands of the densely packed inner areas.

A critical factor here will be the distribution of jobs in the zone of black ghettoes and in the grey belt. More than one-fifth of the New York region's jobs are concentrated in this zone – the so-called core of the region, excluding the CBD – stretching from 5 to 21 kilometres (3 to 13 miles) from Times Square. Here are found the activities which need close contact with the centre but which cannot afford the highest central rents. They include many types of wholesaling and storage, distribution and service centres for the local market, and manufacturing industries like the production of the less fashion-conscious types of clothing, printing and specialized electronics. These industries need a great deal of unskilled labour which is increasingly drawn from the black and Puerto Rican populations. So they set up increasing flows of 'reverse commuters' out of Manhattan and inner Brooklyn, where much of the labour force still has to live (map 6.3). More and more, these people will try to find homes nearer their jobs. The same stimulus will come from the outward shift of the suburban population, generating a demand for local services which can often be kept going only with the help of the non-white population. And eventually, as the more dynamic types of industry grow in the outer suburbs, their demands too will influence the distribution of the black work-force.

Dispersal of the ghetto populations must, therefore, be one answer. But, as the Regional Plan Association stresses, it is not alone sufficient; the older cities, in this region as across the United States, must be spared the crushing burden of poverty-related public services, Federal funds need to be channelled into the cities, helping to reduce poverty and to release city funds for other urgently needed purposes, at the same time reducing the incentive to migrate. But the so-called Moynihan plan for guaranteed Federal welfare benefits, proposed by the 1968 Nixon administration, which would have achieved some of this, was rejected by Senate; and though the new emphasis in the 1973 Budget on revenue-sharing is helping to achieve a similar effect by giving massive Federal funds direct to the cities, which will themselves determine their use, President Reagan's New Federalism will move in a reverse direction by transferring the main welfare burdens back to the states.

Westchester, Nassau, Suffolk, Fairfield: suburbs and exurbs
Almost every part of any city was at one time a suburb. Fleet Street in London, the Châtelet in Paris, Unter den Linden in Berlin were all once *in*

suburbio. In the United States, the word suburban connotes something different from the common European meaning. It refers directly to areas outside a city; it tends therefore to describe development in the recent past – since 1945; development based on the universal possession of the private automobile; development at a density which is extraordinarily low even by generous European standards.

So the interwar housing of the grey belt, the suburbs based on subway transportation and built at densities of 25 to 125 dwellings on each hectare (10 to 50 on each acre), are not what New Yorkers mean by suburbs; suburbs start where the city ends. By 1945 the City area was more or less fully built-up, and suburban developments were started on a wide scale. They were built at lower densities, averaging 17 houses to each hectare (7 houses to each acre), which allowed generous garage and garden room: Levittown on Long Island, dating from the late 1940s and one of the classic homes of William H. Whyte's Organization Man, is the model. Though almost all families in Levittown own cars, many of its commuters into Manhattan go by public (though privately owned) transportation. Just as the interwar suburbs depended on the subway, so the suburbs of 1945–70 – 25 to 70 kilometres (15 to 45 miles) from Times Square – depend on longer-distance commuter railroads like the Long Island, the New Haven and the Jersey Central (map 6.5).

But since the late 1950s a profound change has come over New York suburbs. As development progressed farther and farther from Manhattan, so the new houses were spaced farther and farther apart from each other. By 1962 some 200 municipalities had undeveloped land in the New York Metropolitan Region, and almost all were zoning it at fixed maximum densities. An analysis by the Regional Plan Association showed that no less than 67.2 per cent of all the vacant residentially zoned land was zoned in lots of 0.20 hectare (half an acre) or more; 47.5 per cent in lots of 0.40 hectare (one acre) and more. Allowing for the usual tendency for some development to take place on lots bigger than the zoned minimum, the Association calculated that the average developed lot of the future might be over 0.27 hectare (two-thirds of an acre). In 1950 by comparison, the average was less than 0.10 hectare (one-quarter of an acre).

The result may already be seen in the most recent developments at the fringe of the present built-up area, some 40 to 50 kilometres (25 to 30 miles) from Times Square, in areas like northern Westchester County in New York or Fairfield County in Connecticut. Here is evolving a type of urban area without parallel in eastern North America: an importation from the universal urban sprawl of Los Angeles. It depends almost wholly on the automobile, for a finely developed railroad net, or even adequate express bus transportation, is no longer economic. The commuter bound for Manhattan must drive

155

long distances to a suburban railhead; his wife needs a second car for the long journey to the shopping centre. The early developments are tending to cluster round the infrequent junctions on the freeways; but this will be possible only for a privileged few. And losing the traditional advantages of urban life, the new suburbanites will not gain complete rural seclusion either. True, they will not usually be able to glimpse their neighbours' houses through the trees; but they will still live at ten times rural densities. This new type of suburbia needs a new name. Some Americans call it 'exurbia'. The Regional Plan Association has christened it 'spread city'.

Exurbia tends to be occupied only by the most fortunate members of American society. The 1980 Census shows that here are the highest proportions of households with very high incomes, of white-collar workers and of owner-occupancy (map 6.4). But rich as these people are, the communities they inhabit are in a chronic state of financial anxiety. They find it increasingly difficult to bear the heavy burden of local expenditure, especially school expenditure, which results from the immigration of young people with children. The structure of American government being what it is, they get relatively little help from State or Federal authorities in meeting these expenditures. And here, in pure anxiety, lies the origin of exurbia. It is not something that anyone appears to want; scatteration restricts choice even for the better-off, increases travel distance unnecessarily, and further raises the cost of essential public services. For fear that more families will strain municipal resources, the communities of exurbia create the zoning laws to limit the numbers of newcomers. The spread of light industry, research organizations and routine office functions into the suburbs helps; but many small municipalities do not get much benefit. The Regional Plan Association has suggested ways out of this impasse – larger tax districts, to avoid the present highly localized tax burdens, and greater aid from the States. What is certain is that, unless a change comes, spread city will go on spreading.

The implications of this are disturbing. In 1968, out of a total of 33,400 square kilometres (12,900 square miles) in the New York Metropolitan Region, 6,087 (2,350) were developed or committed to some public use like open space. Another 24,000 square kilometres (9,300 square miles) were given over to parks, reservoirs and military camps, leaving 2,979 square kilometres (1,150 square miles) – over 70 per cent – completely rural. At the space standards of recent development, by the end of the century the developed areas could cover 14,500 square kilometres (5,600 square miles) and the open spaces 6,860 square kilometres (2,650 square miles), leaving only 11,700 square kilometres (4,500 square miles) (35 per cent of the total) still open. But given the likely increase in population between 1960 and 1985, and given the present zoning arrangements, development could eat up another 7,250 square kilometres (2,800 square miles). Thus within thirty-five years the New York region could use up more land than in all the years since 1626, when Manhattan was bought from the Indians for $24. The result would be a continuous urban sprawl stretching on average 70 to 80 kilometres (45 to 50 miles) from Times Square – much farther than that along certain transport lines.

Then, the concept of the American Megalopolis will threaten to take on a new dimension. Megalopolis, in the description of the geographer Jean Gottmann, is 'an almost continuous stretch of urban and suburban areas from southern New Hampshire to northern Virginia' – a stretch of some 700 kilometres (450 miles) of Atlantic seaboard. But though over 30 million people lived here in 1960, in the greatest extended urban agglomeration in the world, they did so on only about 26,000 square kilometres (10,000 square miles), or 20 per cent of the land area of the region. If, however, the rest of Megalopolis proves as land-hungry in the coming decades as its New York regional heart threatens to, then there is a real prospect that by the end of the century a majority of the land area of Megalopolis will be urbanized.

Will the new pattern of living prove tolerable to the New Yorkers of 2000? The Regional Plan Association is reasonably sanguine – provided the spatial pattern of development is right. Much will depend on the location of jobs then. Exurbia will be occupied predominantly by decision-taking executives and their families. If in 1990 there are many more executive jobs in Manhattan, the length and strain of commuter journeys will surely increase. If there is rapid growth of decentralized office and laboratory jobs, the dweller in exurbia may make more cross-trips round the periphery to his work. And here the emphasis on the automobile, and the relatively low densities of people and jobs, may help – especially if the highway pattern is developed to provide better links around the edge of the region. The strong probability, according to the detailed projections made for the Regional Plan Association, is that both trends will occur: alike in Manhattan, in the 16 to 40 kilometre (10 to 25 mile) ring and in exurbia, the highest-paid, most responsible white-collar jobs will grow. So it is likely that some exurbanites will be comparatively badly served by the sort of city they have to inhabit; some less so. Nevertheless, it is fairly clear that intelligent planning could produce an arrangement which would suit almost everyone better. The Regional Plan Association argues strongly for the build up of about two dozen major metropolitan centres throughout the region, containing concentrations of office jobs, college and hospital facilities, stores, museums and galleries, and high density apartments. They would thus house a substantial proportion of the big expected growth in white-collar jobs. They could draw on big local labour pools because they would be strategically sited in relation to highways and at major public transportation nodes. First priority would go to centres in the core of the region just outside the CBD, which could hold residents who might otherwise move out: Downtown Brooklyn, Downtown Newark and

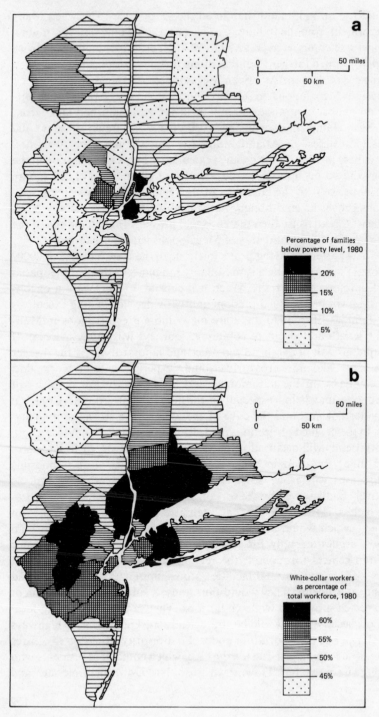

a

Percentage of families
below poverty level, 1980

20%
15%
10%
5%

b

White-collar workers
as percentage of
total workforce, 1980

60%
55%
50%
45%

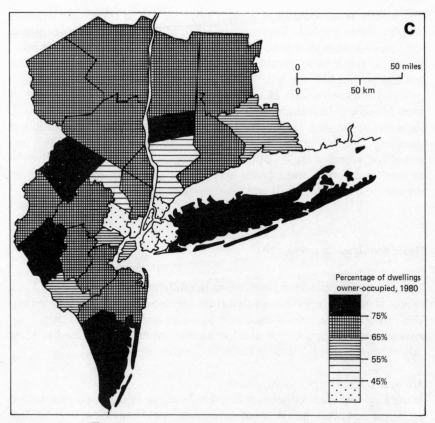

Map 6.4 *New York region: socio-economic indices, 1980.* (a) Percentage of families below poverty level: this is high (more than 20 per cent) in the core, where it is closely associated with the concentration of non-whites (compare map 6.3c), but is also relatively high in the rural periphery. The suburbs generally record less than 10 per cent. (b) Percentage of workers in white-collar jobs: this is high throughout the region, reflecting the character of its economy; it is highest (more than 60 per cent) in Manhattan and the middle suburban counties. (c) Percentage of owner-occupied dwellings: this is high, more than 45 per cent, throughout the region except for the New York City boroughs and inner New Jersey. In the suburbs the proportion is generally above 65 per cent.

above all the proposed major centre at Jamaica, on Long Island near Kennedy Airport within the New York City borough of Queens. This centre, astride the Long Island Rail Road and on the new subway connection from Manhattan to the airport, would draw on an estimated 285,000 white-collar workers within half an hour by railroad or subway, as well as 700,000 potential shoppers within 20 minutes' travel time; and it is only 12 minutes from Midtown Manhattan by train. Such new centres could be coupled with more flexible zoning, so that the higher densities occurred closer to job or shopping opportunities, or at least closer to the transportation systems that would give access to them; in this way, the region's people could be offered a rational trade-off between better accessibility and more space. But, given present local government structures, the prospects seem questionable.

Basic problems in perspective

Underlying the particular problems in the different parts of the New York region, it now becomes evident that there are two deeper, extremely intractable problems. And one of these is in part an expression of the other. They are the government problem and the transportation problem: and of these that of government is the more basic.

Multiple governments - 1,400 or more

In the Regional Plan Association Harvard Study of 1959–60, Professor Robert Wood described the system of government within the New York Metropolitan Region as perhaps the most complicated ever devised. At the last count, there were 1,467 governments each with the power to raise and spend money. That is not to say that the region is divided into 1,467 separate geographical units of government, for a feature of the American local government system is that it multiplies special-purpose or *ad hoc* authorities in addition to the normal units of local government. In fact at least three separate types of government may be distinguished. First, there are the elected local governments at several levels, including cities, counties, boroughs, towns and villages. The precise role of each of these units varies from State to State. In Connecticut, which follows the New England tradition, the town is the important unit; in New York the county is more important than in New Jersey. Secondly, there are the local *ad hoc* authorities which usually represent unions of several municipal governments, such as school districts, water supply districts and fire districts. Lastly, there are region-wide *ad hoc* authorities which have jurisdiction over a substantial part of the whole metropolitan region, such as the Triborough Bridge and Tunnel Authority within the City of New York, or the Port of New York Authority. This is quite apart from the State governments, whose departments play an important role in the performance of some functions.

This summary description merely concerns the forms of government. Their actual working is conditioned by government traditions, which vary greatly from State to State, and in particular between New York and New Jersey. New Jersey has an extremely restricted tax base with no personal income tax and in general much more restricted than that of New York State. Thus in 1966–7, in different school districts within the region, State aid for education varied from less than one-quarter to more than one-third of the total cost. Statewide, New York provided 40 per cent on average of local school costs, New Jersey 30 per cent and Connecticut less than 30 per cent. Within New York State, the City gets less than its needs would call for; so it relies on a variety of its own taxes, including sales and service taxes. But out of these, it has to bear a heavy burden of welfare and educational services for the poor. In 1966–7, out of New York City's total budget of $4.6 billion (US), $3.1 billion came from the City's own funds; within this total, the $1.5 billion spent on poverty-related services included $1.0 billion from State and Federal funds and $0.5 billion from the City treasury. The Regional Plan Association suggested that, to achieve needed improvements in services, the total budget should go up to $7.2 billion and the poverty-related budget to $3.0 billion; nearly half the former, and all the latter, should be met from outside funds. This would permit a marked improvement in the City's general, non-poverty-related spending programmes, making it a more attractive place to live in.

In practice the different major authorities find rich sources of conflict with each other. The State of New Jersey is at loggerheads with the State of New York, over the taxation of New Jersey residents who work in New York; New York State with New York City, over the allocation of State aid; New York City with the Port of New York Authority, over the failure to co-ordinate transport investments; the Port Authority with the State of New Jersey, over proposals to pool transit revenues. Pollution control is another rich source of confusion; most of New York City's effluent is treated before it goes into the Hudson, but a much higher proportion of New Jersey sewage is untreated; car emission control standards are in part a State matter; solid waste disposal, and the location of power stations, engender conflicts between the City and distant rural areas. Nevertheless, they find it possible to co-operate over some major metropolitan issues. The most outstanding case is perhaps the Tri-State Transportation Committee, set up by the governors of the three States in 1961, which has created a permanent system of regional transportation planning. The complaint is still that such examples of co-ordination are too belated and too few.

To non-American eyes, the most logical solution would be to create an effective unit of local government covering the developed area, like the Greater London Council in Britain. But this is hardly a realistic prospect in America, where one of the most persistent features of twentieth-century life is the apparent failure to reorganize metropolitan government in line with metropolitan development. Few major metropolitan areas have witnessed extensions of territory by their central cities since 1890. Meanwhile, especially since 1940, these central cities have become increasingly the home of the recent immigrant, who brings disproportionately great problems of housing, education and employment. Not surprisingly, the suburbs do not want to share these problems. And the Federal Government is powerless to intervene to force annexation through.

The likely trends are two. First, the Federal Government will play an increasing role, through its interest in major spending programmes like transportation, mortgage financing, urban renewal, water supply and open space – and, from 1973 on, through its revenue-sharing programme. But the present weakness is the failure of local governments to shape the Federal programmes for regional ends. With 551 municipalities and county governments, possessing limited powers, Federal money may be uselessly dissipated. Federal government may therefore increasingly press for more effective region-wide special-purpose authorities to administer Federal or State aid. In the New York region there already exists the Metropolitan Regional Council, which was formed in 1956 and which could play an important role as a central co-ordinating council for such regional agencies.

Secondly, it seems certain that outside New York City the county governments will assume greater responsibility, especially in co-ordinating arrangements for public health, welfare and correction. But existing governments are poorly suited for this role: they are pure State agencies with limited powers, no right of special tax assessment, and governing bodies which are virtually impotent. To succeed in bigger roles they must have more effective governments, must be recognized by the State as municipal corporations and must be given power to make ordinances. Nassau and Westchester counties in New York State have gone some way towards this ideal: they are relatively free of routine administrative duties but they have greater legal powers than usual, and they are run by Boards of Supervisors which represent constituent towns and cities.

In this way, gradually and with the least possible violence to existing institutions, a more viable system of government may emerge. At the lower level, democratized counties could take a broader view of such problems as the rapid rise in suburban population, and the means of providing for it. They would be less readily stampeded into low-density zoning as an expedient to keep down school taxes. At the higher level, the counties could be associated in maintaining democratic region-wide control over special authorities receiving Federal and State aid to deal with problems like transportation planning, land use, water supply, water and air pollution, waste disposal, slum clearance and public housing, recreation and civil defence.

Transportation: ageing infrastructure, mounting deficit

Transportation in the New York region is only one area where, apparently, the existing administrative machine is defective. But so important is transportation to the whole pattern of development of the region, that it is worthwhile to focus special attention upon it.

Like other major world cities, New York is an urban region with a highly centralized urban economy: more than one-third of all the workers of the Metropolitan Region find their living in Manhattan south of 61st Street. This labour force depends on the most highly developed system of public transportation in the United States. In 1963 on a typical working day (more recent figures are lacking), 1,627,000 people entered the Manhattan CBD to work. Of these, 111,000 or 7.1 per cent came by car; another 74,000 or 4.7 per cent came by miscellaneous modes (e.g. taxi, ferry or truck) and 73,000 (4.7 per cent) walked. That left 1,306,000, or 83.5 per cent, using public transportation – of whom 1,098,000 (70.2 per cent) used the subway, 63,000 (4.0 per cent) the railroad and 145,000 (9.3 per cent) the bus. In New York City, outside the CBD, the percentage of public transportation commuters fell to 43.4; in the Transportation Study area outside the city, it fell to 10.8 per cent, and here 76.5 per cent commuted by car. The dependence of the CBD on public transportation in fact has no parallel elsewhere in the United States; it reflects the much greater capacity of rail transport to carry big flows of people within a relatively short time to the same destination. It has been estimated that cars on a normal New York street can handle about 1,300 people in each lane per hour (assuming an average of 1.75 people in each car), and cars on an urban motorway can handle 3,200 persons per lane per hour on the same assumption; but a commuter railroad could theoretically carry 43,200 passengers per track per hour with all passengers seated, and the subway with its standing capacity could take 60,000 per track per hour. It is also estimated that, if all Manhattan's commuters arrived by automobile, five levels of parking space would be required over all the usable land from the Bowery to 52nd Street. Whatever the future curve of Manhattan employment, it is certain that by 2000 the great majority of workers there will still rely on the public transportation system to get to work (map 6.5). But conversely, the more the hold of Manhattan is loosened, the more workers are likely to turn to their private cars for travel to work.

Yet within the New York region, until recently there has been no authority to see that the transport system, and investment in future transportation, make a coherent whole; still more seriously, there has been no body looking at the relation between transport and land use. Decisions on investment and charging have been taken independently by dozens of authorities, of which only the most important are the Port of New York Authority, the Triborough Bridge and Tunnel Authority, the State and Federal Highway Authorities, toll highway agencies, suburban railroads, private suburban bus lines, the New York City Transit Authority, the three State Transportation Regulation Authorities, the Interstate Commerce Commission, County and City public works officials and planners. Finally, at the instigation of the Regional Plan Association, the governors of the States of New York, New Jersey and Connecticut agreed in 1961 to set up the Tri-State Transportation Committee in order to consider the future development of the public transportation of the region. Though the Committee was strictly concerned only with public transport, it has published total transportation studies of its area. In a study of development alternatives for the region in 1985, the Tri-State planners stressed the clear relationship between transportation and economic activity patterns. Since employment in Manhattan is expected to grow and the commuters' homes will be even more dispersed than now, heavy investment for better rail public transportation to the CBD must be a priority in all plans. But for the six in ten of the Tri-State region's workers who will find employment outside the CBD, much will depend on whether employment opportunities are strongly concentrated in a few major centres based on public transportation, or dispersed. The more concentrated alternatives would need good mass transit to be workable; but on the other hand they could exploit it more effectively. Later the Committee was transformed into a wider-ranging Tri-State Regional Planning Commission – though in 1982 Connecticut withdrew, thus putting an end to the Commission and leaving the metropolitan area without any official agency for regional planning.

Meanwhile, despite the planning studies of the Tri-State Commission, the making of transport policy is fragmented to an extreme degree. Despite the great preponderance of public transportation into Manhattan during working hours, all the major improvements in access to Manhattan since 1945 have been in the private sector: notably the opening of the third tube of the Lincoln vehicular tunnel from New Jersey in 1957, and the completion of the second deck of the George Washington Bridge, connecting the nothern tip of Man-

---

Map 6.5 *New York region: commuting, 1970.* (a) Percentage of resident workers commuting outside county of residence: the outer parts of New York City and the suburbs are the principal dormitory areas, while residents in Manhattan and the fringe counties tend to find work locally. (b) Percentage of resident workers in cores and rings of Standard Metropolitan Statistical Areas (SMSAS) commuting by car: generally, the great majority of workers in the rings commute by car; for workers in central cities, especially New York, the proportion is much lower.

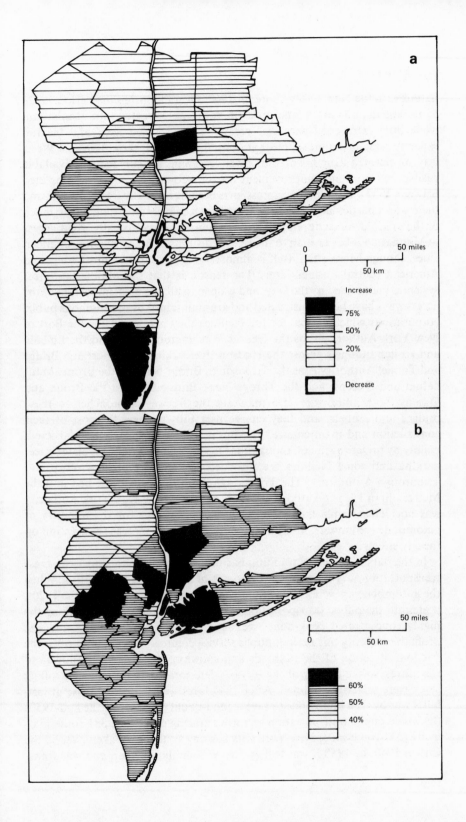

a

0 _____ 50 miles
0 _____ 50 km

Increase

75%
50%
20%

Decrease

b

0 _____ 50 miles
0 _____ 50 km

60%
50%
40%

hattan with the New Jersey shore, in 1962. Overall, during the period 1932–58 no less than 34 extra lanes of expressway were created into Manhattan, while little extra roadspace was created on the island itself and the rail capacity remained almost constant (map 6.6). Indeed, the collapse of Westway, an elevated structure on the Lower West Side, actually reduced available roadspace. No major improvement on the subway system was completed between 1932 and 1970; the express lines became seriously overcrowded, and there was a particular deficiency on the east side of Manhattan, where much of the postwar office development has occurred. Paradoxically, road access to Manhattan is better than to the central districts of many smaller American cities, though Manhattan itself is almost without doubt the most congested American central business area. The reason is that the Manhattan street system is maintained by the City, and is open to all: the most important of the access ways have been constructed and are maintained by autonomous public corporations which charge for the facilities they provide. Thus the Port of New York Authority runs the George Washington Bridge and the Lincoln and Holland tunnels across the Hudson river, while the Triborough Bridge and Tunnel Authority runs the Triborough Bridge between the Bronx, Manhattan and Queens, and the Throgs Neck Bridge between the Bronx and Queens; both authorities also maintain the freeway approaches to these bridges and tunnels, and they charge user tolls to meet the cost of their construction and maintenance. Parking is in turn separately administered, mainly by private agencies, though the Department of Traffic regulates street parking and some facilities are provided by the Port of New York and Triborough Authorities. The Triborough Authority was embodied into the Metropolitan Transit Authority in 1968, but the Port of New York Authority was not. Thus, while the system generously provides for the minority of automobile commuters, at a price, it actually acts to increase congestion on the city streets.

In the public sector the tradition has been quite opposite. American mass transportation was the product of an era of monopoly, before 1918. When the automobile arrived in large numbers on New York streets, in the 1920s, it ate into the public transportation system's off-peak revenues, making the highly concentrated peak-hour weekday commuting services less and less profitable. During this period, public service commissions circumscribed the freedom of action of the railroads and subways: they were not allowed to raise fares, so the quality of the services deteriorated as stations and rolling stock were under-maintained. After 1945 fares were allowed to rise at last, but it was by then impossible to save a good-quality service. By the mid-1950s the whole public transportation sector was facing crisis. The 381-route-kilometre (237-route-mile) New York City subway system was taken over by the City in 1940; by 1953 it was losing over $100 million a year, and was trans-

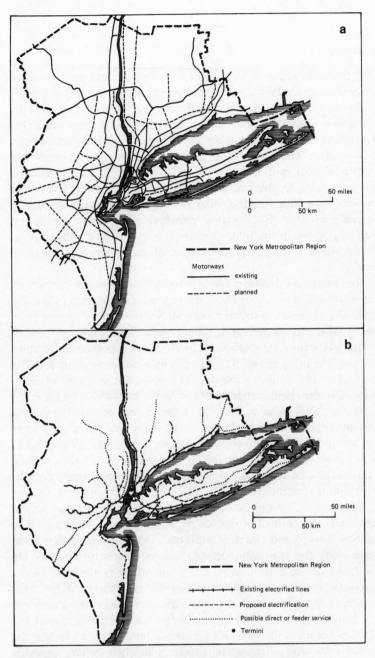

Map 6.6 *New York region: transportation projects.* (a) The major
expressways down to about 1970, mainly toll facilities built by the States or
special agencies, improved access to Manhattan and thus increased
congestion in the CBD. In the 1960s the Interstate Highways (particularly 287)
and the Verrazano Narrows Bridge offered circumferential links aiding
decentralization of factory and office jobs. (This map shows only heavy
freight-carrying highways.) (b) By the 1970s major rail projects were also
underway in the region.

167

ferred to the semi-autonomous New York City Transit Authority so as to relieve the city finances. In 1968 it was transferred to the Metropolitan Transit Authority. By this time the annual deficit was $132 million – all met by the City. And two authorities, McLelland and Magdovitz, have suggested that it would take the staggering total of $50 billion to bring the mass transit system up to scratch. The new arrangement made it possible to issue state bonds to cover almost half the cost of a $13 billion (US) construction programme, especially on the east side. New cross-Manhattan links were another priority; extensions in the outer boroughs, to serve a dispersing population, were another. But by 1972 eventual costs were estimated at $2.5 billion (US) of which the State contribution was fixed at $0.6 billion. Meanwhile ridership, stable throughout most of the 1960s, had begun to decline again.

The short but important Hudson and Manhattan Tube system, connecting the New Jersey railroads with the central district, went bankrupt in 1954 and by 1962 faced abandonment, though it carried 29 million passengers a year; in September 1962 it was taken over by a Port Authority subsidiary, the Port Authority Trans-Hudson Corporation or PATH, which has spent large sums on regeneration. The Long Island Rail Road, which carries heavy commuter loads from Nassau and Suffolk Counties, had long been a subject of bitter New York jokes; it went bankrupt in 1949 and by the early 1950s had reached a point of near physical collapse. In 1954, a twelve-year rehabilitation programme was announced, based on help from all sides: tax concessions from the State, City and County governments; a waiver by the Pennsylvania Railroad (the parent company) of interest dividend and principal payments; and a $60 million investment programme. This work has continued, and the railroad is being extended into east Midtown Manhattan to give direct access from Long Island to the new office concentrations there; in 1965 the system was brought under the control of the Metropolitan Transit Authority. The New York, New Haven and Hartford Railroad, bringing commuters from Westchester County and from Connecticut, was also bankrupt by 1961. On this system – part of the Penn Central Railroad, which is now part of the national AMTRAK system – the Metropolitan Transit Authority has now assumed responsibility. The New Jersey railroads can finance their commuter services from freight operations, but they suffer from lack of direct Manhattan access and from competition from long-distance buses which can use the Lincoln Tunnel; their total patronage fell catastrophically from 1951 onwards and several services are now being kept open only with the help of State subsidies.

The future outlook is confusing. The Federal Government has financed a 66,000 kilometre (41,000 mile) $41 billion (US) programme of Interstate and Defense Highways, started in 1956 and largely complete by 1980; in the New

York region some of the most important projects have given extra capacity in radial freeways like the New Jersey Turnpike or the Long Island Expressway, so bringing more automobile commuters to the Manhattan approaches. But it is now accepted policy that no extra highway capacity in the inner city should be provided, and plans for the cross-Brooklyn and Lower Manhattan Expressways, which were vigorously supported by the Tri-State planners, have been abandoned by the City. The big increase in population in the exurban zone, 40 to 80 kilometres (25 to 50 miles) from Manhattan, coupled with the growth of executive jobs in Manhattan, will throw an extra strain on the longer-distance commuter railroads – though the investment now in hand should help to cope.

In 1962, the local governments of the region spent 32 per cent of their capital budgets on highways and only 5 per cent on mass transit; the Tri-State interim transportation plan for 1985 would demand a shift in these proportions, with rail transit receiving one-third of the capital expenditure on transportation. Meanwhile, the Metropolitan Transit Authority's deficit escalated from $64 million in 1969–70 to $400 million in 1975. Only a small part would be met by Federal funds, through the 1974 Mass Transportation Assistance Act; and the danger was that the city would be tempted to fill the operating gap by raiding the available construction subsidy, thus postponing much needed developments like the Second Avenue subway and the 63rd Street tunnel. Yet the move towards transit is occurring: by 1972 the three States of New York, New Jersey and Connecticut had together devised programmes for spending $1.5 billion (US) on suburban railroads and $2.3 billion (US) on subways. The New York programme will involve modernization and extension of the suburban railways; the New Jersey programme concentrates on the suburban railroads. And at last, on the New York side of the Hudson, the Metropolitan Transit Authority took over responsibility for investment and fare-setting on the subway, buses and commuter railroads. In 1981 the governor of New York State and the mayor of the City agreed on a $5.6 billion (US) investment package as part of an agreement that gave $100 million in operating aid but raised subway fares from 60 cents to 75 cents; by the start of 1983, another rise was in the offing.

Overall, by the end of the 1970s there was thus a real determination to invest in improved rail service into the Manhattan CBD. This could not only improve service levels for existing commuters, but also help extend the commuter field and make the Manhattan CBD more attractive to employers and employees alike. But by 1981, the Reagan administration was threatening a two-year phasing-out of all urban mass transit operating aid and a large cut in capital budgets. This was bound to have a particularly serious effect on the New York region, which counted one-third of all bus and rail passenger transit miles and three-quarters of all commuter rail passenger miles in the United States. It was estimated that the effect would be a further $168 million drain on a Metropolitan Transit Authority already seriously in deficit.

The biggest question, however, concerns the increase in jobs outside the central core, especially the growth of factory and wholesale jobs in the outer suburbs. This must lead to a big increase in reverse commuting, against the main central tide, and even more to the growth of cross-trips round the periphery, which can be satisfactorily undertaken only by automobile. If this could be accompanied by a concentration of highway construction on concentric lines, round the edge of the region, it might be a wholesome trend. By the mid-1970s, there was a well-developed network of freeways which bypassed the congested core, such as the Garden State Parkway of New Jersey, the Cross-Bronx Expressway from the George Washington Bridge to the Throgs Neck Bridge, the Cross-Westchester Expressway farther north and above all the circumferential highway, Interstate 287, around the entire western periphery of the region from Perth Amboy on the Atlantic coast in the south to the New York State Thruway's Tappan Zee Bridge in the north; it may be expected to attract fast-growing types of factory industry, just as the circumferential Route 128 has done so dramatically on the western side of Boston. A similar project is the Triborough Authority's Verrazano Narrows Bridge, which since 1964 has provided a critical link across the southern coastal periphery, linking Staten and Long Islands (map 6.6a).

The Tri-State plans provide for big extensions to the region's expressway network, which already totalled 1,770 kilometres (1,100 miles) in the late 1960s, to give better circumferential access from suburb to suburb. Many of these planned highways were in fact blocked by protest movements in the mid-1970s; some seemed unlikely ever to be built. In any case the extra non-CBD workplaces cannot and should not depend exclusively on the private car. The Regional Plan Association has called for its new planned metropolitan centres to be linked by efficient mass transit lines, giving very rapid reverse commuting facilities from Manhattan and Brooklyn. In many cases these would be the existing services which have spare capacity in the reverse direction to the peak flows. Centres nearer the Manhattan CBD would be served by rail; more distant centres would depend on buses (map 6.6b).

One feature of the New York pattern of transportation will not greatly change. Manhattan will still remain almost unbearably congested. Average traffic speeds there in working hours are estimated at 6 to 10 kilometres (4 to 6 miles) per hour; far below most European cities. It is calculated that, even if 50 per cent of the present automobile commuters between New Jersey and New York shifted to other means, the total street usage in Manhattan streets would drop by only about 3.5 per cent. For most Manhattan traffic is commercial traffic which is firmly rooted there. It could be displaced only if Manhattan were deserted by much of its present business activity; and that, we have already seen, seems an unlikely prospect.

The region's future: two views

The optimistic future of the 1960s

In the late 1950s, the Regional Plan Association took a pioneering world lead in analysing and forecasting the progress of an urban economy, by commissioning a team of Harvard economists to study the main facets of the New York region's economy with a projection of employment and population down to 1985. Updated and extended in the late 1960s, these forecasts gave a picture of growth of the region as far as the year 2000, as seen during a period of expansion and optimism.

During the period from 1965 to 2000, the Association estimated (in 1967-8), employment in the region as they define it would nearly double, from 7.7 million to 13.2 million; this growth would be dominated by white-collar jobs, already 55 per cent of total employment in 1965, which would double from 4.2 to 8.4 million. This growth of 5.7 million jobs would naturally trigger an even bigger population growth – an estimated increase of 11.2 million, from 19.0 to 30.2 million. Of this, a mere 13 per cent was expected to represent net immigration, as compared with 28 per cent for the quarter century 1940 to 1965. Much would depend here, of course, on the future characteristics of the New York labour market: the great majority of the black and Puerto Rican immigrants of the 1940s and 1950s were unskilled, but the needs of the regional economy for such labour now seems to have dried up for ever.

The population would divide itself into more and smaller households: there might be 9.7 million of them in 2000, compared with 6.0 million in the mid-1960s, and the average size would have fallen from 3.19 to 3.12, with a notable increase (from 43 to 49 per cent) in the percentage of one and two person households. This in itself was bound to generate a buoyant demand for new apartment construction. Households would be richer on average, with a dramatic increase – from 26 per cent to 71 per cent of all households – in the proportion with incomes over $10,000 a year in constant 1965 terms. But the poor, and above all the non-whites, might fail to share in this growing affluence – especially if they live in large households. Thus the problem of relative deprivation in comparison with the affluence of the majority, already glaringly evident in the New York of the 1960s and 1970s, might escalate in the last decades of the century. And affluence would bring with it problems of

171

greater mobility, with total distances driven increasing by perhaps 85 per cent between 1965 and 2000.

For traditionally trained urban planners, perhaps the most spectacular resulting problem would be the implications for land development: as already shown, the Regional Plan's own estimates suggest that open land may fall from over 70 per cent of the total area of the region in 1965, to only 35 per cent in the year 2000. Thus more land would be needed for the 11 million extra people expected between 1965 and 2000 than was required for the 19 million living in the region in the mid-1960s. Nevertheless, the Regional Plan Association argued, with proper regional planning this would be acceptable. Without it, spread city would mean lengthening commuter journeys, a steadily more segregated society, lack of access to the services a large urban region like this ought to be able to provide, poor transportation services, a feeling of being shut off from nature and the countryside, and a lack of a clear community focus.

To counter these dangers, the Association's Second Regional Plan, published as a draft for discussion in 1968, suggests five basic principles of regional planning. First, as already outlined, is the creation of new major urban centres to provide for a lion's share of new jobs – above all in the white-collar sector, where 65 per cent of new office jobs are expected to locate outside the Manhattan CBD – and provide needed concentrations of higher level community services – health, entertainment, retailing, the arts, education. They would cut the length and the strain of commuter journeys, provide better services to the growing suburbs, and provide an alternative location to the CBD for many employers and employees alike; they would convert the New York region into a polycentric metropolis, which has already been shown to offer such striking advantages in agglomerations such as Randstad Holland. Secondly, and associated with the first, zoning policies for new housing would be revised to provide a much greater variety of new housing types and densities. Above all, people would be given a better choice to trade off accessibility against space, and people of lower incomes would get better access to the general housing market.

Thirdly, the Regional Plan Association suggests, the older cities must be relieved of the crushing burden of paying for poverty related public services so that they may spend necessary resources in raising their general level of service provision – thus, finally, improving their general environment so as to make the cities once again attractive to a mixture of income levels and social groups. At the same time, if welfare burdens were shouldered by the Federal government, the pressure of in-migration by further poor groups could be greatly eased. Training programmes should be developed to allow the poor to move up the ladder of skills; and more unskilled jobs need to be provided for the populations that could benefit from them, near the heart of the cities.

Fourthly, the new urban development should be channelled so as to keep substantial parts of the region still in a state of nature. About 25,000 square kilometres (10,000 square miles) of the Appalachian Mountains, stretching from Vermont to Virginia, should be acquired as a vast regional park, while the remaining open coast and many river areas should also be reserved for recreation and conservation. It would be prudent, the Regional Plan Association suggests, to buy this land now before the prospect of development raises land values.

Lastly, the draft Regional Plan makes important proposals for transportation. If the new major metropolitan centres are built as the Association suggests, then they will both demand much better public transportation if they are to work properly, but at the same time will make good public transportation possible. The three innermost of the proposed centres – Brooklyn, Newark and Jamaica – can tap the existing rail network through reverse commuting from the centre of the region; but the outlying centres will depend mainly on much improved bus transportation, which must include built-in priority over private car traffic. Within each centre, good planning plus new mechanical aids (such as travellators) should guarantee much better movement than people now enjoy, with an emphasis on easy pedestrian routes. And, by grouping higher density housing around these new centres, there will be a good transportation alternative for those who do not want or cannot use the private car – the young, the old, the sick and the poor. But at the same time, planning must cope with the big expected increase in car use, by new expressways which would cater for as much as one-third of all the region's vehicle travel.

The draft plan was under intensive discussion in the late 1960s and early 1970s. It demanded the co-operation of many different agents both private and public – City and County planning agencies, transportation agencies, State and perhaps Federal park authorities, private developers. Some parts indeed would require major changes in national policies – particularly the idea for relieving the financial burdens of the cities, which has been partly met by President Nixon's 1973 revenue sharing plan. But though the proposals may seem utopian for a private organization lacking any powers, past evidence suggests that the Association may perform a remarkable catalytic function in co-ordinating the actions of different organizations for the mutual good of all. It may seem unusual to the citizenry of countries which have more highly developed formal regional planning machines, but the only final test will be whether it achieves its stated goals.

The changed world of the 1970s and 1980s

This was the outlook in the late 1960s. But then, within a very short time, a complete change occurred in the region's future prospects – and though part

173

of this resulted from the recession of the 1980s which might soon be remedied, another more important part looked like being structural and perhaps permanent.

Population growth in the region first levelled off – an expression partly of a dramatic fall in birth-rate (by 25 per cent in the years 1970–3 alone), partly of a new trend of migration out of the region – and then began to fall. The region's fertility rate, always well below the national average, fell by 28 per cent from 1970 to 1976. Average growth, which had exceeded 200,000 a year throughout the 1950s and 1960s, turned into decline after 1972. As a result, future expectations of demographic growth had to be reduced: against a 1973 base of 19.8 million, from 30 million in the year 2000, as forecast in 1968, to a stable 27 million by the year 2020. And even this, in the light of 1980 figures, may be optimistic.

The internal mechanics of population distribution were significant too. By the early 1970s not merely the core of the region as defined by the Regional Plan Association, but also the inner ring, were experiencing out-migration. Thus the new forecast, made in the mid-1970s, was that by 1990 the population of the core might have fallen by as much as one million; the inner ring might have suffered modest decline; while the intermediate and outer rings might have increased by a million or more. Significantly, the biggest projected increases in the poulation were in the 25–34 age group, who were the major homebuilders and child rearers – and hence the prime candidates for further suburban sprawl. Coupled with a continuing process of division of the population into smaller households, this meant that future land demands might still be heavy: the Regional Plan Association was predicting an increase in the total urbanized area from 7,300 square kilometres (2,830 square miles) (in 1970) to 9,920 square kilometres (3,830 square miles) in 1990.

Secondly, and associatedly, economic growth had drastically tapered off. Against an increase in employment of 2 million (30 per cent) during the period 1950–70, the period 1970–6 saw a decline of 375,000: a happening unprecedented since the great depression of the 1930s. Manufacturing, static during the 1960s, now suffered a massive loss. The losses in employment were particularly marked in New York City, which recorded a fall of over half-a-million – mostly in manufacturing. By this time, the only potentially dynamic sector in the city was white-collar employment; but even there the early 1970s had seen an accelerating loss of corporate headquarters offices.

The reason, as George Sternlieb put it, was that New York had become an historic anomaly. It had provided a convenient location for immigrant entrepreneurs, and immigrant labour, in an era when strong cultural and institutional barriers restricted flows of capital and labour. But by the late twentieth century, the United States has an increasingly homogeneous labour force, a national capital market and uniformly good transportation and communication systems. In this world, New York City's traditional features – high densities of activity, congestion, difficult travel conditions, high wages, strong unionization – are a positive disadvantage for many firms. Manufacturing, in contrast, is tending to locate in the environmentally superior areas of Florida or the far west, or alternatively in the formerly depressed rural areas of the old south. The last place to do effective business, it now increasingly appears, is in the older, bigger cities of the east – of which New York is the archetype.

One major emerging problem, common to other large world cities, is a mismatch between available jobs and the labour force. Though New York City offers a uniquely large and diverse labour market, it is increasingly dominated by the tertiary sector: 80 per cent of jobs are in finance, insurance, real estate, government and other services, and 60 per cent of all jobs are white-collar jobs. But the increasingly black and Puerto Rican population of the inner city – especially the male element – are unsuited for these jobs: only one-third of blacks, and 27 per cent of Puerto Rican males, were in white-collar occupations in 1970, though around half their female counterparts were. So it is unsurprising that, since the 1970–1 recession, New York City unemployment has exceeded the national rate.

In consequence the City has a huge – and increasing – problem of welfare dependency. Within a stable population of roughly 8 million, welfare recipients rose between 1960 and 1980 from 328,000 to 1,400,000, or from 4 to 20 per cent of the entire population. These welfare dependents tend heavily to belong to ethnic minority groups (around 80 per cent, against 30 per cent in the whole population), to be less educated than the average New Yorker, to have come to New York from outside (especially from the South or from the Caribbean), and to suffer from physical or mental illness; there are many multi-problem families. Ironically, then, a city that is increasingly dependent on high-skill, high-salary jobs can make less and less use of an increasingly unskilled, poorly educated work-force.

The crisis of New York City

The fiscal crisis of New York City, which made world headlines during 1975, had one immediate cause: a massive loss of confidence in the City administration on the part of the major financial institutions that had previously been willing to lend money on the city's bond issues. But at root the crisis lay much deeper: in the evolving economy of the City, in the political response to a growing structural crisis, in the power held by different interest groups in the City.

At bottom was the decline in the City's economy. A loss of 400,000 jobs between 1969 and 1975, some 11 per cent of the total employment – a decline that occurred right across the manufacturing and service sectors – meant a massive erosion of the tax base and a simultaneous increase in the City's welfare burdens. But simultaneously, through this entire period – though less rapidly than in the era of Lindsay's mayorship, from 1966 to 1973 – employment in the City's own labour force continued to grow: by 244 per cent overall in the decade 1966–76. In fact, by the mid-1970s the City was the second largest employer in the United States after the Federal government, with some 350,000 on its payroll.

There are many possible explanations; but they fall into two main schools. One, the conservative, holds that the villains were the City politicians – and behind them the City labour unions. The City had traditionally been a profligate spender: on the City university, on the public hospital system, on public housing and on transit subsidies. The taxes to pay for these services came for the most part from business; the services, for the most part, benefited the really poor less than the average middle-class voter. And it was these services, plus welfare, that showed the biggest increases in spending over the 1966–76 decade; basic services, like sanitation or police, grew much less. But the well established public service unions, such as the teachers, also benefited hugely – especially through generous pension agreements, which led to a massive funding problem for the City.

The alternative explanation holds that the City has been wronged. When the comparison is fairly made, it is argued, New York is no more profligate in most services than comparable cities. It spends less on welfare per head, for instance, than Philadelphia or Baltimore. One reason for the City's crisis, according to this school, is that the City has an exceptional concentration of social problems such as drug addiction. Another is that, unlike cities in many states, the City has to provide more support for its services because the state provides less. The City has no county aid for courts or hospitals, no tax district for its schools. It must raise one-third of its welfare budget itself, because it gets no benefit from the rich counties that ring it to the north and east. Since the government structure is unitary, the trouble-ridden components drag all the rest down. Such is the counter argument.

Whatever the true explanation, the evident fact is that the City embarked on a potentially very dangerous fiscal path. From the mid-1960s onwards, it issued short-term bonds to meet the increasing gap between income and expenditure. As these became due for payment, it was forced to roll them over: that is, to issue new bonds to pay the interest and principal on the old ones, and to meet the continuing expenditure gap. By 1976, it had $2.6 billion

(US) of such debts, while its current account deficit for the year was expected to be $726 million.

At this point, for whatever reason, the financial institutions lost confidence. In March 1975 the City found for the first time that its bond issues would not sell. The resulting crisis led in June 1975 to the formation of the Municipal Assistance Corporation – or, as it soon became known in tribute to a famous hamburger, the Big Mac. MAC was a State corporation pledged to borrow on behalf of the City, with a cover provided by state taxation and a promise to reform the City's fiscal practices. But the market remained nervous, and in September the State was forced to pass a Financial Emergency Act whereby $2.3 billion (US) was raised to meet the City's immediate cash needs, with an emergency Financial Control Board to set the City's fiscal practices on a sound basis by mid-1978. Yet collapse still loomed, to be stilled only by a Federal act guaranteeing funds in December 1975.

By 1982, through a combination of economies, State aid and Federal subsidy, the City could announce an actual budget surplus. Thus, temporarily, the City's crisis has abated. But the root causes are still present; and they interact. The likelihood is that the tax base will continue to erode as manufacturing – and even white-collar jobs – desert New York for other cities and regions. Yet this can only cause the burden of dependency to increase further; while inherited problems like the funding of the World Trade Center, or the deficits of the Long Island Rail Road, will not go away. Nor has the political sociology of the City altered: the great public service unions retain their power, and in a city so dependent of public services as New York the threat of a strike is not taken lightly. Many argue that the only answer is for the Federal government to intervene, by diverting investment from the southern and western states where so much of it has gone since 1945. Yet much of that Federal spending has been on defence, and it is difficult to see how in the short run it could readily be channelled into the City. Pessimistic commentators, like McLelland and Magdovitz, point out that the budget is limited only in a technical sense and that several of the basic problems – an ageing population needing greater welfare expenditure, a decaying infrastructure – will not go away. The only ray of light is that in contrast to the early 1970s, the period since 1975 has seen a revival of business activity in the heart of the City.

The history of New York City in the 1970s, some pessimists say, is the fate of many other world cities in the 1980s and 1990s. Earlier than other great metropolitan areas, they argue, New York experienced the chill effects of major shifts in the geography of basic industry – shifts that can now also be seen beginning to affect the fortunes of London and Paris, Amsterdam and perhaps even Tokyo. Truly, also, New York has its unique features – not least the American tradition of forcing cities to stand on their own without central government aid, now somewhat dented by necessity. But the New York crisis certainly bears pondering by planners and politicians in other world cities. It might happen there too.

7 Tokyo

Of all the world cities, Tokyo is richest in paradoxes. In terms of population it is the largest city authority, and the second largest metropolitan area, in the world; but its public services are structured for a city some one-half the present size. Its factories produce some of the most technologically sophisticated products in the world; yet, despite a rate of economic growth almost without parallel during the 1960s and 1970s, its physical living standards are still noticeably below those of most of the other world cities considered in this book, and they contrast sharply in turn with relative poverty in Japan's provincial agrarian regions, only a few hundred kilometres away. Its rate of population growth compares with those of the newly-industrializing cities we shall study in the following chapters; it shares with them enormous problems in accommodating the extra millions of people. It is a metropolis, in the 1980s, where an elaborate network of urban expressways was virtually complete, but where only half the city's 11.5 million people were connected to main drainage. Of all world cities, it is the one whose citizens have devised the most varied and original solutions to their own problems; yet it remains a city where these problems still strike at the ordinary citizen every waking hour.

Many of these problems reflect Tokyo's size; but this, as with almost every other world city, presents a nice problem in definition. There is the *historic* Tokyo, or ward area; enlarged many times, the city numbered twenty-three wards in 1980, with 8,351,893 people at the census of that year. There is the *administrative* Tokyo: the area of the Tokyo Metropolitan Government (TMG) which provides local government services for the ward area and for the suburbs immediately around it. This is almost, but not quite, identical to the Tokyo *prefecture*: one of the basic units into which Japan is divided for the purposes of central government. At the 1980 Census of Japan, the ward area had a population of 11,471,892, having become the first city authority in the world with over 10 million people. But between 1975 and 1980, for the first time, it declined; while outside the TMG limits, rapid population growth has already created a Tokyo *agglomeration*: a continuous urban area having close functional links with central Tokyo. There are at least three ways of measuring this area. The United Nations, using figures supplied by the Japanese Census, have defined an area containing an estimated 20,045,000 people in 1980. The

179

Japanese Census itself, on the basis of 'densely-populated enumeration districts' (with more than 4,000 people per square kilometre, 10,360 per square mile) has come out with a slightly smaller population: 20,355,888 (in 1980), distributed in sharply radial fashion along the major railway lines, with some isolated concentrations up to 50 kilometres (30 miles) from central Tokyo. And two Japanese geographers, Teruo Ishimizu and Hiroshi Ishihara, have used commuting ties to define a Tokyo Metropolitan Area extending up to 55 to 65 kilometres (32 to 40 miles) from the centre and including a 1975 population of 25,090,000. Lastly, there is the *planners'* Tokyo: the area which it is necessary to consider as a whole, if a more viable structure is to be found for Tokyo in the future. The area defined in the National Capital Region Development Law of 1956 extends up to a radius of 100 to 125 kilometres (60 to 75 miles) from Tokyo Station; it had a population of no less than 35,701,559 in 1980. These definitions of Tokyo are shown in table 7.1 and map 7.1a-b.

Table 7.1 The Tokyo region: definitions and constituent parts, 1980

	Area (square km.)	Population (thousands) 1980	Population change (per cent) 1970–80
Tokyo Ward Area	518	8,351.9	− 5.5
Tokyo Metropolitan Government (TMG)	2,145	11,471.9	+ 2.8
Agglomeration (census definition)	2,204	20,355.9	+ 20.7
National Capital Planning Region	36,834	35,701.6	+ 18.7
(UN definition)		(20,045.0)	+ 34.9

Sources: Census, 1980; United Nations, *Patterns of Urban and Rural Population Growth* (*Population Studies* 68), New York: United Nations, 1980.

Tokyo in history

Tokyo is no newcomer among the world's great cities though it achieved world city status late in its history. As long ago as 1785 it had a population of 1.4 million people, and was almost certainly the biggest city of the world in terms of population; London, its nearest west European competitor, had less than 900,000 at that time. Yet Tokyo, then known as Edo, could not claim to be a world city for the simple reason that the city was almost completely shut off from the world. Both the size and the isolation result from history. By Japanese, if not by world standards, Tokyo is a young city; the empire dates

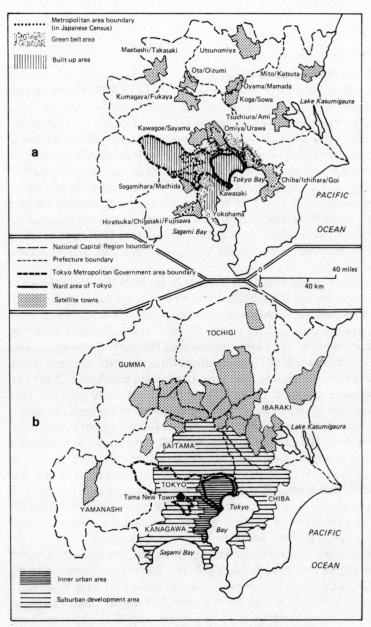

Map 7.1 *The Tokyo region.* With continuing rapid growth, Tokyo presents a problem of definition. In 1980 the 'Ward Area', with a population of 8,351,893, and the larger Tokyo Metropolitan Government area, with 11,471,892, were both losing people; the Tokyo prefecture is almost, but not precisely, equal to the TMG. Far larger is the National Capital Planning Region, with over 35,701,559 people. (a) The main planning divisions pre-1965: the green belt and satellites were heavily modelled on Abercombie's 1944 Greater London Plan. (b) Post-1965: the previous scheme having proved ineffectual, Tokyo planners distinguished a suburban development area and another more distant zone (unshaded on map) where development would be controlled.

from about AD 300 and the ancient capital of Kyoto from 794, but the first fort on the site of Tokyo was established only in the twelfth century and the permanent fort of Edo – which became the nucleus of the later city – was built by the warrior Ota Dokan as late as 1456-7. Yet less than a century and a half later, Tokyo was the *de facto* seat of power in Japan. When the fort at Edo was built, power had already passed from the Imperial Court at Kyoto to warring lords and their bands of retainers. One such lord, Tokugawa Ieyasu, occupied Edo in 1590 and established a territorial governorship, or shogunate, there in 1603. In 1615 he rose in revolt against Toyotomi Hideyori, the son of Toyotomi Hideyoshi who had managed to achieve nominal national unity thirty years before, and defeated him. From 1615 onwards, then, Japan was unified peaceably under the Tokugawa regime; and the seat of that regime was Edo.

The Tokugawa regime effectively isolated Japan from the rest of the world for over three centuries. It established also a peculiar system of power which was directly responsible for the size of Edo's population. The individual lords, or *daimyo*, had to stay in Edo for part of the year, leaving hostages when they went to their own fief. Thus large numbers of retainers, the *samurai*, were quartered in Edo. As late as the mid-nineteenth century the *samurai*, then a superfluous and parasitic class, numbered two million people or 6.25 per cent of the Japanese population; but in Edo they made up 30–40 per cent. They created there a big luxury demand, which was satisfied by a complex economic organization including merchants, craftsmen and a putting-out system using cheap agricultural labour. This system was well suited to rapid and supple adaptation to changes in demand; and it proved an extremely favourable structure for the rapid development of consumer-goods industries of a specifically metropolitan type, as soon as western technology could be applied. So the conventional view – that the Tokugawa period was economically backward and provided an unfavourable background for further development – could in this instance hardly be further from the truth.

After the collapse of the Tokugawa regime, indeed, the Japanese adopted western techniques with remarkable speed. The Tokugawa regime collapsed, the Emperors were restored (no longer at Kyoto but in the fort at Edo, which became the Imperial Palace of the renamed Tokyo), in 1868. Telegrams arrived in 1869, a postal service in 1871, a steam train in 1872, the gas lamp in 1874 and the electric lamp in 1878. Under the new Meiji regime, industry grew and with it population. Tokyo's own population had fallen in the latter days of the Tokugawa shogunate because of the gradual dispersion of the *samurai* class: it was 596,000 in 1873. But then it rose rapidly to 810,000 in 1878 and to 1,370,000 in 1889, at the birth of the new administrative city of Tokyo. By 1920 the population was 3,358,000; the disastrous earthquake and fire of 1923 did little to halt the city's progress, but rather helped to decentralize the city. Its population spread westwards, on to the higher land away from the bay, while industry developed especially southwards along the bay coast between Tokyo itself and the old but rapidly expanding port city of Yokohama. By 1942 the city population had reached 6,916,000 and the entire area of the prefecture (which embraced the city, together with outlying cities, counties and islands in Tokyo Bay, and which became the area of the new TMG in 1943) was up to 7,358,000. Wartime bombing reduced the population of the metropolitan government area to just over 3 million in 1945; the population did not exceed the pre-1945 record until 1953 when 7,448,562 was recorded. Yet in 1962 the metropolitan government became the first administrative city in the world with a population to pass the 10-million mark, and by 1980 the population was 11,469,000.

It is common to think of this extraordinary growth in population as being due to rapid natural increase. But that overlooks the fact that natural increase in Japan reached a maximum in the late 1920s and early 1930s, since when the reduction in the birth-rate has been much steeper than the continued fall in the death-rate. In 1980 natural increase in Japan was 7.5 per thousand, closely comparable with the United States and considerably higher than any European country. During the 1950s and 1960s, indeed, no less than 70 per cent of the growth of the Tokyo population represented net migration, chiefly for jobs and for higher education. However, during the 1960s the rate of growth of the TMG area progressively declined; over 4 per cent a year in the late 1950s, it was down to 2.4 per cent a year in the early 1960s, 1 per cent a year in the late 1960s and only about 0.45 per cent a year in the early 1970s. By 1978 the Tokyo planners were anticipating a static or even a declining population for the early 1980s, and the 1980 Census showed that that decline had already set in. By this time, more people were leaving the Tokyo area than were migrating into it.

Tokyo's functions

It should not be imagined from this that Tokyo is losing its dynamism. What is happening is that Tokyo's growth is now extending well beyond the boundaries of the metropolitan government; here are the areas that are gaining rapidly by migration from Tokyo itself. Overall, the migration trend is still strongly towards the Tokyo region – a fact that is chiefly to be explained in terms of a very rapid structural shift in the composition of the Japanese labour force. As almost everywhere else, agriculture employs a decreasing section of the population, though in the 1960s there was still too much underemployment and low productivity in agriculture which was a principal cause of Japan's low per capita income. Manufacturing accounted for only 24 per cent of the Tokyo work-force by 1975.

The impact of these changes can be seen both in Tokyo's booming inner business districts and in the factory areas of the northern and southern suburbs. Services accounted for over 40 per cent of the Japanese labour force in the early 1980s; but in Tokyo they made up over 70 per cent, and they are sharply concentrated in or near the centre of the city. South of the Imperial Palace, the old Edo fortress, is the administrative quarter; east of it, near the central station, the Marunouchi area is the centre of Japanese financial life, with the headquarters offices of banks and big industrial corporations. Many of these firms moved here from Osaka after 1945, especially those concerned with foreign trade. Farther east again is the main retail district, including Tokyo's two chief shop windows, Ginza and Nihonbashi streets. And north of these again, in Asakusa, the wholesale quarter is concentrated.

The industrial economy

But this is not the only cause of Tokyo's magnetism. To the north-east of the core, on the low-lying flats along the numerous watercourses of the Sumida river, is a great factory zone with more than three-quarters of a million workers in the late 1960s. To the south, along the bay shore towards Kawasaki and then again between Kawasaki and Yokohama, are further great industrial concentrations. Here there is some division of function. Despite the deepening of the channel into Tokyo Bay in 1923, and the subsequent major development of the port of Tokyo, Yokohama remains Tokyo's outport; and most of the industries near it are logically the heavier types depending on bulky raw materials – refineries, primary metals, chemicals, cement. The inland areas of the north tend to concentrate on lighter and more complex products which are perhaps most typical of the evolution of the Japanese economy since 1945. The fastest-growing industries in Japan in the 1960s and 1970s were the science-based, consumer durable industries like cars, transistor radios, tape recorders, electronic calculators and cameras. And in Japan, perhaps even more than in other countries, these tend to be specifically metropolitan industries, which depend on the existence of big manufacturing complexes embracing large plants and a host of smaller suppliers of materials, components and specialized services; two-thirds of Tokyo's labour force is still in small and medium-sized businesses.

Structural shifts in the economy, coupled with the continued existence of a depressed agrarian class in the rural provinces, explain much of the attraction of Japan's big cities but above all the two giants of Osaka and Tokyo. Average per capita income in Tokyo is nearly twice the national average and about three times the average of the poor agricultural communities of Southern Kyushu. Such large regional income disparities are unusual in a developed country and they are bound to lead to continuing labour flows into the metropolitan region. They help to explain Tokyo's overwhelming problems – the problems of over-rapid growth.

Growing pains

The rate of growth of the Tokyo agglomeration has few parallels in the world in the period since the end of the Second World War. Between 1955 and 1960, population in the TMG rose by an average of 329,000 a year; from then to 1965, by 237,000 a year, thence dropping to 108,000 a year between 1965 and 1970 and to 49,000 from 1970 to 1975; from then to 1980 it actually fell by 14,000 a year, by which time the rapid growth had shifted to the outer parts of the region. Hardly any urban agglomeration could bear such a rate of growth without strain. But Tokyo's structure of public services happens to be singularly ill-adapted to deal with the problem.

A disproportionate part of the employment generated since 1945 is in the industrial zones but above all in the Central Business District (CBD) Yet ever since the 1923 earthquake Tokyo's population has been spreading into ever more distant suburbs, and above all on to the higher ground west of the centre. Between 1923 and Pearl Harbour the highest rates of growth were recorded in the outer wards of the city proper; since 1945 they have been in the areas outside the city, and even outside the area of the TMG. True, the Japanese have long kept a tradition of close in-city living – the Toshima ward in north-west Tokyo recorded 22,179 people to the square kilometre or 57,444 to the square mile in 1980 – but the central wards have been losing population as new offices and shops have displaced homes, and, while the Tokyo ward area suffered a slight population loss after 1965, suburbs have sprawled ever farther from the centre. The process has been generated by rising land prices at the centre, by the traditional Japanese preference for the single-family house, and by the anti-earthquake building regulations, in force until recently, which limited multi-storey dwellings to 31 metres.

The great growth in population, but above all its outward spread, was responsible for three overwhelming problems in the Tokyo of the 1960s and 1970s. They concerned housing; basic public services like water and sewerage; and transportation.

Housing
During the Second World War 768,000 dwellings, or 56 per cent of Tokyo's housing stock, were destroyed, leaving 51 per cent of the population homeless. This tremendous problem had been met by 1960, though even then too many

185

people were still living in temporary accommodation – boats, old railway trains, abandoned factories – which they had occupied after the war. But the housing programme continued unabated. In Tokyo prefecture, by 1978, of the total housing stock over 94 per cent had been built since 1945 and 71 per cent since 1960; the total of post-1960 housing represented a completion rate of some 150,000 a year. These are impressive totals. But less than a quarter of the new dwellings were built by public bodies, like the Metropolitan Government Bureau or the Metropolitan Housing Supply Corporation, for rent. Public housing made up only 10 per cent of the total in Tokyo in 1968; and by the late 1970s, local authorities and public corporations were supplying less than 5 per cent of new housing. These public dwellings are small and by western standards some of them lack essential facilities like bathrooms. But they are relatively cheap, and the demand for them far exceeds the supply. Another public agency, the Japan Housing Corporation, builds bigger dwellings, usually flats; since it must break even on each project it charges higher rents, but its flats too are heavily in demand. Paradoxically, therefore, more public housing is provided for middle-income than for low-income groups. Private luxury apartments are built in big numbers near the city centre but their rents are more than the average family's monthly income. So the great majority of families must look to private housing in the suburbs. Some try to obtain public help through a loan for house buying: a public body, the Japan Housing Finance Corporation, will advance 80 per cent of the standard cost both of land and of construction. (The standard cost is, however, lower than the real cost.) But this means a large problem of finding land, and even so there is again severe competition, resolved in the last resort (as with the publicly rented housing) by a lottery. Land is expensive because it is scarce; farmers on the edge of the city are determined to hold on to it until the last possible moment so as to realize the best price for it, and as compared with prewar days land prices had risen 1,600 times up to 1967. (The general wholesale price increase was only about one-quarter as great.) From 1955 to 1965 alone the increase was tenfold, and Professor Shibata has estimated that land prices in Tokyo may be as much as ten times as high as in New York or London. Indeed, by the mid-1970s, land prices in Tokyo were reported to be the world's highest. In the 1970s it was calculated that to buy a plot of 150 square metres (1,600 square feet) within commuting distance would take the average Japanese worker 6½ years, against 290 days in France, 174 days in Germany or 45 days in the United States. Interestingly, this indicates that weak planning controls, which make building land quite freely available, do not necessarily reduce the rate of inflation on that land.

Thus there is a continuing housing crisis. In 1968 45 per cent of Tokyo's families were living in tenement buildings, often with shared toilet and kitchen; typically, a tenement family would have only 10 square metres (107 square feet), one-tenth its European equivalent and two-fifths the very modest official norms of the Metropolitan Government. Further, since most tenements are wooden, they are a serious fire and earthquake hazard. And typically, a single privately rented room may cost as much as a whole flat from a public corporation. Average housing rentals per square metre in 1967 were nearly twice those in Osaka, Japan's second city; they had increased sixfold between 1955 and 1965, while incomes only doubled.

There are no easy remedies. In a 1968 survey, 834,000 households (28.1 per cent of the total) were classified as living in sub-standard accommodation, while another 1,017,000 (34.2 per cent) considered themselves inadequately housed. (There was a 17.6 per cent overlap between these two groups.) The main complaint was lack of space. According to a 1966 survey, more than 50 per cent of the lowest income group of manual workers required rehousing. The TMG's five-year housing plan, announced in 1967, aimed at building more than 10,000 units a year. But this is miniscule in relation to needs, and its achievement will depend on funds which may be swallowed up by the ever-rising cost of land. Achievement will depend on funds – the traditional stumbling block in all schemes for the improvement of Tokyo over a long period.

Basic services
Coupled with the housing shortage is a dire deficiency in basic public services. In 1967, 10 per cent of the population of the Ward Area did not enjoy a piped water supply, and had to use wells. Even in some of the areas of piped supply, water was only available for two hours a day in the summer peak period. And there are local disparities; in the Nerima Ward for instance only 26 per cent of the population was connected. Outside the Ward Area the position was worse: only 64 per cent had piped water supply. Per capita water consumption is still well below American levels, but it is increasing rapidly with more and more bathrooms and washing machines; and by 1980 maximum daily consumption was expected to be double that of 1962. An acute water shortage in the early 1960s was overcome by 1970 through the construction of dams on the rivers Tone and Arakawa; this increased the supply capacity by nearly one-third, but it was estimated that between 1970 and 1985 demand would further increase by two-thirds. There is an obvious need to allow the TMG to supply water outside the Ward Area, which is not the case at present.

Even more alarming is the deficiency of the sewage system. Within the Ward Area proper, in 1975, 37 per cent of the population still had no sewerage, and had to depend on the collection of excreta by gangs of nightmen; in 1967 only 35.5 per cent had the use of flush toilets. In 1950, as a temporary measure, it was arranged that a fleet of contractors' boats should dump waste into the Pacific Ocean; and in 1962 the ironically named 'Honey

Fleet' was still disposing of 44 per cent of the total collection of night soil in this way. This was costly both in labour and in equipment, and it increased the already serious traffic congestion; it was abolished only in the late 1960s. The plan was to extend 100 per cent sewerage to the Ward Area by 1980; in Tama new town, where only 14.5 per cent were served in 1974, the target was 1985. Still in 1975, over 70 per cent of the population of the suburban parts of TMG had sewers; the percentage for the entire TMG area was just over 50 per cent. Similarly, 46 per cent of Tokyo's house garbage was being dumped into Tokyo Bay for reclamation purposes, in the mid-1970s; but if this policy continues there will soon be major problems for fishing and for shipping fleets, and the earlier plan – to incinerate 100 per cent by the end of 1970 – was badly delayed. The dumping of untreated sewage causes serious problems in the Tama river and in Tokyo Bay, where it contributes to the notorious summer problem of the 'Red Tide'.

Pollution was a growing problem, too, in the air above Tokyo. Petrochemical smog warnings increased dramatically from 1970 to 1973, by which time Tokyo was competing for the title of one of the world's most smog-ridden cities; proposals for tougher emission controls were successfully fought off by Japan's powerful car makers.

Transportation

By the late 1970s the population of the entire TMG area was declining while that of the surrounding ring was rapidly increasing. While the most rapid growth between 1960 and 1965 was in the ring 20 to 30 kilometres (12 to 18 miles) from the centre, by 1965–75 it was 30 to 40 kilometres (18 to 25 miles) distant and by the late 1970s even farther than this. Factory employment, too was dispersing; but headquarters office employment continued to increase in Tokyo. Commuter traffic thus continued to rise – at an average of 5 per cent per annum – and by 1975 Tokyo registered one of the biggest commuter movements in the world: the central area (conventionally defined as the three wards of Chiyoda, Chuo and Minato) was taking in 1,880,000 people daily, of whom well over half came from outside the twenty-three-ward area. Hence the forecast in the mid-1970s was that by 1985 commuters into this central area might increase further to 2,200,000, of whom again about one-half might travel relatively long distances from outside the Ward Area. Total commuting into the Ward Area, 1.8 million in 1970, might increase to 2.8 million by 1985. Already, as early as 1970, within a 40-kilometre (25-mile) zone, 40 per cent or more of resident workers commuted to the Tokyo Ward Area.

Yet until recently, the physical infrastructure of Tokyo's transportation system was ill-equipped to meet such phenomenal pressures; virtually all of it dated from the period between 1920 and 1940. And its geography is curiously ill-related to today's commuting patterns. By a government decision of 1935 (impelled by the need to co-ordinate the rail system during the war with China), the area within the so-called Yamate loop line (operated by the National Railway System) was monopolized for the Tokyo Metropolitan Traffic Bureau. But a very large proportion of the commuters travel from the western suburbs by the so-called private railways, which were built in the 1920s and 1930s, and which have to terminate at stations on the Yamate loop line, 5 to 7 kilometres (3 to 4 miles) from the CBD (map 7.2a). This in turn throws an enormous strain on the National Railways, which carry many of the passengers into the centre, as well as on the underground railway, bus and streetcar systems. The National Railways' Chuo line is the only radial line from the western suburbs which connects directly with the CBD; in 1972, during a typical morning rush hour, its passenger load was 260 per cent of capacity. This was a record; but many lines recorded double their capacity or more.

Despite the celebrated army of 700 student pushers, therefore, Tokyo's problem gets steadily worse. The short-term answer is simply more capacity; and, out of necessity, this is being provided. A plan for eleven new subway lines, totalling 278 kilometres (178 miles) was being energetically executed by 1976: eight lines totalling 166 kilometres (103 miles) were open. Critics, however, complained that, during the 1960s, roads had a disproportionately large share of the total construction budget (map 7.2b). The medium-term answer is to integrate the different parts of the system under one authority, on the London model, as was recommended by the Metropolitan Transportation Advisory Council, appointed by the Governor of the TMG in 1960. This would permit more effective use of investment funds and would put fares on the same basis everywhere. But the long-term and finally the only effective answer is not the reform of the transportation system alone, but the reshaping of the pattern of economic activities and land uses which is responsible for the present impasse.

Still, a small proportion of Tokyo's commuters travel by private car, for registered cars in Tokyo prefecture totalled only 1.7 million in 1979, one for every 6.75 persons. But the total stock of vehicles has been increasing by 5–7 per cent a year; and Tokyo's traffic snarl-up is in any case already one of the worst in the world. For street space in the Tokyo Ward Area is only 12.7 per cent and, in the entire TMG area only 6.3 per cent, of the total area, compared with 23 per cent in London, 26 per cent in Paris and Berlin, 35 per cent in New York and 43 per cent in Washington. Again, the immediate response of the Metropolitan Government has been investment in new facilities – this time of a spectacular order. Remembering the scenes of chaos which accompanied the Asian Games of 1956, when some spectators failed to reach the stadium all day, the authorities determined on the construction of 71 kilometres (44 miles) of four-lane metropolitan expressways on eight main routes, to be completed in time for the Olympic Games in October 1964. Though not

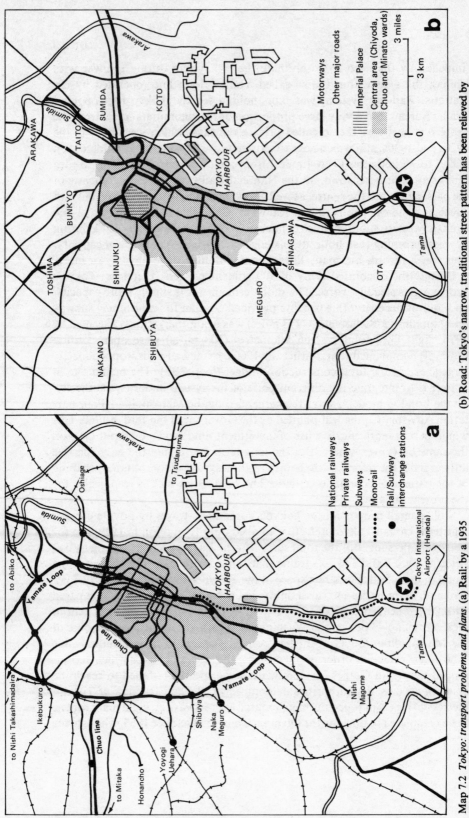

Map 7.2 *Tokyo: transport problems and plans.* (a) Rail: by a 1935 government decision, the private railways all stop short of the CBD; the Yamate Loop offers Must transfer to the Japan National Railways' Yamate loop or subways to reach the central area. (b) Road: Tokyo's narrow, traditional street pattern has been relieved by a major programme of toll expressways, one of which even penetrates the grounds of the formerly sacred Imperial Palace. But a good highway

Within the map, legends read:

(a)
National railways
Private railways
Subways
Monorail
● Rail/Subway interchange stations

Tokyo International Airport (Haneda)

Place names: to Nishi Takashimadaira, to Abiko, Ikebukuro, Oshiage, to Tsudanuma, Yamate Loop, Chuo line, Sumida, Arakawa, to Mitaka, Honancho, Yoyogi Uehara, Shibuya, Naka Meguro, Nishi Magome, Yamate Loop, TOKYO HARBOUR, Tama

(b)
— Motorways
— Other major roads
||| Imperial Palace (Chiyoda,
▒ Central area (Chiyoda, Chuo and Minato wards)

0 3 km
0 3 miles

Place names: TOSHIMA, NAKANO, SHIBUYA, MEGURO, OTA, SHINAGAWA, SHINJUKU, BUNKYO, ARAKAWA, TAITO, SUMIDA, KOTO, Sumida, Arakawa, TOKYO HARBOUR, Tama all of the network was completed in time for the games, by the end of 1976 103 kilometres (64 miles) had been opened, and 144 kilometres (89 miles) more were under construction towards a target of 273 kilometres (170 miles). Execution has been held up because of difficulties over compensation, expropriation, astronomical land costs (up to 3,500,000 Yen or £3,460 for 3.3 square metres in the city centre) and difficulties of rehousing the inhabitants of the 59,000 dwellings to be displaced. These expressways have a modest design speed of 60 kilometres (37 miles) per hour, with many access ramps; built by a special Metropolitan Expressway Corporation set up by the Metropolitan Government, they are distinct from the full-scale inter-urban motorways in the suburban fringe areas. Meanwhile, the city traffic department wages a running war aganst drivers of heavy lorries and tourist buses, which jam the city's narrow streets, and against owner-drivers who leave their cars parked in the streets day and night. Regulations insist that new offices and hotels are accompanied by private parking lots, and that private car owners possess garages as a condition of their licences. This last regulation in particular has provoked bitter resentment.

Regional policies: capital and nation

But massive investment alone may merely encourage further growth, so generating a vicous circle. The Japanese almost certainly suffer from one of the most acute problems of metropolitan overgrowth in the world, and since the mid-1950s they have been evolving positive regional policies to try to counteract its worst effects.

First they have devised policies to promote regional growth in the less favoured regions of the country. These measures are embodied in the Law of Promoting Industries in Under-Developed Regions, of 1961, and the Law of Promoting Construction of New Industrial Cities, of 1962. The latter measure is especially interesting because it seeks to develop certain areas in the provinces as major regional cities, so that they may act as effective counter-magnets to Tokyo. Suitable sites are to be proposed by prefectoral governors in the regions and agreed by the central government. Plans will then be drawn up by provincial governments in consultation with advisory councils. The aim is an ambitious one: it is to develop cities of one million people and more, and with a full range of urban services. Only cities of this order, the Japanese think, can counter the attractions of giants like Tokyo or Osaka.

Secondly, though, the fact has to be faced that many of the tertiary functions (in particular) will continue to grow in Tokyo; so it is critically necessary to provide a new structure for the internal development of the metropolitan

191

region, in order to avoid further pressure on the already hopelessly congested core. The National Capital Region Development Law of 1956 aimed to provide such a structure. It applied to the wide planning region within 100 to 120 kilometres (60 to 75 miles) of central Tokyo, including the whole of the TMG, three whole prefectures and parts of four other prefectures; and it was intended that all these authorities would co-operate in the work of a National Capital Region Development Commission, which would prepare a plan of construction programmes to be carried through by the Metropolitan Government and the individual prefectures. In practice, however, the Commission proved a weak body with virtually no powers or financial resources of its own.

The 1956 law

The basic principles of development under the original 1956 law were based on Sir Patrick Abercrombie's plan for Greater London in 1944. First the plan delineated a built-up area extending about 16 kilometres (10 miles) in any direction from Tokyo Central Station, and incorporating all the twenty-three wards plus the cities of Yokohama, Kawasaki and Kawaguchi. Here further outward urban sprawl should be prevented. To this end a second zone – the 11-kilometre (7-mile) wide green belt zone – was intended to encircle the development area: but in fact planning powers proved inadequate to hold this belt against pressures for development. A considerable potential population growth would have to be accommodated elsewhere, in the peripheral zone between 27 and 72 kilometres (17 and 45 miles) from central Tokyo; here the plan proposed satellite towns to absorb decentralized population and employment (map 7.1a). The Law for Town Development in the National Capital Region (1958) provided a specific method for developing the satellites. The central government would provide funds, subsidies for local authorities and technical assistance; individual government departments might also help local authorities and the Japan Housing Corporation; and the government would advance funds to developers if they were recognized by the National Capital Region Development Corporation. By 1967 a number of these satellites had been designated; though originally termed new towns, they did not represent self-contained communities as the British model and one of the largest – the so-called new town of Tama – was in fact a giant commuter development designed for 400,000 30 to 40 kilometres (18 to 25 miles) west of the city centre and built by a number of different agencies including the TMG, the Japan Housing Corporation and four different local authorities (map 7.3a). It is linked to Tokyo by new private railway extensions. By 1977 it had a total population of 49,000. Eventually it will contain twenty-three neighbourhood units of approximately 100·hectares (247 acres) containing 12,000 people and a full range of services, grouped in zones.

The original plan worked on the basis of a 1975 population, for the entire

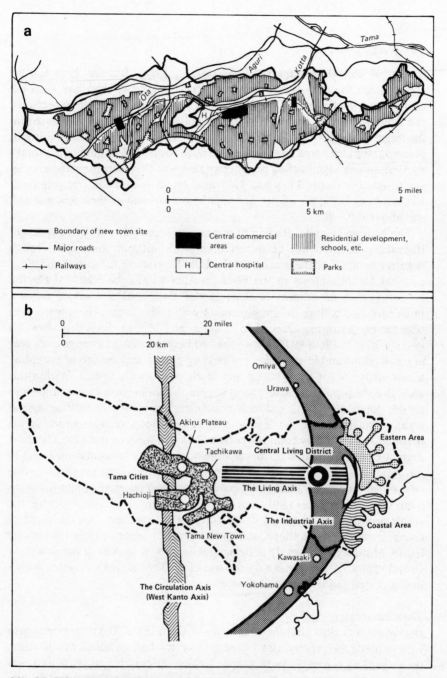

Map 7.3 *Tokyo: new urban structures.* (a) Tama new town: designed for 400,000 people, this town, 13 kilometres (8 miles) long, and 30 to 40 kilometres (18 to 25 miles) west of Tokyo, will form the nucleus of a polycentric urban complex. (b) Bi-polar Tokyo: the Tama complex will form the western end of an east-west 'living axis' connected to the centre of the region by good transport; it is thus hoped to develop it as a counter-magnet to Tokyo proper, with a special stress on higher education, research and culture.

region, of 26,600,000 (against 19,800,000 in 1955). But the 1960 Census showed that the population was increasing even faster than had been expected, and the figures had to be revised. Population was then expected to rise from 22,520,000 (in 1960) to 28,200,000 (in 1975), to be distributed: in the inner built-up area, 12,250,000; in the outer area, 15,950,000. (Without planning, the inner area might sprawl so as to contain 16 million of the total.) By 1963, fifteen satellites had been designated, and they were expected eventually to number thirty. They had 1975 final target populations ranging from 150,000 to 670,000; the additional population for each of them, on average, was about 100,000.

The National Capital Region Plan was a positive plan for regional decentralization; it could not be expected to work without some fairly tough negative controls at the centre. So the Law Restricting Industrial and Educational Establishments in the Built-up Area within the National Capital Region (1959), an adjunct to the regional plan, restricted major factory, university and college building projects within the twenty-three-ward area plus the neighbouring cities of Musashino and Mitaka. But even after this law, by the mid-1960s 80,000 new jobs had been created on average each year in small plants and in extensions of existing plants, and the job of providing a new structure for the built-up area itself was equally urgent. Within this area, the Metropolitan Government sought to channel investment funds into the development of office and retail subcentres away from the existing central area, especially along the line of the Yamate loop railway which is the destination of so many commuters from Tokyo's western suburbs. The most dramatic project so far is the development of the Shinjuku subcentre next to the important railway station on the Yamate loop, 5 kilometres (3 miles) due west of the Imperial Palace. Here removal of the Yodobashi water filtration plant freed 107 hectares (240 acres) for development as a business centre; the whole project was completed in the early 1970s, creating a major island of CBD activities – offices, shops, and entertainment – separate from the historic Ginza–Marunouchi core. It is being followed by a similar development at Ikebukuro; a 7.5-hectare site on the site of the former Tokyo prison, with a business area and transportation interchange.

The revised law of 1965
By 1965 it was clear that the main lines of the original Tokyo regional plan – particularly the preservation of the green belt – had no hope of realization; the powers to achieve it were simply lacking. Population increase and new development were very marked in the green belt ring; it added over 2 million to its population between 1955 and 1965. Therefore, in 1965 a revision of the National Capital Region Development Law (which extended the boundaries of the National Capital Region) recognized a *fait accompli*; it abandoned the

green belt and substituted a new suburban development area extending beyond 50 kilometres (30 miles) from the centre. Within this zone, population
growth would be encouraged at suitable points; these would include most of
the former satellite towns (the term itself was eliminated) which would be
fewer in number, but larger than in the original plan. The new suburban
growth areas would be physically contiguous with the existing urban area,
but an effort would be made to preserve open space between them; in this
respect the 1965 revised plan somewhat resembles the corridor or axial plan
for Washington, or the even earlier finger plan for Copenhagen, in which
lines of urban development are separated by sectors of open land (map 7.1b).
Then, in 1968, a revision of the basic City Planning Law gave further sub-
stance to the concept by distinguishing urban promotion areas (with provision
of infrastructure) and urban control areas where there would be no development in principle. But, significantly in the Tokyo case, these were to be at the
far periphery where there was least pressure for development; here, as not in
the past, Tokyo planners seemed to be accepting the inevitable. Efforts have
however been made to keep green space. Under the Greenery Conservation
Act of 1973, the TMG declared a Greenery Conservation Zone of 79 hectares
(195 acres). More significantly, under an act the following year - the Production Greenery Conservation Act of 1974 - it designated a much larger so-
called Production Greenery Zone of 3,586 hectares (8,861 acres) consisting of
farmland to be protected against the threat of development. Whether this will
hold way is of course a matter for speculation.

These are official, legal responses to the immediate problem of controlling
growth. But Tokyo probably has a greater wealth of original and unconven-
tional expert ideas for its future development than any other major world
city. They reflect the extraordinary technical ingenuity that is typically
Japanese, allied to a passionate interest in the problems of metropolitan
growth. One set of solutions is based on a major extension of Tokyo eastwards
into the bay. The technical means range from reclamation through the sinking
of piers to create a 'Venice of the East', and the construction of a series of
bridges, to a city built on rafts. Another school sees the solution in building
upwards. With an average building height in the twenty-three-ward area of
only 1.35 storeys, Tokyo must be the lowest-rise major city of the world, and
during the 1960s the Ministry of Construction lifted the 31-metre (102-feet)
height limit imposed after the 1923 earthquake. Yet another idea is the
development of a Japanese Brasilia 145 kilometres (90 miles) from Tokyo,
built on 300 square kilometres (116 square miles) of state-owned land at the
foot of Mount Fuji. A super-highway would connect the two centres within
one hour and 180,000 civil servants and their families would be decentralized
from Tokyo. This last scheme neatly accords with official policy, for in 1961
the government announced a plan to move seventy-eight government offices

and institutions out of the capital; and they estimated that the total numbers affected, directly and indirectly, would also be 180,000. Interestingly, though, the proposed move has met with a great deal of rooted opposition. Despite the problems of overgrowth currently facing Tokyo, it appears that some of its citizens prefer it with all its faults.

More likely – because eminently practicable – is a fairly modest proposal by the TMG: to create sufficient new jobs in the Tama new town area, particularly in the public sector through new universities and cultural institutions, so as progressively to give the whole region a bi-polar structure. At first this will be fairly limited: only 80,000 out of 200,000 Tama workers are expected to find jobs in the new town area itself. But, coupled with the development of strong two-way transportation links, the proposal could create a new axis along a roughly east–west line, some 32 kilometres (20 miles) in length between the present centre, via the Shinjuku subcentre, to Tama (map 7.3b).

Tokyo government: a growing fiscal crisis

By 1976, Tokyo was fast joining New York as a world city in crisis. Throughout the boom years of the 1960s and early 1970s, economic buoyancy had produced a steady and substantial growth in tax yields, which the TMG needed to support an ambitious programme of improvements; in 1975 alone, this increase was 14.5 per cent. But by 1974–5 TMG was on the verge of a fiscal crisis produced by a combination of sharply rising costs – partly a result of inflation – and declining revenues. For the fiscal year 1976 the budget was back to 8.7 per cent: fairly spectacular by western standards, but producing an expected deficit of 100,000 million Yen.

Officials were agreed that the remedy lay in two directions. First, there had to be administrative streamlining, which would concentrate the city's efforts on the most essential programmes: the growth in the city's work-force, which had proceeded inexorably in the early 1970s, had to cease and even be reversed; and the housing programme would need to be concentrated on essentials, especially homes for low-income groups. Secondly, though, no amount of pruning would suffice unless the city found new revenues to maintain its essential programmes. The present revenues, derived from a combination of income, corporate and residence taxes, might be supplemented in various ways: new business taxes, real estate tax, petrol sales tax, an end to present tax concessions (for instance, to large businesses), extra profit taxes. Above all, property taxes should be restructured so that big corporations paid their share. The city might acquire greater freedom to issue bonds – though that might run the risk of the New York experience. There might be greater central government subsidy – for school construction, and for salaries of police or teachers. And tax assessments might be recast, to give a greater share of revenues for the cities. Above all, therefore, Tokyo needed greater fiscal autonomy. And associated with this, it needed greater powers to tax and acquire land. Without these extra financial powers, the city simply could not maintain its pressing programmes to bring greater order and dignity to the everyday lives of its citizens.

The Tokyo experience

This chapter ends as it began, with paradoxes. Tokyo indicates that great economic dynamism, which attracts population to a major urban area at an unprecedented rate, may create social problems with which the administrative machine cannot cope, leading to a situation of near-breakdown in essential public services. It shows too that, in such an economically buoyant society, considerations of land-use planning are likely to take a bad second place in competition with the overwhelming desire to exploit every economic opportunity; put at its bluntest, most Japanese decision-takers – and perhaps most Japanese people – have little time for planning at present. Lastly, and most tellingly, it shows that a society in a state of relative *laissez-faire*, while undoubtedly imposing considerable social costs on its citizens, does not necessarily bring compensating benefits. It is paradoxical indeed that Tokyo, with an ineffectual planning machine powerless in practice to stop uncontrolled development, suffers a rate of inflation of land prices in excess of London with its tight control of land use. Thus, despite freedom to spread, the citizens of Tokyo remain considerably more crowded, and more short of house-room, than their equivalents in either western Europe or North America. The relationship between planning controls, urban form and life styles is thus a complex one. And lastly, Tokyo's experience shows that, when world recession strikes, the great city in a previously buoyant economy may be stricken most grievously of all; its programmes, based on high expectations of growth, may face unprecedented crisis. Tokyo's recent story, in many ways, is a chastening one for the planners of other world cities – not least for those in the burgeoning metropolitan centres of the newly industrializing world, to whose experience we now turn.

8 Hong Kong

Hong Kong comes into this book because, indisputably, it is one of the few cities of the newly industrializing world to claim world city status. It is a major world centre of trade, transport, finance and tourism. It is one of the great export manufacturing bases of the world. It is also one of a select group of countries – the others include Singapore, Taiwan, South Korea, Mexico and Brazil – that in the brief space since 1950 have leapt from being poor third world countries to being fairly affluent first world ones. So, by any standards, its story is worth telling; its resultant problems and achievements are worth examining.

But any such examination has to start with a set of paradoxes. Hong Kong is not always what at first sight it seems. Some first impressions will not, indeed cannot, be contradicted: the incredible congestion of the 5.1 million people and their activities, crammed into a mere 1,046 square kilometres (404 square miles) of land; the extraordinary energy and dynamism of the place; the feeling of growth and change. But other myths will need modification. True, this economy is one of the freest, the least subject to government interference, to be found anywhere in the late twentieth century; but that does not stop the government investing massively in housing, roads, schools and social provision. True, also, the city is a living testament to the energies and entrepreneurial spirit of the Chinese people; but it also demonstrates a happy symbiotic relationship with British public administration.

Hong Kong in history

All world cities, to be understood at all, need to be seen in the light of their history. But Hong Kong's history is very special, helping explain its late rise to fame, its recent dynamism and some of its present problems.

To all intents and purposes, Hong Kong – the Fragrant Harbour – was born in 1841. In that year the British, concerned to establish a free port under their control to help develop trade with China, established a small settlement on the island opposite the tip of the Kowloon peninsula of the south Chinese

198

province of Canton. Using the convenient pretext of a war with China over the opium trade, the next year they signed a treaty whereby China ceded the island in perpetuity to Britain – a treaty that a later Chinese government was to repudiate as signed under duress. In 1860, another treaty brought them the Kowloon peninsula; in 1898, they obtained an unusual ninety-nine-year lease on the territories extending for about 40 kilometres (25 miles) to the north, which were dubbed the New Territories. Thus, in the vastly-extended Hong Kong of the 1980s, an invisible boundary line through the heart of the city divides that portion which the British regard as firmly theirs from that part on which the lease will expire at the end of 1997.

For a long time – indeed, down to the Second World War – Hong Kong remained fairly small. The population was 225,000 in 1891, 457,000 in the extended Hong Kong of 1911, 840,000 in 1931 and about 1,640,000 at the time of the Japanese invasion of 1941. The centre of the colony was the Central District on the island, which housed the government buildings, the offices of trading companies and banks, and the celebrated Hong Kong club. It was an archetypal outpost of the British Raj, which today can be appreciated only from faded sepia photographs; even the club has gone, razed in yet another property development. Farther up the mountains of the island, on the mid and upper levels, the officials and traders of the Raj had their exclusive and spacious quarters. To this day, a charming Victorian-style mountain tramway takes their descendants direct from Central District more than 500 metres (1,500 feet) up to The Peak.

In sharp contrast, to the west of Central District and just behind the original port, Sheung Wan was the Chinese city: then, as now, a warren of tenements, shops and workshops, where a family of six might live in a cubicle of 3 square metres (6 feet by 4) with perhaps one or two more people in a cockloft above, and where in all twenty-five adults might occupy a single flat, seventy-five or one hundred a tenement building. Kennedy Town to the west was a similar Chinese trading and working-class area, developed in the same way; while across the water in Yaumati and Old Kowloon was another Chinese city, built and occupied at similar densities. Characteristic for both of these areas was – and is – a traditional Chinese urban organization: specialized business clusters, typically of family-owned businesses, who depend for their livelihood on their proximity to one another. Outside these areas, Causeway Bay east of Central District on the island and Tsimshatsui on Kowloon were pleasant residential suburbs, all reached within a few minutes by tram or ferry from the central business cluster.

That was still Hong Kong at the end of the Second World War – a period in which evacuation and invasion had reduced the population to 650,000; by the 1951 Census it had climbed to just above the pre-war peak, 2,015,000. Thence its growth was dizzy: to 3,130,000 in 1961, 4,064,000 in 1971 and

199

5,154,000 in 1981. An apparently unlimited supply of people met an apparently limitless demand. After 1949 refugees poured in from China; by the mid-1950s they were estimated to number about 700,000. And, because most were young, they produced large numbers of children. Though by 1981 the birth-rate was down to 17 per thousand – a level typical of an advanced industrial country – the much higher rates of the previous decades had made their mark.

As the population poured in, so inevitably – given the constraints of space – it redistributed itself. Since there was virtually no room to expand on the limited flat land of the island or on the Kowloon peninsula, increasingly after 1970 the growth took place in the New Territories leased from China, and liable to be returned in 1997. The main vehicle of that growth, the new towns, are simultaneously Hong Kong's supreme planning achievement and also – because of the political uncertainty – its major potential problem (table 8.1 and map 8.1)

Table 8.1 Hong Kong and its constituent parts, 1981

	Area (square km.)	Population (thousands) 1981	Population change (per cent) 1971–81
Hong Kong Island	78	1,183.6	+18.8
Old Kowloon	9	799.1	+11.6
New Kowloon	37	1,651.1	+11.7
New Territories	938	1,303.0	+95.7
Marine population	–	49.7	−37.8
Total	1,062	4,986.5	+26.7
(UN definition)		(4,085.0)	+15.6

Sources: Census, 1981; United Nations, *Patterns of Urban and Rural Population Growth* (*Population Studies*, 68), New York: United Nations, 1980.

The modern economy

Yet the extra millions were employed: the rapid growth of the economy saw to that. Superficially, the outlook in the early 1950s could not have been worse: the economy, traditionally based on the entrepôt function, was threatened with virtual collapse by the Korean War. But accumulated trading capital united with refugee funds and entrepreneurial talents – above all from the millowners of Shanghai – to create a new export manufacturing base, directed first at Britain, later to the United States and other advanced industrial countries such as Germany, Japan, Canada and Australia. As the new manufacturing economy grew, it progressively became more sophisticated;

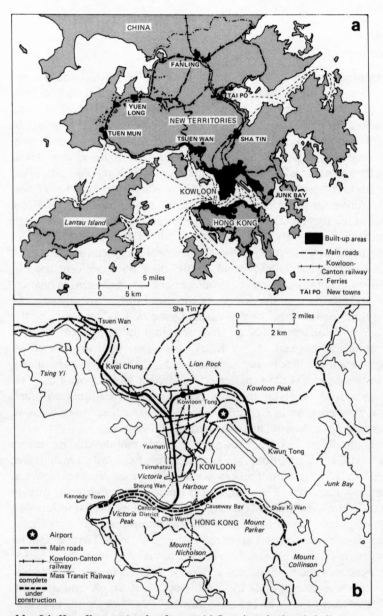

Map 8.1 *Hong Kong: main urban features*. (a) Overview: the densely built-up
inner areas on the north shore of the island and on the lower Kowloon
peninsula are hemmed in by mountains which are crossed by rail or road
tunnels; the harbour itself is crossed by a road tunnel and the new Mass
Transit Railway tunnel. Beyond the mountains in Kowloon, in the New
Territories, the new towns now under construction will help relieve the
colony's chronic overcrowding. (b) The central area: the improved Kowloon–
Canton Railway, serving Sha Tin new town, and the Mass Transit Railway,
serving Tsuen Wan, interchange at the Kowloon Tong station close to Hong
Kong's constricted Kai Tak airport.

heavily oriented towards textiles in the 1950s, it evolved into clothing in the 1960s – and increasingly towards fashionable goods – and then into toys, dolls and finally a bewildering array of electronic products. Though clothing still accounted for 35 per cent of manufacturing exports in 1977 against 14 per cent for electronic goods, the latter was growing much faster. Entrepreneurship, originally highly concentrated among the Shanghai merchants, spread to their workers who became manufacturers in their own right, often as subcontractors. Start-up capital was readily available through kinship ties.

Manufacturing for export still remains the main economic base of Hong Kong. But in recent years the colony has followed the usual economic path towards tertiary activity. By 1982, only 41 per cent of the work-force were in manufacturing. Nearly 16 per cent were in personal and social services, over 19 per cent in trade, restaurants and hotels, close on 8 per cent each in construction and in transport and communications, and 5 per cent in finance, insurance, real estate and business services. Financial and commercial services accounted for close on 20 per cent of Gross Domestic Product (GDP) by the late 1970s, and wholesale and retail trade for close on 24 per cent, against manufacturing's 27 per cent. Hong Kong's economic structure, therefore, increasingly resembles that of any advanced industrial country. Particularly notable, in this regard, is the rapid growth of higher-level service functions such as international shipping, tourism and the regional headquarters office blocks that now burgeon in Central District – a token that Hong Kong is now among the dozen leading financial centres of the world.

But there are differences. Both the manufacturing and the trading sectors are still organized on a traditional small-scale family basis, with a high degree of reliance on subcontracting. Three in five plants have less than ten workers, nine in ten less than fifty. These small firms succeed through good quality labour, easy access to capital and their ability to exploit the newest technology as soon as it appears – as witness Hong Kong's extraordinary grip on digital watch manufacture as soon as it appeared in the early 1970s. There is a subtle and constantly shifting boundary between the bazaar economy of the casual street workers, and the more formal economy. There is no minimum wage rate; the wage level is set purely by the interaction of supply and demand. And the government firmly eschews any form of macro-economic intervention in the economy. Though wages are the highest in Asia outside Japan, they are still only about one-quarter the level there; and they have not risen as fast as productivity during the 1960s and 1970s. The combination of high productivity and relatively low wages, then, is a hard one to beat.

Yet the government is not as anti-interventionist as popular legend would have it. It is true that there is freedom of trade and of exchange, a balanced budget, low taxation for individuals and businesses, maximal freedom for private enterprise and relatively low small public spending (about 15 per cent of GDP, against 40–60 per cent in most advanced industrial countries). But the government invests generously in basic infrastructure, builds and rents factories, provides business loans and export credit finance, organizes technical education and assists technological development, and actively promotes Hong Kong exports. The result has been impressive. Hong Kong's per capita income stands just behind its rival Singapore's at about half the level of Japan or about one-quarter of the United States. But its rate of growth of GDP per capita (between 5 and 7 per cent a year during the 1960s and 1970s) is such that, projected, would cause it to catch up with these more advanced countries within the next three decades. Its exports per capita are 50 per cent greater than Britain's and four times those of Japan. The only threat would seem to come from those neighbouring countries that are less developed but are also growing – and are determined to catch up.

The major problems

But Hong Kong's explosive growth has brought in train some epic problems for its planners. The most notable are industrial building; housing; and transportation.

Industry
One of Hong Kong's first resultant planning problems is precisely the consequences of its economic success. A 1971 survey found that close on 70 per cent of all manufacturing premises, with 27 per cent of factory employment and 20 per cent of sales, were in homes. Of the small firms – defined as those with less than one hundred workers – which comprise 95 per cent of the total, fully 72 per cent were in domestic buildings. The great majority of these were very small: more than two-thirds of them had working capital of less than $HK50 (about £6). Generally they were former employees who had used their own meagre savings to set up on their own. More than half lived in their workplace, and almost invariably the unit – like almost every unit in Hong Kong – was small.

Clothing, plastic products, textiles, electrical and electronic goods are the industries where this small-scale domestic production is the norm, accounting for between 70 and 90 per cent of all premises but for a much smaller proportion of employment. Much of the work consists of subcontract for import–export houses – the same system, essentially, as prevailed in the sweated industries of London or New York at the end of the nineteenth century. Logically, the home workshops are heavily concentrated into the worst slum areas close to the centre from where the orders come: the clothing district of Shumshuipo and the noxious industries of Taikoktsui just to the south in Kowloon, the miscellaneous workshops of Tokwawan just south of the airport, the tourist-serving workshops of Tsimshatsui at the tip of Kowloon, Sheung Wan and neighbouring Sai Ying Pun on the island.

Though legally tolerated, two-thirds of these premises are unregistered with the authorities – mainly because they would not meet their standards, for instance of fire risk. Since 1976, the regulations have stipulated that non-industrial buildings completed before that date may have industry only on the ground floor, while such buildings subsequently finished may house only service trades such as tailors, bakers and bicycle repair. These regulations could affect as much as 70 per cent of all the industrial undertakings in the city, and it is still unclear as to how they can be made to work. Victor Sit, a Hong Kong geographer who has made a close study of these industries, concludes that the long-term answer to the problem would be for the government to provide alternative flatted factories on an unsubsidized basis, as it already has in the case of resettlement estates.

Associated with this is however another, deeper, problem. These small workshops are clearly operated by entrepreneurs who are both poor and not very sophisticated. Considering the circumstances, their achievement in developing progressively higher-technology industries – office machinery, watches, TV sets, electronic games, computer components – is nothing less than miraculous. The question, however, is how long it can continue unless the whole economy acquires a more secure base in scientific and technological training. Hong Kong's chief rival, Singapore, has recognized this problem and has started to develop positive government policies to this end. Without doubt, if it is to keep one jump ahead of its less-developed Asian competitors, Hong Kong will need to do the same. The Polytechnic, opened in 1972 and expanding, is a start in this direction.

Housing

Though Hong Kong may now be a middle-income country, that income is still very unequally distributed; indeed, observers have concluded that the colony has one of the widest spreads of income of any country in the world. Successive waves of refugees – from China in the 1950s and 1960s, from Vietnam in the 1970s – have arrived often virtually destitute, and have had to build up their fortunes from nothing. One result has been another continuing paradox: a country, which in statistical terms seems poised to enter the ranks of the advanced industrial nations, nevertheless exhibits some characteristic features of the third world city. Among these, the most evident – even to the casual visitor – is a squatter housing problem of awe-inspiring magnitude.

The paradox lies in the fact that the government has made equally awe-inspiring efforts to solve the problem. It has not so far succeeded, simply because each effort is apt to be followed by another refugee influx. In the mid-1950s 700,000 people, 30 per cent of the then population, were refugees; by the early 1980s, after the influx of the Vietnamese boat people, there were still 750,000 squatter households. Yet, in the intervening period, Hong Kong's housing programme had made the government the biggest public landlord in the non-Communist world: another rich paradox for an administration so committed to the principle of non-intervention.

This story started on Christmas Day 1953, when a disastrous fire in squatter housing on Kowloon rendered 53,000 homeless and necessitated a crash housing programme. The result was the Mark One and Two resettlement estates of 1954–64. Twelve in number, housing eventually some 544,000 people, they consist of extremely simple seven-storey H-plan blocks, divided into flats usually of 11 square metres (118 square feet) for a family of 4 or 5: a minimal 2.2 square metres a person, with communal toilets and washrooms and cooking on open balconies; schools, elementary children's playspace and open-air market sites were provided within the estates. They are now well below contemporary norms, and are being rebuilt to provide private washing and toilet facilities.

Resettlement estates, nevertheless, are still one important element in Hong Kong's gigantic public housing programme with over 1 million tenants, 30 per cent of the total. Essentially they cater for those who are most needy and have the most restricted choice, including the squatters – who now consist mainly not of refugees, but of Hong Kong people displaced from private housing. Unlike many other governments of developing countries, Hong Kong takes a very firm line on squatter housing: it patrols and clears new squatter areas systematically, moving for instance nearly 31,000 people in 1979 alone; it makes no attempt to improve existing squatter areas; it rehouses squatters only when the sites are cleared; it then houses only those who are already registered, the rest being sent to temporary accommodation, which takes the form of a shell within which the inhabitants can make their own improvements. The result is that resettlement of squatters is still a major concern of the Housing Authority in the mid-1980s, thirty years after it first took on the task.

A second category of public housing, government low-cost estates, caters for over 300,000 low-income tenants. In these two categories, the rents amortize the capital costs and – in the case of the low-cost estates – maintenance and administration. A third kind of housing is provided by the Hong Kong Housing Authority for middle-income families at higher space standards – though still cramped by the standards of other industrial countries. Here the rent, which averages 13 per cent of the tenants' incomes, provides a small surplus to finance future construction. All these kinds of public housing benefit from cheap land, provided by the government in its capacity as sole landowner. In addition the government helps a Housing Society with land and low-cost loans to provide higher-quality accommodation for low- and middle-income groups.

It all adds up to an impressive picture. The Hong Kong Housing Authority, which since 1973 has administered also the programme of the former Re-settlement Department, is landlord to over 2.25 million people: some 44 per cent of the total population. Consisting of twenty members appointed by the Governor and chaired by the Secretary for Housing, in the early 1980s it is building a regular 45,000 new homes each year for rent and – a new and increasing element of the programme – for home ownership.

Necessarily, it achieves this programme only by building dense and high. The height is new, but the density is traditional. Though Hong Kong extends over a total area of more than 1,000 square kilometres (400 square miles), 77 per cent of the entire population live on only 11 per cent of that area. In Mongkok, the most congested district, densities rise as high as 155,000 per square kilometre (400,000 per square mile); net densities in parts of the city rise as high as 1.2 million per square kilometre (3.1 million per square mile), or about twenty-five times the density of the Barbican in London, which is regarded as a high-density development. A working-class family will typically have between 1.5 and 3.25 square metres (16–35 square feet) per person: little more than the space needed to lie down in.

As Frank Leeming has pointed out, these densities are not simply a reaction to the present population levels; they were true when Hong Kong was much smaller, and they appear to be typical of Chinese cities generally. Leeming himself, after a long discussion, cannot quite resolve the question of whether poverty plus high rents produce crowding, or whether Chinese social customs produce crowding and thus high rents. Some evidence for the latter is pro-vided by the fact that, as well as crowding within their homes, the Chinese in Hong Kong crowd the streets outside them: here congestion arises because everyone is concerned to use space to make money. Thus everyone tries to encroach on public space: restaurant sculleries spill out into back alleys, storage on to common staircases, hawking on to the pavements and streets. The government does what it can, by regulation, gradually to restrict these practices; but it is necessarily slow work.

What can be said is that life in a typical 51-square metre (554-square feet) Housing Authority rented flat in a new thirty-five storey block, crowded as it may seem to the British or American visitor, represents an extraordinary degree of spaciousness to the middle-income family living in it. Furthermore, it takes only between 4 and 6 per cent of this family's income, as against 25–6 per cent for the less fortunate half of the population that still live in privately rented housing. In this sense, Hong Kong housing standards are certainly changing in the direction of affluence.

Solving the housing problem: the new towns

By 1970 available space in inner Kowloon, and on the facing shore of the island, was to all intents and purposes exhausted. Hong Kong faced a difficult problem: mountain barriers made both the south shore of the island, and the northern part of the New Territories, relatively inaccessible to the employment opportunities of the central and inner city. The government's reaction was typically bold. Under the direction of the New Territories Development Department it began the construction of seven new towns for a total population of no less than 2.5 million people: one of the biggest urban housing programmes ever attempted anywhere. And it had to find ways of linking these towns to the centre of Hong Kong by new roads and public transport connections.

By the mid-1980s the prodigious planning effort has already begun to yield impressive results. Tsuen Wan new town – the planning of which began in the early 1960s, well before the 1973 scheme – had about 660,000 people out of its projected total of no less than 885,000. In 1982 it was linked to the new Mass Transit Railway, providing a fast connection to lower Kowloon and Central District (map 8.2) Sha Tin, reached across the mountains by a dual road tunnel and by a rail tunnel on the Kowloon–Canton Railway, had reached about a quarter of the way to its target of 756,000, to be reached by the end of the 1980s – 450,000 of them in public housing. These two new towns, only 10 kilometres (6 miles) from the tip of Kowloon, are the nearest and so are the earliest to be developed. Of the others, four – Tuen Mun, Tai Po, Fanling and Yuen Long – are in the northern part of the New Territories between 25 and 30 kilometres (15 and 18 miles) from the centre; they have population targets ranging from 135,000 to 547,000; they should all be completed by the early 1990s. The last – Junk Bay on the east side of the Kowloon peninsula – was still being planned in the early 1980s.

Like everything else in Hong Kong, the new towns are big, high and dense. Superficially, there is no conceivable resemblance to Ebenezer Howard's garden city model – except for the conscious effort to plan homes, factories, shops and community facilities in concert. The new towns are planned to be self-contained, with a full range of jobs, shopping opportunities and community facilities provided from the beginning in step with the development of housing. But, like their British or Swedish equivalents, they are also planned with excellent communication links to the city for those who need them. When they are finished in the early 1990s, particularly if the planned extensions of the Mass Transit Railway take place, they will give a new structure to Hong Kong: it will become a planned polycentric agglomeration, in which nearly half the total population will live in a series of interlinked new towns. So, despite the superficial lack of similarity, Hong Kong by then should

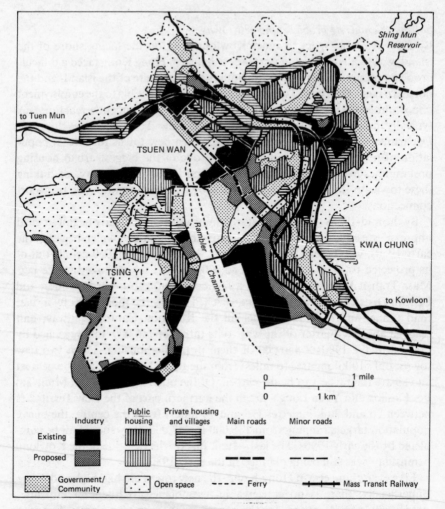

Map 8.2 *Hong Kong: Tsuen Wan new town*. First of the new towns to begin construction, Tsuen Wan will reach its planned population target of 885,000 in the mid-1980s. Densely built-up because of the shortage of flat land, it has high-rise residential areas close to new industry and is the terminus of the extended Mass Transit Railway.

provide a dramatic realization of Ebenezer Howard's original 1898 vision of Social City.

Transport

Hong Kong's notorious congestion expresses itself in another obvious way: on the streets, in the buses, on the trains. Five million people, getting to jobs and friends and recreational opportunities, represent a tremendous problem of physical movement. But density also has its advantages: it means very high numbers of passengers along the main corridors, guaranteeing an effective and economical public transport system. Along the island waterfront, the antique green double-deck trams – which have run since the early years of the century, and are almost a Hong Kong institution – follow each other at intervals of a couple of hundred metres (or yards): a kind of horizontal Paternoster lift, perhaps the densest system of public transport in the world.

Given the basic fact of congestion, Hong Kong has been remarkably effective in dealing with it. In comparison with most other cities of the newly-industrializing world (save only its Chinese rival Singapore), and even in comparison with London, its traffic moves smoothly. Traffic regulations are strictly enforced on the main roads by an army of British-style traffic wardens. The Public Works Department has completed a prodigious series of grade separations at all the major bottlenecks, many of them hanging like concrete sculptures from precipitous hillsides. Out in the New Territories, a fast-growing network of urban motorways connects the new towns to lower Kowloon. Major road tunnels – at Lion Rock south of Sha Tin new town, under the harbour, and through the mountain heart of the island between Happy Valley and Aberdeen – penetrate the colony's mountain and water barriers. Hong Kong, in fact, has a far more impressive and modern road system than any British city – but it certainly needs it.

The traffic planners' job is also eased by the fact that car ownership, by the standards of other middle-income cities, is remarkably low: a total of only 212,000 in 1981, one for every twenty-four of the population. The simple reason, of course, is that there is hardly any place to park a car. In addition, the public transport system is so good that there is hardly any need. Hong Kong is thus an extreme version of what we earlier observed for Manhattan Island.

Until 1980 the whole of this demand for public transport, apart from a few passengers on the Kowloon–Canton Railway and the Peak Tramway, has had to be met on the streets. Conventional British double-deck bus services, belonging to private companies – the China Bus Company on the island, the Kowloon Bus Company on the peninsula and in the New Territories – compete with a fleet of 4,350 public and 900 private light buses: minibuses which collect and set down passengers on request for a slightly higher fare than their conventional competition. Along the island waterfront, the trams rumble slowly but reliably from Kennedy Town to Shau Ki Wan. The famous Star Ferry plies every few minutes across the harbour between Kowloon and Central District, while thirteen bus routes pass underneath via the Cross-Harbour Tunnel.

The early 1980s, however, saw the most momentous developments of Hong Kong's transport system for many decades. In 1980 the Mass Transit Railway was opened along a 15.6-kilometre (9.7-mile) initial section linking Central District under the harbour to lower and East Kowloon. In 1981 it carried 223 million people; the 10.5-kilometre (6.5-mile) extension to Tsuen Wan was opened in 1982, while the third line, following the line of the tramway along the island waterfront, will be complete in 1986. Like almost everything in Hong Kong, the system is supposed to pay for itself; it has been built by a specially constituted company with borrowed money. However, during the early 1980s it has been badly hit by high interest rates and has had to be rescued by government purchase of equity – a most un-Hong Kong-like operation. For the future, the idea is that the construction of the island line can be financed by property development profits – a device already used for several of the stations on the first two lines.

The other major development was the electrification of the Kowloon–Canton Railway, coupled with the double-tracking of the tunnel south of Sha Tin new town and the purchase of completely new rolling stock. The new railway, for this is essentially what it is, connects with the Mass Transit Railway at Kowloon Tong station at the north end of Kowloon. Completed in 1982, it was expected to double its passengers by 1990 – not least because of the expansion of Sha Tin, which it serves.

By the early 1980s, therefore, Hong Kong had perhaps the most modern and efficient public transport system of any of the great cities of the world. It may have had rivals for that title, but few could claim better than equal place. True, conditions were uniquely propitious for the development of the system – but much of the credit must go to the government, which despite its policy of non-intervention had in fact master-minded it. And particularly impressive was the integration of the reshaped public transport system with the planning of the new towns, thus creating a totally new multi-centred, inter-linked metropolis. Stockholm in the 1950s and 1960s pioneered this kind of integration; Paris in the 1960s and 1970s developed it on a vaster scale; but Hong Kong's achievement is fully equal to either of these.

How it is done: planning and public administration

Like most things about Hong Kong, its government is unusual. Constitution-ally it is a Crown Colony of the United Kingdom, under a Governor appointed by the British Crown, whose authority in principle is absolute. He is advised by an Executive Council, also appointed by the Crown, but can disregard their advice if he pleases; laws are passed by a Legislative Council in which, however, the Governor's representatives have an absolute majority. There are elections to the Urban Council, but these make up only half the members and the chairman; and it controls only the 106-square kilometre (41-square mile) urban area. The New Territories are administered by District Officers on a traditional colonial model; there are elected local authorities, but few people ever vote.

In practice, however, it is more complex. The colonial government has to have regard for at least three sets of interests: those of the United Kingdom, those of a powerful and influential Chinese business élite, and those of the ordinary people. The British tradition of free speech has produced a powerful independent press which vigorously discusses proposed policy changes. What is especially strange about Hong Kong from a western viewpoint, however, is the pragmatism of the culture. It is often said about the Chinese in Hong Kong (and perhaps anywhere) that they want a strong, efficient, mandarin-style government to provide a safe framework within which they can pursue their main life interests: making money and enjoying family life. Certainly this is not a bad description of how, in practice, Hong Kong actually works. There is a remarkable degree of political apathy, or acquiescence; the average citizen does not seem very interested in politics. Government in practice arises from pressures, suggestions and representations within a bureaucratic-mer-chant ruling group.

Another paradox concerns the style of government that thus arises. Hong Kong prides itself on having the least interventionist government in the world. But that claim must be subjected to certain important modifications. The government regulates conditions of employment, particularly of women and children, and - increasingly - the location and establishment of polluting industry. It protects the consumer. It tries to help industry by disposing of land cheaply. As seen, it has one of the biggest public housing programmes in the world. It intervenes positively to build a highway infrastructure and to establish a modern, integrated system of public transport. These functions have rapidly increased during the 1970s; in the short period from 1970 to 1977 alone, the size of the Hong Kong civil service rose by 46 per cent. It might be better to characterize the Hong Kong style, again paradoxically, as *laissez-faire* underpinned by municipal socialism.

This is well seen in the colony's planning system. An outline plan, first developed in the late 1960s, is regularly reviewed to provide a framework for the preparation of statutory outline zoning plans, departmental planning guides, outline development and layout plans. Statutory outline plans, for both existing and new urban areas, are prepared under the direction of a Town Planning Board. They show the distribution of future land uses and, after consultation, they acquire statutory force. By 1982, in the urban area three of the thirty-nine planning areas had approved plans and another twenty-three draft plans; in the New Territories, plans were ready or being developed for the new towns and other important growth areas; for other areas in the New Territories, planning guidelines are laid down.

All this means that the new areas of Hong Kong, particularly the new towns, are subject to planning down to a minute level of detail. In other areas of very rapid renewal of the fabric, such as the commercial districts of Nathan Road on Kowloon, Central District and Causeway Bay on the island, the planning authorities obviously intervene positively in what are often very large urban redevelopment operations. But, in contrast, the authorities have not concentrated nearly so much attention so far on the renewal of the more outworn and congested areas of the city, where slum housing and small industry live cheek by jowl. A start is being made, in the Hollywood Road area of Sheung Wan, but it is a very modest one. This is only too understandable; the government's first preoccupation has necessarily been to build the new towns to cope with the rapid increase of the population, and only when equilibrium is reached will attention shift to renewal. With an estimated three-quarters of a million still living in squatter housing, that point is still some years away.

So, in the mid-1980s, there are increasingly two Hong Kongs: the dense, bustling, congested, unruly but buoyant older city and the more regulated and planned world of the new towns. What distinguishes both is the extraordinary press of humanity, the hard work and dedication of the people, and above all the extraordinary capacity to build order out of apparent chaos. It all makes for one of the most dynamic, the most exciting and above all the most forward-looking great cities of the world.

Life after 1997

British colonial rule, then, seems to have been good for Hong Kong. Of course, after 1997 it may be good no longer; all increasingly depends on the ability to reach accommodation with the People's Republic on a new formula to run the city after that time. But any pessimist on the score should reflect on two things: first, even during all the uncertainties of the Cultural Revolution, China continued to supply Hong Kong with its basic needs of fresh food and fresh water, without which it could not survive many days; second, the Chinese government is itself investing heavily in Hong Kong development. China needs Hong Kong as much as Hong Kong needs China – so the most likely outcome is a new and extended territory, extending into the new export processing zones China is establishing just across the border, and enjoying some special status guaranteed by itself and Britain. Perhaps, by the early twenty-first century Hong Kong will be like now – but, by courtesy of the Chinese, bigger.

9 Mexico City

There is a certain logic in coming last to Mexico City. For truly, towards the twentieth century's end, it is the ultimate world city: ultimate in size, ultimate in threat of paralysis and disintegration, ultimate in the problems it presents for its politicians and planners. And these problems are of interest not merely to the people who live and work in the Valley of Mexico, but also to the whole of the world. For if by some miracle Mexico City's growth can be controlled and serviced and planned, then perhaps any other city on earth has hope too.

Size is the first overwhelming fact about Mexico City. But it is a very recent fact. At the start of the present century, the population of Mexico City was 541,000: not quite double the size of the ancient Aztec capital of Tenochtitlan, which Hernan Cortez and his *conquistadores* had conquered and razed in 1521. In 1941 it had trebled to 1,760,000: a respectable national capital for a medium-size developing nation. Then, with rapid industrialization during and after the Second World War, came its truly dizzying rise. Its metropolitan area population almost doubled, in effect, every ten years: to 3.5 million in 1950, 5.2 million in 1960, 8.8 million in 1970 and 14.1 million in 1980. Already in the 1960s, indeed, the reality of the metropolitan area's growth began to outgrow the administrative framework of the city: the Federal District (*Distrito Federal*) that had been designated in 1928 as a special area of government for the capital city. But even the metropolitan area, vast as it was, only constituted the heart of a larger and more complex system of cities spreading out 100 kilometres (60 miles) and more into the Valley of Mexico: the so-called Conurbation of the Centre of the Country, the responsibility of a special commission set up by government in 1978 to try to bring some order into the regional planning of the national capital region (table 9.1).

The metropolitan area, though it is perhaps already not a complete definition of the reality, is nevertheless a starting-point since it is close to the definition employed by United Nations statisticians for their population projections down to the end of the century. In 1980 these experts concluded that by the year 2000 Mexico City would number some 31 million people: the greatest mass of urban humanity the world will have ever seen. And, though such projections in urban planning are notoriously liable to error, no one

214

Table 9.1   Mexico City: alternative definitions, 1980

	Area (square km.)	Population (thousands) 1980	Population change (per cent) 1970-80
Distrito Federal (DF)	1,499	9,370.7	+40.1
Metropolitan Area (AMCM)	2,000	14,125.1	+69.9
Conurbation of the Centre of the Country (CCP)	15,435	18,416.0	not known
(UN definition)		15,032.0	+67.1

Sources: Census, 1980; United Nations, *Patterns of Urban and Rural Population Growth* (*Population Studies*, 68), New York: United Nations, 1980.

seems seriously to doubt that such an increase will occur; the only question is whether it will be a little before or a little after the millenium.

We do not know, and we find it hard to imagine, what a city of this size would be like to live in or to work in or to govern. But we are fairly certain, as we saw in chapter 1, that by the year 2000 Mexico City will merely be first in a new group of super-cities in the newly-developing world. In them, super-size will breed super-problems – and the paradox is that this will happen to nations of limited means, simultaneously struggling with other problems of rapid development.

That is obvious enough, if we look even at the Mexico City of today (map 9.1). Already twice the size of Greater London or New York City, and just behind New York or Tokyo in its total metropolitan population, Mexico seems to be permanently on the edge of urban collapse. As the incoming traveller flies into the international airport, his first impression is one of endless sprawl: a parody, reach-me-down version of Los Angeles. Uniform, shack-like structures, thrown up on vast rectangular grids, stretch in all directions until halted by mountains or water. To the immediate left is Nezahualcoyotl, a settlement that hardly existed before 1960 but that now – with between 2 and 3 million people – is, unbelievably, the second city of Mexico.

Nezahualcoyotl, and indeed the whole metropolitan area of Mexico City, are almost lost in a vast haze of pollutants that seems to fill the whole valley of Mexico. On one side are the remains of a vast, stagnant, apparently polluted lake: all that is left of the great Lake Texcoco, on which the Aztecs built their island capital, and into which today comes much of the sewage of the world's third city. From January until May, the dry season, the lake dust blows into Nezahualcoyotl, choking its inhabitants and filling their lungs. Its children suffer twice the amount of respiratory disease as their more fortunate counterparts in the affluent south and west of the city.

Once through the airport and into the streets, the visitor's first impression

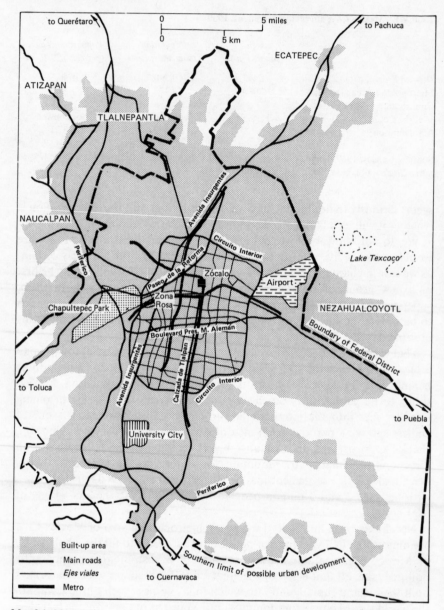

Map 9.1 *Mexico City: general view*. Explosive urban development has now far outrun the administrative boundaries of the *Distrito Federal* – yet the extensive improvements to the city's chronically congested transportation system, such as the new Metro and the one-way streets (*ejes viales*) all stop at the boundaries of the *Distrito*.

– as so often in the cities of the developing world – is one of imminent paralysis. Despite an impressive network of freeways laced together by broad arterial avenues, huge streams of traffic are congealed, their exhausts rising into the mountain air – the city has an altitude of over 2,000 metres (6,500 feet) – to add their contributions to the smog haze. It appears that every person in the city owns a car, as often as not an ancient American gas-guzzler. And catching a view of the prices at the state-owned filling stations – where, until recently, it was always said that a litre of petrol cost less than a litre of Coca Cola – he may begin to understand how.

Arriving at last in the city centre, the traveller may catch a faint hint of the vanished city of only thirty years before. The great central arteries – the Paseo de la Reforma, the Avenida de Insurgentes – still show, here and there, the magnificent residential mansions that characterized them as recently as the 1950s. But they are rapidly being buried under the curtain-wall architecture of the international office-block and international hotel. Mexico, first city by far of the Spanish-speaking world, has now become not merely capital of one of the world's larger nations, but in some ways the natural capital of Spanish Latin America.

The penalties of success: Mexico City's problems

Mexico City is the archetypal metropolis of the developing world. As with Hong Kong, so also here, explosive growth has produced almost unmanageable problems. The most pressing, for the average citizen, in logical order, are earning a living; finding shelter; occupying and servicing the land; and moving about the city.

The economic base

Mexico City is thus unique. It is, nevertheless, an archetype of the third world metropolis. Its recent growth comes from two interlinked sources: the concentration into the capital city of a disproportionate part first of the nation's higher-order governing and managing and cultural functions, and second of the nation's modern industries. And these have a common cause: it is that in a country in the course of development, both physical and human capital tend to be disproportionately concentrated in the region around the capital. This produces what the development economist Gunnar Myrdal called a process of circular and cumulative causation: a circle, vicious or virtuous according to your prejudices, whereby success leads to further success. In countries like Mexico, all roads lead to the centre: here is the best transportation infrastructure, the most highly-trained work-force, the greatest variety of specialized services – and above all, access to government officials whose help is invariably needed to get things to happen. Mexico, like many third world countries, has developed with powerful state aid – and this aid comes from the capital city.

Thus the city had, in 1975, 191,000 out of 516,000 – or some 40 per cent – of all government employees in Mexico. Adding in employees of other public agencies, the total may have been nearer 500,000. It had 220,000 higher education students – nearly two-thirds of the national total – in thirty-seven institutions. It had all important newspapers and periodicals, and four in five of all the publishing houses. It had six television stations and sixty-four radio stations. It had 45 per cent of the higher managerial and 40 per cent of the professional and technical expertise in the whole country. Its banks had nearly 70 per cent of the total capital stock and reserves in the whole system. Its people represented over half the national demand for industrial products – and, logically, it had over half the national industrial production. Its average per capita income was double the national average – though, as so often in developing countries, that average concealed an extraordinary spread between rich and poor: the top 10 per cent received nearly 40 per cent of income, the bottom half less than 20 per cent.

These two main urban functions were very differently located. Logically, the national and international high-level services crowded into the Central Business District (CBD). More precisely, as they grew so they caused a massive outgrowth of this district: away from the historic Zócalo, the great central square which the Spanish conquerors had placed directly over the ruins of the Aztec temple, westwards towards the Reforma and the Insurgentes. In this, they followed a very European pattern: there, characteristically, the rich had put their mansions close to the royal palace and park (St James's, the Louvre), and there, centuries later, commercial functions took their place. Mexico's zone of luxury had similarly developed around the Chapultepec Palace, which Emperor Maximilian had built in the 1860s; and here, according to a seemingly inexorable law of urban development, the offices and hotels and luxury shops followed in the 1950s and 1960s. The *Zona Rosa* (Pink Zone), as late as the 1950s a charming bohemian resident quarter, was already a tourist zone by the 1970s; in a metropolis growing as fast as this one, the geographical processes of invasion and succession occur with breathtaking speed.

With the industry, it was different. Modern, highly-capitalized industry has the same needs the world over, in developed and developing countries alike: it seeks plenty of cheap, flat land at the urban periphery, easy access to motorways that offer low-cost distribution to the rest of the national market, and good services. Logically, the multinational corporations and their Mexican counterparts went north of the city, astride the main motorways that

218

were being built northwards to Huehuetoca, north-eastwards to Pachuca. Thus they went outside the boundaries of the Federal District, the unit of government that had been created in 1928 to manage the territory which – just as in the United States – had been carved out of the federal structure of the nation to house its capital. The main areas of modern industry are thus in the neighbouring State of Mexico.

Modern, centralized services and modern, decentralized industry only employ about half Mexico City's work-force. The other half find work, of a sort, in that part of the economy that characterizes the metropolis of the developing world: the informal sector. True, this sector is often discussed but is difficult to define. Essentially it consists of casual jobs with little or no security and with no links to the power structure of formal labour organizations. In Mexico it embraces a vast army of female domestic servants in hotels and in private homes, male construction workers, porters and security guards, lower-paid workers in small-scale industry – particularly subcontractors to bigger firms – and small traders, especially street traders. These workers are found all over the city, including the CBD and the inner suburbs where much of the small-scale workshop industry and petty trading tends to concentrate. Because of the need to be close to casual job openings here, many new migrants to the city traditionally sought homes in the same crowded areas. And, because such workers have to find some kind of work in order to live, characteristically developing cities like Mexico City have fairly low rates of registered unemployment – itself a feature of the formal economy; instead, they suffer prolonged underemployment at a very low average daily wage rate.

Housing, segregation and sprawl
The division between formal and informal economy, plus long-inherited wealth, plus a traditional Spanish class structure that elevates non-manual work, together help to produce in Mexico City one of the most segregated societies on earth. The rich, displaced from their former haunts by the commercial invasion, now live in their palatial villas or condominiums in the more attractive areas of the south and west, where basic services are readily available. The poor and the fairly poor live in the north and north-east, sprawled out for endless miles along the radial freeways, often interspersed with the factories where many of them seek work; and in the east, where the dried-out bed of Lake Texcoco offers vast tracks of poor but relatively cheap building land. Here, they live in scores of self-built settlements (*colonias*), some – such as Nezahualcoyotl – gigantic: they include Neza itself and Ecatepec east of the city, Tlalnepantla and Naucalpan to the north. Others live in the west, but in places where the upper and middle classes would not deign to go: in sandpits and narrow ravines, hidden away from sight.

219

The dispersal of the poor is relatively recent; it is a direct result of the city's phenomenal growth. Down to the 1950s, the low-income immigrants from the countryside sought shelter close to the informal-sector job opportunities of the central and inner city, in rent-controlled apartments (*vecindades*) which soon degenerated into slums. Then, during the 1950s, they began to erect flimsy squatter settlements, 'lost cities' (*ciudades perdidas*), anywhere that they could find space, on vacant sites behind existing blocks. Finally, in the 1960s, as the city authorities moved to tear these down and rehouse the poor – a move that was generally unwelcome, since it meant higher rents – they made their final move: out to the peripheral *colonias* in the State of Mexico, where by 1980 no less than one-third of the total population was living. Here, only a minority live in true squatter settlements, illegally occupied: the areas the Mexicans piquantly call 'parachutists' colonies' (*colonias paracaidistas*). The great majority, those in the *colonias proletarias*, believe themselves to be the legal owners of their land, which they have paid for. The problem is that they paid these sums to subdividers who, in most cases, lacked legal rights over the land and had obtained control over it by graft and fraud. The buyers also thought that they were getting promises that the land would be serviced – promises honoured, more often than not, in the breach.

In Nezahualcoyotl, the most notorious case, it was almost impossible to establish who really owned much of the land. And this, ironically, is because under Mexican law much of it had been collective land, on which – as on so much similar land around the city, on which nine in ten of the *colonias* were built – it was legally unclear as to whether sale to individuals was possible. Whatever the case, wholesale disposal of the land began in 1951, after a ban on sales was lifted, and mushroomed in the 1960s; the buyers understood that services would be forthcoming, as provided by a law of the State of Mexico of 1958, but they were soon disappointed. As a result, by 1970 39 per cent of residents had no drinking water, 53 per cent no sewerage, and 88 per cent no sanitary installations. (Ironically, Neza is named after a great Aztec king, among whose accomplishments was water engineering.) There was elementary schooling for only a quarter of the children, secondary schooling for a mere 14 per cent; basic services like pay telephones and post offices were equally lacking. After protests, the State of Mexico in 1973 achieved a compromise: in return for further payments, the people would get the services they had thought they were buying originally; 40 per cent of these payments would go to the subdividers, who in return would provide firm title to the land. At least, this solution achieved results; by the early 1980s, Neza was undergoing transformation into something like an ordinary suburb, and the inhabitants were obviously investing a lot in the improvement of their own houses.

That, some experts argue, is a good argument for letting such irregular settlements flourish. Close on 70 per cent of Mexico City's total population cannot afford to enter the formal private housing sector and are unlikely to qualify for the meagre stock of public housing; therefore, informal self-built housing is really the only option open to them. Further, most of these people do not represent depressed marginal classes, but a great variety of different conditions including factory workers, white-collar employees, shopkeepers, small business people and even some professionals. Their main concern is to own their houses and to invest their own time and energy in improving them. By buying unserviced land at relatively low prices, they can achieve this. And the eventual result can be a reasonable standard of housing: the poor in Mexico City have space standards not notably worse than the rich, though both live at relatively high densities compared with their Anglo-American counterparts – a product of high land coverage and lack of open space rather than high-rise building, since rich and poor alike inhabit single-family, often single-storey homes.

They, and the entire community, pay a price. Such areas are frequently unserviced because the land is unsuitable for occupation – as in the case of Nezahualcoyotl on the old lakebed of Lake Texcoco. Services may thus prove disproportionately expensive to put in after the event. When they are, the paradoxical result is a further rise in land values – and this is reflected in the regular payments which the inhabitants must pay for the legal title and for the servicing of their land. Some cannot meet the higher costs, and thus sell out. They move away on to cheaper land, where also they pay no property taxes, or they become renters. The paradox is that, for those who remain as owners, the inflation of property values may be beneficial – so long as they can keep up with it.

Land and services
The problem of shelter in Mexico City – and, by extension, in so many cities of the developing world – is at heart a problem of land and service provision. The problem of land, which has been intensively studied by experts from the World Bank, has various possible solutions – all of which, according to the iron law of planning, may carry snags. The state might try to put the burden of servicing the land more fairly on the subdividers; but in the past such attempts have tended to fail, because of collusion between corrupt officials and subdividers. It might try to discourage speculation through some form of taxation on speculative gains, including special taxes on land held idle. Better, it might develop a programme of gradual land release. Most promising of all, perhaps, it could try to devise an urban equivalent of the rural land reform of 1910, which in effect collectivized the peasants' land. Such an urban *ejido* would be established through trust deeds which made individual sale of the land null and void. It might just be possible – but it would meet objection

because speculation in land, in an economy suffering from regular double-digit inflation, becomes almost a popular pastime and a recipe for survival.

The other problem is that of service delivery. This does not merely mean their final transmission to the door of the consumer, difficult as that may prove; behind it, there is the deeper problem of how to keep up with the apparently insatiable needs of the population for water, power and the removal of waste water. Still, in 1980, 20 per cent of the entire population of the Federal District, about one million people, had no direct supply of water and had to depend on neighbours or carriers; outside, in the State of Mexico, the position was even worse. Two million people, or over one-third of the population, lacked connections to the sewer system; and, for those who had it, the efficiency of the system was falling because of the pressure upon it. Both water supply and drainage were threatened by the progressive sinkage of the porous volcanic soils that make up the floor of the Valley of Mexico, arising perversely from the extraction of underground water from wells, which had caused the general surface level to fall by no less than 4 or 5 metres (13 to 16 feet) since 1900.

The authorities have calculated that, between 1982 and 2000, total demand for water would more than double, even without any increase in per capita consumption. To provide even for half of that extra demand would mean extremely expensive tapping of progressively more distant rivers – the Cutzamala, 100 kilometres (62 miles) distant and 100 metres (328 feet) lower down, to the west, and the Tecolutla, 200 kilometres (124 miles) distant and 2,000 metres (6,562 feet) lower, to the east – at a cost estimated to be as much as $500 million. The marginal cost of supplying this extra water, it has been calculated, could be as much as six times the present amount. Energy demands are rising even more rapidly; they are doubling each four to six years. And, since the new water schemes will necessitate pumping from lower levels, they will further increase the strain on the power generation system.

These basic services are not the only ones that will come under strain. At the start of the 1980s, there were close on 200,000 children at the basic and middle levels for whom no school places could be found. Public clinics fell short of requirements by 50 per cent. There was a grievous lack of open space – and, outside the Federal District, the problem was if anything worse. Further, growth of the city can only exacerbate the chronic air pollution, which – according to the *New York Times* of 1973 – meant that living in the city centre was equivalent to smoking 40 cigarettes a day. For 60 per cent of this pollution is estimated to originate from cars, and – unless something can be done – will simply rise with the total amount of traffic on the streets.

Transportation: escape from paralysis
Thus, since 1970, much of the residential growth of Mexico City, and also

222

much of the industrial growth, has taken place outside the boundaries of the Federal District, in the neighbouring State of Mexico. No less than one-third of the metropolitan area population – over 5 million people – live outside the Federal District. The problem is that the homes and the factories tend not to have been built in the same places: many of the homes are in the east and south-east, many of the factories in the north and north-west. In an urban mass the size of Mexico City, that spells a commuting problem of epic proportions. Because petrol is so cheap, car ownership is much higher than might be guessed from the income level of the population: in the entire urban area there are more than 2 million vehicles, meaning that on average four out of five households have cars (though, since many rich families own more than one, the actual figure is lower). Hence congestion is chronic: speeds average only about 15 kilometres (9 miles) an hour and fall as low as 4 kilometres ($2\frac{1}{2}$ miles) an hour – slower than walking pace – during the four long peak periods of the day. Further, because of the lack of good outer orbital connections, most of the through traffic from south to north, and from east to west, actually passes through the city centre. The planners in the Federal District estimate that by 1988 the average speed will have dropped under 8 kilometres (5 miles) an hour and the system will be completely saturated.

The paradox is that, though 97 per cent of total traffic consists of private cars, four in five of all personal trips are on public transport. And, despite the construction of a Metro which began in the late 1960s, the great majority of the public users have to depend on the bus system. The Metro system in 1982 reached a total length of some 82 kilometres (51 miles): an extremely modest network for such a huge city. Further, because it is part of the transportation system of the Federal District, it stops sharply at the boundaries of the District. It, and the Federal District bus system, do nothing directly for the journeys – one in four of all in the Federal District – that begin or end outside it. The citizens of Nezahualcoyotl, for instance, have to ride on feeder buses to reach the Metro terminus. And, if their destinations are the factory zones to the north-west, they will need another bus at the far end to reach them. Small wonder then, that, including lunch trips – a feature of the Spanish-culture day, that anomalously survives in such a vast city – the average Mexico City commuter is supposed to spend four hours of his or her day just in getting to and from work.

It may not get better very fast. One immediate result of the economic crisis that hit the country during 1982 was an abrupt stop to major public works, including Metro construction. Also threatened is further extension, into the outer parts of the Federal District, of the so-called *ejes viales* – the system of one-way streets, with reserved bus lanes and co-ordinated traffic signals, that had brought about a notable improvement in traffic flow during the 1970s. And in any case, until some way can be found of integrating the public transportation systems inside and outside the District, as the city grows so its transportation problems seem likely to increase exponentially.

Curbing the monster: planning for Mexico City

It might be argued that Mexico City, of all places on earth, is almost beyond the aid of planners. That seems to have been the implicit attitude of the politicians for a long time, for they did not even make a semblance of trying. But, relatively recently, Mexico City has made a spectacular attempt to come to terms with itself.

The task, admittedly, is complicated – as so often in the world's great cities – by administrative geography. In 1824 the Federal Constitution of Mexico, in obvious imitation of the United States, established a Federal District – then a circular area, of radius 8.8 kilometres (5.5 miles), around the Zócalo – as the area of the capital city; in 1928 an Organic Law established that this area, by then extended, should be governed directly by a *Jefe* appointed directly by the President of the Republic. Until 1960, or later, the 658 square kilometres (254 square miles) of the Federal District provided a reasonable definition of Mexico City. But, since then, growth outside – in the State of Mexico – has led to all kinds of anomalies: in taxation and revenues, in housing policies, in transport systems. Thus a ban on new subdivisions in the Federal District, during the 1960s, merely transferred the problem into the State of Mexico where no such limitation existed, creating the vast *colonias* of today. And, as just seen, the failure to co-ordinate public transportation unnecessarily adds to the stresses and strains of commuting.

These problems are familiar from many other world cities. What is impressive is the recent efforts of government to overcome them. The governments of Presidents Echeverria (1972-6) and of Lopez Portillo (1976–82) saw a concentrated attempt to create a new planning system at the national, regional and urban scales. The Law of Human Settlements (*Ley de Asentamientos Humanos*) of May 1976 was followed by the establishment of a Sub-Secretariat of Human Settlements (*Secretaria de Asentamientos Humanos y Obras Publicas*, SAHOP) within the Secretariat of Public Works. By 1978 SAHOP had already produced a National Plan of Urban Development, with a broad strategy for decentralization of activity and guidelines for developing more detailed plans at State level. Almost simultaneously, the Federal District created a General Planning Agency (*Direccion General de la Planificacion*, DGP) to develop a master plan and develop land-use regulations. By 1980 this too was ready, with both a general plan and more detailed plans for each section (*Delegacion*) within the Federal District.

The central aim of SAHOP's 1978 National Plan of Urban Development is to put a brake on the growth of Mexico City by encouraging the development of counter-magnets in many other cities of the country, in major ports and in the United States border area. By this strategy, SAHOP suggests, the population of the conurbation area around Mexico City in the year 2000 could be cut back from the trend projection of between 32 and 43 million, to a little over 20 million, implying – an heroic assumption, this – that in-migration could be cut to zero; the population of the wider Central Region, which takes in a number of surrounding cities up to 100 kilometres (60 miles) distant, could be reduced from 60 million (45 per cent of the national population total) to perhaps 39 million. Within this latter region, the aim would be to build up more distant cities, thus creating a more polycentric system: Puebla, 100 kilometres (60 miles) east, would have 2.1 million people; Toluca, 80 kilometres (50 miles) west, 851,000; Cuernavaca, 80 kilometres (50 miles) south, 750,000. To this end, new highway links would be developed which would tangentially by-pass the existing built-up mass: the *Libramiento Norte* some 80 kilometres (50 miles) north, and the *Libramiento Sur* a similar distance to the south. New rail links would parallel these. In 1982 the World Bank announced a loan to the government of Mexico to start work on a study of the *Libramiento Norte*.

Within this framework of national decentralization and regional deconcentration, the Federal District's 1980 plan in turn represents an ambitious scheme to create within the city itself a polycentric metropolis. Nine high-level, largely self-sufficient urban centres for civic, administrative, cultural, recreational and commercial functions are to be intensively developed around major interchanges on the new Metro system. In turn they will be linked by urban corridors along the Metro lines and new expressways, where redevelopment at higher densities will be positively encouraged. But, in contrast, peripheral sprawl will be controlled by establishing buffer zones, within which government agencies will develop uses 'compatible with conservation and economic improvement' such as farming, villages and parks. Beyond this, the land will be designated as conservation areas within which all development – including even village extensions – will be strictly controlled (map 9.2).

It is all very impressive. The objectives are clear and sensible, and they are accompanied by specific statements saying which agency is responsible for implementing which part of the plan. Further, many of the elements of the plan – the centres, the corridors – seem readily capable of being achieved through private investment, given the right basis in public infrastructure. The only problem is that once again, the plan – including the subcentres and the corridors – stops sharply at the borders of the Federal District. Anomalies of administrative geography, it seems, have triumphed again.

To help meet that charge, there is yet another agency and another plan.

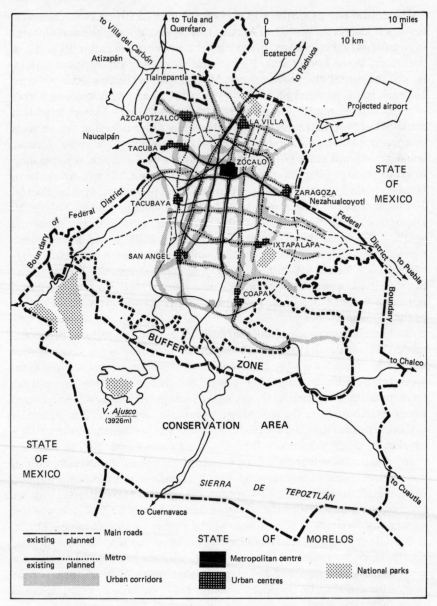

Map 9.2 *Mexico City: plan for the* Distrito Federal. The plan provides for deconcentration of
the capital's higher-order functions from the historic metropolitan centre into nine urban
centres at nodal points, linked by corridors of higher-density development following the new
Metro lines. Further sprawl will be limited by a buffer zone and a conservation zone in the fine
hill country to the south of the city.

226

The *Comision del Conurbacion del Centro del Pais* (CCCP) is one of six, set up under the 1976 Law, to co-ordinate planning as between cities and states within major urban agglomerations. Like the others, it consists of State governors, mayors and officials, chaired by the Secretary of SAHOP. It has produced – in 1981 – its own *Plan de Ordenacion* and accompanying programme, which aims to develop peripheral areas and cities as counter-magnets to the growth of Mexico City itself. It suggests two 'crowns of cities', including cities for priority development, with enhanced service provision levels, linked by several hundred kilometres of circumferential highways: one 20 to 40 kilometres (12 to 25 miles) distant, north and west of the city, including a major new transportation interchange at the city of Huehuetoca, with development eastwards to Teotihuacan and then southward to Chalco and Amecameca; the other 70 to 130 kilometres (45 to 80 miles) distant, linking the capitals of the five states that surround the Federal District (map 9.3). It endorses the plan for polycentric development within the Federal District itself.

All this, of course, is totally in line with SAHOP's national plan. The question must be how it is going to happen. The CCCP suggests that it can be achieved through a combination of selective public investments in service provision and transportation infrastructure, plus a policy of industrial deconcentration to be achieved by differential pricing of water and power supplies. The end result, again, would be a polycentric system of cities among which the most important – the state capitals of Puebla, Cuernavaca, Toluca, Pachuca and Tlaxcala – would become very important centres in their own right, forming the nodes in turn of smaller systems of cities, all within a two-hour commuting distance of Mexico City.

It all adds up to a consistent set of policies. The remaining question is how far it can be implemented. Mexico is a federal state, and achievement of a regional plan for deconcentration must depend on the agreement of the five states within the CCCP. Fortunately, it appears that the different bodies may to some degree have interests in common. The central government, through the Federal District, is definitely committed to stemming growth there – at least on paper. Several of the peripheral states, such as Hidalgo and Tlaxcala, happen to be among the poorest in Mexico and so are desperately interested in getting greater resources from the centre. And the central government can take a strong lead through provision of crucial infrastructure such as highways or water.

Yet there are still question marks. In the past, the Federal District has shown an impressive capacity to gobble up available central funds for investment. It needs more to complete the interior beltway (*periferico*), the subway system and sewerage systems. And it has the inestimable advantage that it is itself the Federal government. On the other hand, the plans – especially those

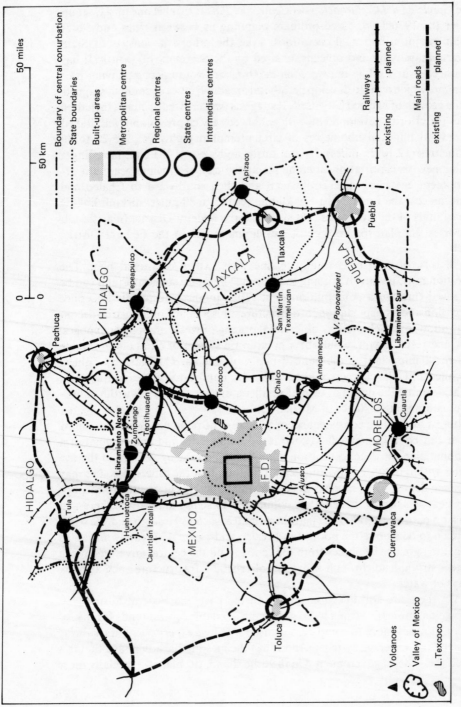

Map 9.3 *Mexico City: principles of regional planning.* The regional plan seeks to turn Mexico City into the heart of a polycentric city region with a system of cities linked by new highways and railways, thus taking the pressure off the core of the city.

for the Federal District – assume an elegant articulation of different sectoral plans on the part of various Federal agencies, which has not always been evident in the past. Then there is the problem that, in the past, the best of intentions in Mexico have tended to founder in the sea of influence and corruption that has become almost a way of life. At least, the administration of Miguel de la Madrid promises a clean break with those traditions – and, given Mexico's parlous economic condition, austerity may well be the order of the day.

A final and crucial question concerns planning powers. All the plans rely on a combination of incentives – public infrastructure, subsidies to industry – to deconcentrate industries, plus fixed population targets and urban containment policies for the central urbanized area. The problem is that the buffer zone and conservation areas are not spelt out in detail, and until they are – and until they are seen to be working – the risk is that the incentives may achieve the very reverse of what is intended: they may result in a massive low-density extension of the present urbanized area, rather than the development of a true polycentric region.

Here, administrative geography may again prove crucial. The main pressures for development, almost without doubt, are going to be felt in the State of Mexico just outside the Federal District, especially in the north of the urban area. What would make sense is a radical reorganization of powers to extend the Federal District to take in these areas of potential growth, so as to make the containment policies more effective right round the urban fence. But this would raise major constitutional issues, from which any Mexican government – however radical – may well draw back.

The question then is whether, in these circumstances, the government can take the necessary steps, perhaps unpopular, to divert resources out of the city and into the periphery to achieve its stated aim of decongesting the world's ultimate metropolis. It is also whether it can match the positive measures of deconcentration with negative controls on further urban sprawl: controls which, since they will directly threaten speculative profits, are bound to meet with at least passive resistance. For any Mexican government, that is a daunting prospect. And it has not got much time.

10 The future metropolis

We have looked at the development of eight among the great city regions of the world in the recent past and the present time, and have speculated on their immediate future. It is now time to attempt the really difficult: to sum up, to generalize, to try to determine what in the experience of the world cities is particular and special, what on the other hand is part of a general set of urban processes. And – an equally difficult, closely associated, question – to ask how far, and in what ways, the planner can hope to influence, guide or change these processes.

In this task, we need to start with a caution. Nothing is more fatally easy, in the study of social and economic processes, than the fallacy of extrapolation. The present trend is so pervasive that it becomes persuasive: it is inconceivable that growth will not continue, that deconcentration and decentralization might reverse. Yet, within an alarmingly short time, the surest and the apparently best-founded statements may prove to be without foundation. This book provides a salutary example. The first and second editions repeated with confidence the accepted wisdom: that all the great metropolitan centres had shown, and would show, continuous population growth both absolutely and in relation to their countries. This rule, it was said, was true of countries large and small, densely and sparsely populated, capitalist and communist, *laissez-faire* and interventionist. And, despite many attempts to limit or reverse the process, still it continued. Now, with the usual benefit of hindsight, we can see that this statement – like almost any of its ilk – was too sweeping and too specious. In some of our case studies, we have discovered a recent and fundamental change: in the world cities of the first world – in London and New York and the cities of the Randstad, perhaps soon in Paris – growth has ceased: not merely in the inner city but in the wider city region, out-movement of people and jobs is the new order of the day. One American geographer, Daniel Vining, has argued that in the advanced industrial (or post-industrial) nations we are now witnessing a clean break with the migration trends of the last two centuries: the movement, traditionally from farm to city, is now from city to small rural town. So the previous argument is now stood almost on its head. The questions now are whether the clean break is truly occurring; whether, if so, it is a general phenomenon or destined to become one; and whether, in that case, the planner could do anything to stop it, or whether it is not some inevitable phase through which, eventually, all cities must pass.

In this final chapter, therefore, the most fundamental question must be whether the eventual general trend is towards urban growth or decline. But this cannot be answered meaningfully without looking also at the internal trends in the organization of the great metropolitan cities; it may be that, as has apparently occurred in New York and in London, today's deconcentration is tomorrow's city-regional decline. We need to start, therefore, with the basic building blocks of the city's structure – any city's structure. We need to ask, first, how and where the people earn their living; second, how and where they live that part of their life which does not consist in working; third, how and where they travel between these elements of their lives. Thus we need to look at the role of the Central Business District (CBD) and its relation to the wider metropolitan economy; at the distribution of manufacturing industry and associated goods-handling activities; at the spread of the residential suburbs and their associated facilities; at processes cf urban renewal or residential succession in older, inner urban areas; at the rise of car ownership and its impact on mass transportation fares and service; at traffic congestion and its impact on commuting; and a hundred other questions concerned with patterns of working, living and travelling around. We need to look at these elements, not only separately and analytically, but as parts of a possible general model of urban growth and change, that – so far as can ever be possible – can be applied alike to cities greater and smaller, more or less developed. Therefore, we need constantly to ask: how far is this trend a general one, applicable to cities in different places, at different times, in different stages of development? This indeed is one of the two fundamental questions with which we started this chapter: how far is such a general model meaningful and real? The other is equally important to keep in mind in what follows: how far can deliberate planning action have any influence on it?

The building blocks of the metropolis

Working
As already noticed in chapter 1, the economic base of the metropolis has fundamentally changed within the last century, and even within the last quarter-century. Up until 1850 or even later, though precise statistical evidence is lacking, much of the growth of metropolitan cities seems to have been occasioned by an increasing concentration of the *goods-handling* activities within the central and inner areas. Here, raw materials and finished goods

231

were transshipped, traded and stored; here a variety of raw materials, often imported, was worked up into finished goods. The typical metropolitan activities were commodity trading, both wholesale and retail, and a variety of industries ranging from the bulk processing of imported basic materials like flour or sugar, to the handicraft production of luxuries for the rich. Only belatedly, after about 1650, had these physical functions begun to produce forms of service industry which were not directly concerned with goods handling: activities like banking, insurance and dealing in business stock and shares. In this period down to about 1850, cities grew most rapidly where goods were readily traded, around seaports and river ports, or at natural junctions of the new railway routes of the nineteenth century.

But, as seen in chapter 1, after 1850 a profound change came over the centres of the metropolitan cities: the traditional activities were joined, and then even sometimes displaced, by new types of activity which were characteristically carried on in offices. This was no sudden once-for-all process; it has gone on happening ever since, and it threatens to be a major feature of the development of the great metropolitan centres in the immediate future. Indeed, the process may be speeding up; the 1960s and 1970s have seen a radical reconstruction of factory industry in most advanced industrial countries, leading first to great advances in productivity that actually reduced total manufacturing employment and, second, to a movement of that employment to suburban and smaller city sites. But, since the process was part and parcel of a profound change in the international division of labour, this decline in the manufacturing base of the advanced industrial cities has no parallel in the cities of the developing world; there, the processes of industrialization and urbanization were still in full swing. Indeed, the same causes that aided industrialization in the third world – a vast, willing, weakly-organized labour force willing to accept work at low wages, coupled with a buccaneer entrepreneurial quality – acted to bring about the contraction of industry in the first world.

It is thus easy enough to understand why traditional urban industries like clothing and printing should have left London and New York either for the smaller cities of the southern United States, or for the teeming factories of Taipei or Bombay. What is more difficult to understand is the countervailing set of forces that help to explain precisely why advertising agencies or finance houses should gravitate towards Manhattan or London's City and West End. Yet the general principle is clear enough. At the very centre of the CBD – alike in the older cities of the first world, and in the burgeoning cities of the developing world – there is found a relatively small nucleus of highly skilled professionals. All these people, in one way or another, live by creating, processing or exchanging ideas. The stockbroker, considering the fortunes of a hundred companies in a dozen countries; the company lawyer, pondering a difficult piece of patent law; the consultant, wondering whether or not to recommend an operation; the university professor, arguing about urban growth in a seminar; the government official, discussing whether to approve new investment in schools or roads or power stations; the editorial director of the publishing house, taking advice on a manuscript; the newspaper features editor, looking for a specialist to write about the latest travel spot in Africa; the television producer, discussing a script on housing problems with a journalist and a university researcher; the advertising copywriter, talking about a campaign with the accounts executive and then with a number of technical specialists; the freelance photographer, taking varied assignments from half a dozen photographic editors; all these people live only on their ideas, on transmitting these ideas readily and economically to others and on receiving their ideas in exchange.

The CBD of the typical world city can therefore be seen as a highly specialized machine for producing, processing and trading specialized *intelligence*. And of all commodities, intelligence has the highest costs of transportation. As American economist Robert Murray Haig pointed out as long ago as 1926 in his classic study of the metropolis, this is why activities depending on transmission of information are compelled, but are also willing, to pay the highest urban rents for the most accessible central sites, displacing other activities from the city centres as they do so.

The process is a continuing one, for the ideas industries are growing many times faster than industry as a whole. As late as 1850, they included only a very small number of traditional professions like banking, medicine or the law. But as increasing mechanization and then automation have reduced the physical agony of growing wheat and turning it into bread, of picking cotton and turning it into shirts, so new types of economic activity have come into prominence. The road to economic advance no longer consists in concentration on the brute processes of physical production, but rather in increased attention to research, to education, to better understanding of the organization of the production and the sales processes. And even the nature of brute production changes. The market for bread or shirts expands less rapidly than the market for fashion magazines or television programmes; bread and shirts, in any case, can be produced more and more efficiently with fewer workers (or with workers in less developed lands), while the production of ideas is impossible to automate; an ever-growing proportion of physical production represents processed ideas. Given this, as Haig said, the question is changed from 'Why live in the city?' to 'Why not live in the city?'

The logic of this argument is clear: as the economy of advanced industrial nations moves progressively into a tertiary or post-industrial phase – with the great bulk, perhaps two-thirds or even three-quarters, of all workers employed in tertiary or service industries – so the giant cities of these nations, as

233

centres of information exchange, should grow. In the early 1960s this logic was first debated between two colleagues at the University of California in Berkeley: Richard L. Meier argued that giant cities in advanced countries were uniquely well-suited to high levels of information exchange, while Melvin Webber countered that new advances in information technology permitted these urban standards of information to spread across the whole country or even across the whole world, creating an urban culture based on 'community without propinquity', in which the 'urban place' was supplanted by a 'nonplace urban realm'. The Meier–Webber debate was never resolved; it continues. On the one hand, Webber proved remarkably prescient in anticipating the world of the 1980s, in which telephones and micro-computers available to almost everyone can communicate at rapidly decreasing real cost over long distances by satellite. Further, his argument has been fortified by the evident trend – noticed for several cities in this book – for office functions as well as goods-handling functions to begin to deconcentrate from the historic CBD. Yet evidently, a very wide range of office-based activities do remain in the major centres; and some, especially the higher-order national and international headquarters functions, seem if anything to concentrate there. The most recent geographical work, notably that by Pred for the United States and Goddard or Daniels for Great Britain, suggests a paradox: in the really great cities, like London or New York, massive outflow of manufacturing and routine office functions is partially compensated by increases in these higher-order functions; but in the provincial manufacturing cities, no such compensating force can be found. This suggests a model of increasing concentration at the level of control of the economy, coupled with increasing dispersion of the functions that are controlled.

The explanation seems to lie in a fact originally noted by Meier: earlier advances in information technology – the penny post, the telephone – actually strengthened the hold of the CBD, by speeding and increasing the number and range of preliminary contacts, so multiplying the need for person-to-person encounters where critical decisions are made. As Aaron Fleischer put it at that time, information technology 'may not be adequate for transactions that would terminate in a handshake – or a fistfight. Clearly, it would not suffice for encounters that culminate in an embrace.' Later work on office communication – by Cowan, Goddard and Reid in Britain, by Thorngren in Sweden – confirmed this: while more routine control processes could be performed by telephone, unprogrammed exchanges involving speculation or exchange of new ideas continued to need face-to-face contact. Many planning processes, both within organizations and also for individuals, involved some mixture of the two – making it difficult, save for very large organizations with a high degree of division of labour, to move away from the face-to-face contact centre.

But there is an evident trend, both in advanced industrial countries and in newly industrializing countries, for organizations to grow in scale through merger and take-over. More and more companies, in other words, can contemplate a process of rationalization whereby they remove their more programmed, routine functions to peripheral locations where office rents and salaries are lower than in the giant metropolitan city centres. For this to happen, though, these peripheral locations must possess the requisite physical and human infrastructure: physical, in terms of transportation and communications facilities; human, in terms of the right kinds of managerial and clerical labour. And such infrastructure is likely to be widely available only in the most advanced countries; therefore, deconcentration is likely to become an option in the course of the development process. Certainly, as the world recession of the 1980s compels such rational decisions, there is increasing evidence that in the developed nations – aided and abetted by advances in information technology – just this process is occurring. The real ideas industries will remain in the centres, and indeed will expand there. They will displace the other activities, long associated with the centres but now no longer appropriate there: many types of manufacturing, wholesaling and warehousing, the more generalized and popular kinds of retail shopping, and those types of office activities that involve the assemblage, processing and storage of data, and even the taking of routine decisions on that data. And it is even possible that some of the ideas industries themselves – those with less-well developed and immediate linkages, such as higher education, research, some parts of the government machine and publishing – will also be displaced from the centre to more spacious and lower-cost locations.

In these advanced nations, this can no longer be seen as an entirely painless process. In the era of growth of the 1960s, such widespread deconcentration was seen as necessary and desirable to relieve the pressure – of new economic activities and new in-migrants – in the heart of the city. Thus, in London, in Paris and in the Dutch Randstad, planners actively sought to promote the decentralization of manufacturing and also of offices from the hearts of the cities. But in the stagnant or declining world of the 1980s, such policies are no longer seen as either necessary or desirable: in London the Location of Offices Bureau, set up to promote office decentralization, has actually been abolished, while similar policies in the Netherlands have been effectively abandoned. This is because, in many of these giant cities of the developed world, the tertiary industries are no longer increasing fast enough at the centre to counter the rapid decline of traditional manufacturing and the out-movement of routine offices. Now, the decentralizing city is leaving an economic hole in the centre. Deconcentration is thus a zero-sum game, in which the gain to the suburbs and the smaller towns must be balanced against the loss to the central city. The questions are whether the planner can do anything to affect the process; and, if he could, whether he should. The answers are not immediately clear.

Living

This argument leads on to another central question of urban organization, which can be put in the form of an heroic generalization: that almost all great cities, everywhere, demonstrate suburban spread. In every modern major city for which we have any kind of precise data, the frontier of building is being pushed outwards; the newer areas at the fringe show more rapid growth of people and activities than the more densely populated inner cities. This statement is true of a capitalist city like New York and a communist city like Moscow, an advanced industrial city like Paris or a developing metropolis like Mexico City; only the form of the suburban outgrowth - speculative single-family housing versus giant public projects, neat villas versus shanty-towns - reflect the underlying economic and social system. Finally - most interesting new discovery of all - the phenomenon is apparently independent of growth; it may as well occur in a newly-declining metropolis like London or New York as in a still-dynamic one like Hong Kong or Mexico City.

It continues to be true, even in the worst recession since the 1930s, and even following a series of energy crises that for a time threatened the car-orientated life style on which most suburban growth is based. It continues to be true even despite the well-publicized phenomenon of gentrification: the reoccupation by the middle class of inner residential areas that they had deserted years before to lower-income groups, coupled with housing rehabilitation and neighbourhood revival. For ironically, this process - first noticed and named in the early 1960s in London, now observable in great cities almost world-wide - is actually identified with further outward movement of people, since invariably the gentrifiers occupy more space at lower density than the gentrifiees they displace. Furthermore, as already seen, in many of the great cities it is no longer simply a question of residential deconcentration; the economic activities, not merely local shops and services but also basic man-ufacturing and warehousing and office functions, are moving out too.

The supreme irony is that the resulting settlement structure corresponds in important respects to the form that planners have been trying to achieve ever since the pioneer of planning theory, Ebenezer Howard. Writing in 1898, without any realization of the change the motor car would bring to urban form, Howard set forth the notion of Social City: a planned cluster of small cities, each with a mere 30,000 people, that would grow naturally as popula-tion increased, to any size that might be needed (figure 10.1). Within each small garden city, any inhabitant would find within walking distance a certain range of jobs and services; if he needed a wider range, then he could travel rapidly and easily to other towns in the cluster, or to a larger central city. To

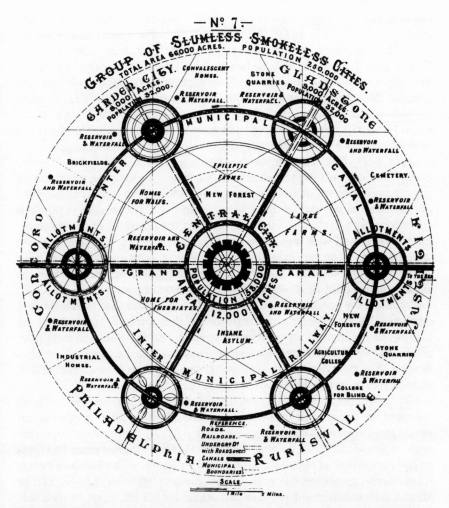

Figure 10.1 *Social City*. Ebenezer Howard's master plan for a polycentric garden city complex, produced in 1898 before the motor car became a factor in urban form. It proves remarkably adaptable to both high-mobility and low-mobility conditions.

this end, Howard suggested what we would today call a rapid transit system, connecting each of the towns in the cluster. Something like this is what the Dutch have proposed for the Randstad, or the French for their extended Paris region. It is a form that hedges bets for the future; it permits personal mobility so long as energy is easily and cheaply available, but provides facilities close at hand should it become scarce; it is also curiously appropriate to the new, dispersed world of cheap information technology. Thus, in many ways, Howard's great intuitive notion may be more appropriate to the last quarter of the twentieth century than it was to the end of the nineteenth.

Much later than Howard, at the beginning of the 1960s in the United States, Kevin Lynch suggested another variant of the dispersed polycentric city region: one based on a triangular transportation grid, coarser at the edges of the urban area, finer in the interior (figure 10.2). Densities within this structure would vary, with intensive peaks at the junctions of the transportation system and with high concentrations along the main routes, but with wide areas of low density in the interior of the grid. Belts and tongues of open land would form another type of grid, penetrating this network. Within the system there would be a hierarchy of central concentrations; the larger the centre, the more specialized the activities. Lynch argued that planners could guide existing metropolitan city regions into this polyform structure by actually encouraging further growth; by constructing the transportation grid; and by allowing rival centres to develop away from the existing main centre. Beyond this, the planning system would largely leave it to economic and social forces to produce the desired structure.

Melvin Webber, at about the same time, argued in similar vein: within large metropolitan regions, the future spatial organization would be very complex, with a great variety of concentrations of activity, and with much dispersion both of people and jobs. Webber suggested that Los Angeles (map 10.1) was an early prototype of the new untraditional structure, with 10 million people spread across a vast freeway grid, 160 kilometres (100 miles) square. Yet, he argued, an establishment on Wilshire Boulevard, in the heart of its linear business strip, would have the same accessibility to other activities, in terms of time, as a similar establishment on Manhattan Island in New York. That may be doubted: an executive on Wilshire Boulevard could hardly make the same boast as the New York businessman described by Haig in 1926, that from his Times Square skyscraper he could reach anyone of importance in the business world within fifteen minutes – particularly since, in the twenty years since Webber wrote, the congestion on the Los Angeles freeways has become steadily worse.

Moving
The Los Angeles case is a particular example of a general law: that different

patterns of urban working and living will inevitably be associated with different patterns and different ways of moving about between the two. Clearly, this relationship cannot be identical for all cities: very advanced and affluent cities, with high levels of car ownership, will be different from poorer ones where the great mass of the population have no access to private transportation. Bearing this in mind, the British transport economist Michael Thomson has classified the great cities of the world into five main types.

The first type, the 'strong centre' city, includes most of the world cities considered in this book. All – as we have seen – are characterized by an extremely large and dense mass of CBD employment: typically more than one million and sometimes (as in New York and Tokyo) nearly 2 million, concentrated in a very small area typically about 25 square kilometres (10 square miles) in area. Most of these workers commute in from outside, sometimes over long distance, by a radial rail system focusing on the CBD; smaller numbers come by bus and only a small minority of commuters (typically 10–15 per cent) can use their own cars. In such circumstances, the rail system is so well developed that it offers an acceptable substitute, in terms of speed and convenience, to the private car.

We have also noticed significant differences as between these cities. London, for instance, has much lower residential densities, especially in its inner city residential areas (within about 10 kilometres, 6 miles, of the CBD) than either Paris or New York. Yet even these densities produce enough passengers along the radial rail corridors to give an effective and economical public transport system. The only difference is that London's underground is less dense, and has more widely spaced stations, than the Paris *Métro*. Non-CBD commuters – a majority, even in such cities – however, make little use of the rail system, and a majority tend to go to work by car. In this respect, strong centre cities in part behave like other prototypes now to be described. This is an extremely important point in considering the future development of such cities; we shall come back to it shortly.

The second type is called the 'weak centre' city. It includes a number of important cities of less than the first rank, including some capitals of smaller countries (Copenhagen, Stockholm) and some provincial cities in bigger countries (Melbourne, Chicago, Boston). It is traditional in having a radial road network and a dominant city centre, which is however much smaller than the CBD of the strong centre cities; typically it offers employment to between one-quarter and one-half million workers. Since this is at least 125,000 or so in excess of those who can commute by car, this centre tends to have a mixture of car and public transport (bus, tram and rail) commuters. A large proportion of the work-force, however, finds employment outside this dominant centre, including a substantial number who work in subcentres, a fairly characteristic feature of this form; and most of these go by car. So this

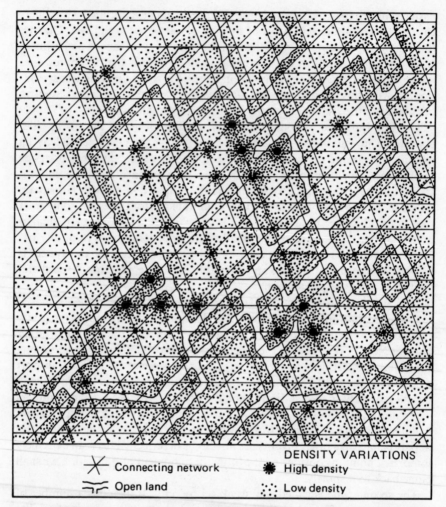

DENSITY VARIATIONS

✕ Connecting network ✳ High density

〜 Open land ∴ Low density

Figure 10.2 *Scheme for a dispersed metropolis, by Kevin Lynch.* Lynch's plan has some affinity with Howard's. It is based on a triangular transportation grid. Densities rise very high at intersections and are high along transportation lines, but there are wide low-density regions within the triangles. Belts and tongues of open land form another intersecting pattern. This is really a polycentric plan with a hierarchy of central concentrations; the biggest centres have the most specialized activities.

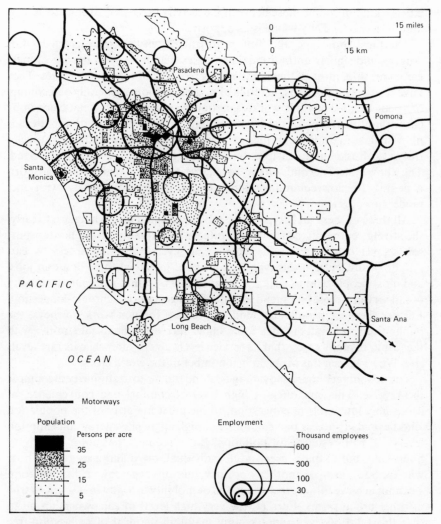

0   15 miles

0   15 km

Pasadena

Pomona

Santa
Monica

PACIFIC

Santa Ana

Long Beach

OCEAN

—— Motorways

Population

Persons per acre

35
25
15
5

Employment

Thousand employees

600
300
100
30

Map 10.1 *Los Angeles*. The southern California metropolis, with a population of nearly 11.5 million in 1980, is the archetype of the loose, dispersed, polycentric city – though it arose spontaneously, not by plan. During the 1970s it developed stronger employment concentrations in its CBD and at some other centres, making it rather more like Lynch's scheme.

city is a kind of compromise between the heavily rail-based strong centre city, and the motorized city which is its opposite.

The third prototype, the 'full motorization' city, is represented by Los Angeles and similar untraditional new cities that grew up in the age of mass car ownership, most of them in the western states of the United States. They have relatively weak CBDs, in terms of numbers of jobs: generally a maximum of about 150,000 daytime workers, about the maximum that can come in by car without unacceptable levels of congestion. The transportation pattern is not radial, as in traditional cities; it takes a grid form, as with the Los Angeles freeways. Residential densities are low and activities are widely dispersed. The whole system depends on car travel, with relatively weak public transport; it permits freeflow communication between all parts of the city, with only moderate congestion.

All three of these archetypes have advantages and disadvantages. Clearly, the strong centre city can uniquely offer a high quality of public transport service; yet it does so at the expense of severely limiting access by car. Paradoxically, even in this type a majority of jobs tend to be non-CBD jobs, and most people tend to use cars to get to them, so that – despite the quality of rail service – these cities tend to suffer from generalized chronic congestion. Further, because people also tend to use cars for non-work journeys, the public transport system tends to be under increasing financial strain – with the result, in many cases, that its service levels deteriorate while its fare levels rise. We have seen this problem in a number of the world cities.

The advantages and disadvantages of the full motorization city are almost the reverse. This city offers a high level of comfort and convenience, at acceptably low levels of congestion, to the great majority of the population who have ready access to a car, albeit at high aggregate energy consumption levels and with resulting air pollution. But it requires that not merely every household, but virtually every adult individual, owns and uses a car. Those who for one reason or another – poverty, infirmity, age, simple disinclination – cannot achieve this are truly deprived of mobility in a way that is not as true of other urban forms. Further, the very high levels of car ownership mean that this kind of city cannot readily maintain its ideal of congestion-free highways – as the recent experience of Los Angeles so clearly shows.

The weak centre city, as already noticed, is a compromise. It has some of the advantages and some of the disadvantages of each of the extremes. Its main problem is that in the course of time it tends to veer towards one or other of these extremes, to become either a strong centre city or a full motorization city. Given the pervasive trend towards deconcentration of people and activities in most cities, the latter is the more likely outcome.

Thomson lists two other kinds of city which are really of a different character. One, the 'low cost' city, is restricted to the developing world; it is characterized by overall poverty (albeit with a substantial very rich car-owning minority), by generally low (though not very low) car ownership and by limited public investment funds. Such cities typically rely on a high-density network of cheap buses, streetcars and low-cost informal transportation (shared taxis, jitneys, public light buses and the like). These tend to run along high-density traffic corridors which in turn connect high-intensity commercial subcentres. These systems are typically cheap and effective, but unfortunately traffic congestion is endemic because of the poor road network, inadequate traffic management and the presence of quite large numbers of cars. Only a few cities of this type, together with a much larger number in the developed world – including both strong and weak centre cities – have managed to adopt effective 'traffic limitation' strategies, thus forming a fifth and rather special type of city. In the developing world, Singapore and Hong Kong are outstanding in this last category; in the developed world, Stockholm, Copenhagen and London provide examples.

Thomson's archetypes, simplified though they may be, offer an invaluable understanding of the structure and functioning of great cities. But, in using them, three related points need to be kept in mind. First, in none of them is the transportation system independent of the rest of the urban system; all these types result from a close, subtle and mutual interaction between the transportation system and the pattern of activities and land uses. Secondly, in none of them is this relationship a stable one; both the system of activities and land uses, and the transportation system, are subject to constant change from a multiplicity of different causes. In particular, virtually all cities of the world are subject to two forces which work in the same direction to change them: on the one hand, the tendency for both people and activities sooner or later to deconcentrate from the core to the periphery; on the other, the curve of rising car ownership which proves incompatible with the traditional notion of the strong centre city and even, in time, the weak centre city. This means, as already noticed, that virtually all cities are not pure types but are mixtures: strong centre and weak centre cities both conform in part, in their suburban tracts, to the full motorization archetype, and it may be argued that the general tendency, expressed in varying degrees and at varying speeds in different cities, is towards this archetype. But thirdly – an important qualification to this last remark – in no case are the systems of land use and transportation completely spontaneous; to varying degrees, depending on the socio-economic and cultural and political traditions of the city and the nation of which it forms a part, both are to some degree open to conscious public planning and control. Further, the planning and control systems here include not merely traditional ones of land use and infrastructure investment, but also a host of other managerial decisions that can affect the cost and quality of the transportation system for the user: public transport fares, service frequency and reliability, traffic congestion and delay. The critical question is whether the two elements – the transportation network on the one hand, the pattern of land uses on the other – are truly congruent with each other. Very often, they are not; but the land-use planner and the transportation planner, always within the limits set by general socio-economic trends, may help to make them more so.

The city in the developing world: is it a special case?

In trying to generalize from the varied experience of the world cities, we have treated them all – alike in the developed and developing world – as subject to similar forces and developing in similar ways. But sometimes this has not been possible: Thomson's low-cost archetype, for instance, is unique to the cities of the developing world, though it may have interesting lessons for more developed cities too. The fact is that developing cities do share some features with developed ones; but in other regards they are distinctly different. This creates a profound paradox for the urban analyst, which is not readily resolved.

The first point is one of difference. Growth, even explosive growth, is still a feature of the great urban areas of the newly industrializing world. It is true that birth-rates in most of them have declined during the 1970s, as a very result of the urbanization process. It is true also that GNP per head may not be growing as it was in the early 1970s – and in one or two cases it may even have shown a temporary stop. But in general these cities are still industrializing and their citizens are reaping the benefits; their gain is precisely the loss of the factory workers in the cities of the older industrialized world.

Secondly, just because they are growing so rapidly, these cities are also spreading. They can only grow outwards or grow upwards, and, though their CBDs are generally experiencing wholesale renewal in the form of a forest of high-rise office towers, their citizens – with a few special exceptions due to physical constraints, such as Hong Kong – tend to house themselves in relatively low-rise, moderate-density structures. The result in most developing cities is epic sprawl, quite dwarfing the equivalent phenomenon that has so worried the planners of the developed world cities.

Thirdly, because the suburbs sprawl while much employment (in services and artisan industry) remains in the CBD and the inner city, and other employment (especially new factory industry) is generated in other sectors of the city, many developing cities suffer traffic and commuting problems which again dwarf those of their first world counterparts. In them, those citizens able to buy cars – the relatively affluent ones who benefit from the skewed income distribution – do so, and then drive them for all purposes at all times; because in such cities public transport tends to be regarded as poor people's transport, there is a strong incentive to use the car. The rest of the population makes do with the low-cost transportation systems described in the Thomson archetype. But because traffic congestion – worsened by the use of cars, coupled with generally poor standards of traffic management and control – is so endemic, and because these cities seldom have well-developed metro systems like their first world equivalents, journeys to work are often extraordinarily slow, long, tortuous and exhausting. Often, because the street and public transport system is radial in form, commuter journeys – even from suburb to suburb – go through the CBD, further adding to the congestion.

A third point, perversely, is that many of these cities have felt the full force of the energy crises of the 1970s. Here the story very much depends on which side of a critical boundary these cities belonged. A fortunate few, such as Mexico City, belonged to the select club of countries with abundant energy – and too often, in consequence, tended to squander their patrimony. Most, however, were subject to the full force of rising bills for their energy supplies, which they could ill afford.

The final point is that, in these cities, planners' energies are inevitably concentrated on the plight of the poor, simply because there are so many of them. However, in the cities of most interest here – those in the newly industrializing countries – there is a paradox: quite rapidly rising per capita incomes are associated with extremely unequal distribution as between rich and poor. Thus the poor can feel that they are becoming richer, even though the rich might be getting richer even faster than they. The result in all these cities is the development in some form of a dual economy and dual society: one very affluent and westernized, the other poor and more traditional. In consequence these cities tend to suffer both the problems of affluence – in the form of pressures for redevelopment, traffic congestion, long journeys to work and pollution – and also the problems of extreme poverty in the form of squatter housing, lack of services, poor public health and a thousand and one other ills. It is a daunting challenge; but in comparison with the giant cities of the developed world the difference is one of degree, not of kind. In London, Paris and New York, too, we have seen that the problems of inner-city deprivation can sit cheek by jowl with the problems that stem from opulence. The difference is that in the cities of the developing world both sets of problems are more acute, the contrast between them so sharp, and the means to tackle them so much less.

What can be said is that good planning principles apply to each and every city, whatever its location, whatever its socio-economic system, whatever its level of affluence. Traffic congestion, albeit a sign of affluence, is a problem; reducing it is a solution. Slums are a problem; removing or alleviating them are solutions. Long journeys to work are expensive and exhausting; bringing work closer to the workers, or vice versa, represents a solution. What may vary is the means to the achievement of a given end: affluent cities can perhaps afford expensive urban motorway or rapid transit systems, if they choose, while poorer cities have to make do with buses and a variety of informal transport; affluent cities can afford to rehouse their poorer citizens in public housing, poorer ones have to make do with site-and-service, self-build solutions.

Poor cities may, however, have lessons for richer ones. Rich cities like rich people may be spendthrift; they may spend their wealth unwisely. However rich you are, the economist will tell you, it makes sense to consider the alternative use of your resources. Before building elaborate highway or transit systems, it is right to consider whether a cheaper solution would suffice. Before launching major programmes for multi-storey public housing, it is right to consider whether it would not be equally as good to encourage people to build their own. The questions for planners always must be: first, what do we want to achieve; second, what is the most economical way of achieving it effectively? These elementary questions are too often forgotten.

Towards a general urban model

To put these apparently contradictory world trends into perspective, we need some general model of urban growth and change, that could be applied to all countries at all times in the two-hundred-year period since the Industrial Revolution. To start, there are three basic questions you can ask about people in cities.

Some basic questions
The first is: how many people live in urban areas, and how many in the countryside? This tells us a lot about how much they earn their living and how they live. It used to tell us whether people were farmers or not, and in the developing world it still tends to do that.

The second question is: how many of the urbanites live in the biggest urban area of the country? (Geographers call this the 'primacy index'.) This is important because the economy, society and problems of big cities tend to be quite different from those of smaller ones. As this book has shown, housing, transport and service provision tend to be a much bigger headache in big cities – even though chances of getting work may be better, which may make it seem all worthwhile, especially for poor people.

The third question concerns the internal organization of cities, that has been discussed in this chapter. How many of the urbanites live in the central, more congested, incorporated city area and how many in the sprawling suburbs beyond? This again is important because suburbanites often have quite different styles of life from city people. They may do different jobs, they live in different kinds of houses, their journeys to work are different, they may shop differently, and often their styles of life are quite different.

So there are three key measurements: the 'degree of urbanization'; the 'primacy index'; and the 'extent of suburban decentralization'. With these, we can really begin to make sense of changing patterns of urbanization world-wide. In order to do it, though, we need to use a metropolitan area framework with core cities and suburban rings around them (figure 10.3).

Five stages of urban evolution

In the first stage of development, which is the one occurring in many less developed countries today, people are flooding from the countryside to find work in cities. There is rural overpopulation because of high birth-rates and much lower death-rates (which have been reduced by medical advances), and besides there is rapidly improving agricultural technology which gives much greater productivity off each hectare of land. The people cannot all find work in nearby local cities, because industrialization is still very concentrated in one key city: generally the capital, or the port. So there is increasing urbanization, but it is heavily concentrated in the first (primate) city system. Other city systems are growing somewhat, but their surrounding, still-rural, rings are experiencing population loss which the core city cannot absorb. So most city systems are losing population but also centralizing it into their core cities. We call this condition 'centralization during loss'. Perhaps only the primate city system is growing at this stage: it shows the same phenomenon of core gain and ring loss, but in this case the core gain is the greater. We call this 'absolute centralization', and it appears to represent a second condition in urban evolution, which the leading city system reaches in this first stage, before any other system.

In a second stage, industrialization (meaning cultural modernization) has spread from the major city to a number of provincial cities, which now provide alternative magnets for the labour that continues to pour off the land. However, the rings around these cities are still taking part in this process of out-migration. Now, other city systems have joined the primate city system in the state of absolute centralization: their core cities are gaining at the expense of the still-rural rings, while metropolitan areas generally are gaining at the expense of the purely rural (non-metropolitan) areas. Meanwhile, in all probability, the primate city system has kept a step ahead by entering a third state of urban evolution: its growth is such that it washes out into the suburban ring, so that core and ring are both growing, though the core's growth is still

247

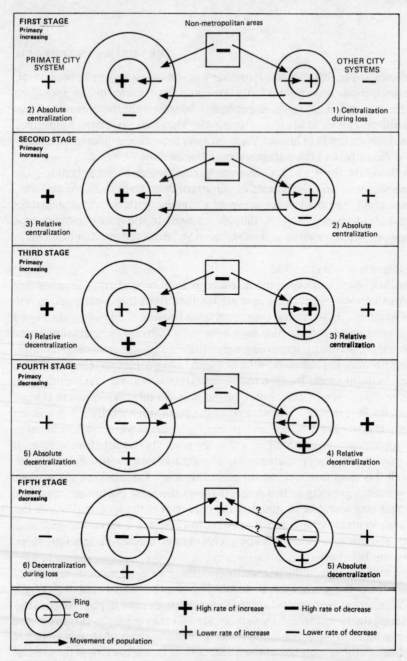

Figure 10.3 *General scheme of urban change.* In this five-stage scheme,
corresponding to stages of economic development, growth first concentrates in the
heart of the leading city. But later, this city leads the rest in decentralization from
core to suburban ring – first in relative growth, then through actual decline of the
city. In the final stage a 'clean break' has occurred: movement has reversed, out of
the cities and into the non-metropolitan part of the country.

faster than the ring's. We can term this third state, appropriately, 'relative centralization'.

In the third stage of development, the flow into the cities continues. Now, however, other city systems begin to follow the pattern earlier set by the primate system: growth spreads into their suburban rings, producing a state of relative centralization of urban areas. But the first city system is as usual one step ahead: its growth and spread are now such that the suburbs are growing faster than the core city, giving a fourth state of urban evolution which we call 'relative decentralization'. This represents a major change: a reversal in the pattern of growth within the primate city system. Up to this stage, as a general rule, the primate city system will tend to grow faster than the other systems; in other words, the primacy index will still be tending to increase.

The fourth stage represents a more general change. Now, the other city systems begin to follow the lead earlier set by the primate system: here, too, the push of the cities out into the suburbs reverses the pattern; while both core and ring are growing, the latter is gaining faster than the city. But, as usual, the first city system is one step ahead: here, the core city itself has begun actually to lose population, while the suburbs are still growing. This is the state of 'absolute decentralization'. Because of this loss from the core city, the growth rate of the whole system is slowed down in comparison with that of the other city systems: for the first time, the degree of primacy begins to decline. But overall, city systems are still gaining at the expense of purely rural, non-metropolitan areas.

In the fifth and final stage, there is a further evolution. Now, the cores of the other city systems also begin to empty out and to decline absolutely, while their suburbs continue to grow; they too have reached the state of absolute decentralization. As ever, though, the first city system is one step ahead: the loss of population from its core is now so great that the continuing weak gain of the suburban ring – if indeed it continues at all – cannot compensate, so we have a situation of 'decentralization during loss'. As this happens, naturally, there is a marked fall in the primacy index. However, by this stage the primacy index has generally been falling for some time, and a more general phenomenon starts to take its place: that of negative returns to urban scale, whereby smaller city systems tend to gain people while larger ones, not merely the largest of all, stagnate or decline. This in turn is associated with a spread of the decentralization-during-loss pattern from the first system to perhaps half-a-dozen or more of the leading second-order urban systems in the country. At this stage, for the first time, the growth of non-metropolitan areas is faster than that of metropolitan areas: the 'clean break' has taken place.

Looking back, we find that the five stages have a neat symmetry. At any time, any one of the city systems in any particular country will always be in one of six states of urban evolution. These are mirror images of one another, so that a system will pass from centralization during loss, to absolute centralization, to relative centralization, then to relative decentralization, to absolute decentralization, and finally to decentralization during loss. However, in this process the leading urban system – that of the capital, or first, city – will in general be one step ahead of the others.

It might be argued that the whole pattern is a little too neat and symmetrical. But it does correspond fairly well to the facts of what has been happening in the world in the last twenty years. Generally, the developing nations are still in stages one or two of the process. The NICS – Korea, Mexico, Brazil – and the nations of southern and eastern Europe tend to be in stages two or three. Those of central, northern and western Europe tended to be in stages four and five, at any rate by the early 1970s. Great Britain and the United States have arrived at stage five. In those countries, it really does appear that the large city is tending to decline. But elsewhere in the world, indeed in a majority of the world's countries, the great cities are still thriving and growing – growing, indeed, at a positively alarming speed.

The role of planning

Thus the typology shows how, and why, the problems of urban areas in the developing countries are almost the precise reverse of those in the developed lands. In the developed countries, we have decaying cities and agglomerations, coupled with contraction of the economic base, and a growth of new activities in suburbs and, increasingly, far-distant rural locations. In the developing world the giant cities are still magnets to the people of the countryside; the resulting problems of urban organization threaten to overwhelm them.

The obvious lesson is that cities, like organisms, have some way of regulating their own growth and form: when they become too big, too congested, they decentralize and finally shrink. But that would be too simplistic. Great cities are the result of actions by millions of human beings; they decide, by their choices as to living and working and schooling and enjoying themselves, how the city shall grow and change. And among these people are planners. By their actions, as we have seen in the case studies of this book, they cannot deny or reverse major trends in the wider urban economy and society; but they can anticipate them, encourage or discourage them, and persuade them to happen in ways less harmful and more beneficial to the citizens of the world cities.

They would do well to start with one of the most fundamental conclusions,

250

perhaps the most fundamental conclusion, of this book: that the general tendency for all great urban areas, wherever they may occur and whatever stage of development they may have reached, is to spread outwards. That rule rule is equally true for the growing cities of the developing world and for the declining cities of the developed world. If this is accepted, then the planner – dependent always on his legal authority, which in turn depends on the socio-political system within which he works – has certain powers, certain levers, to influence the course of changes. He can to some extent influence the size and distribution of centres for office employment, shopping and services. In a number of ways – both by land-use controls and by provision of vital infrastructure – he can influence the provision of location, size, shape and density of new residential areas. He can also help shape the distribution of open space. Finally, and very importantly, he can try to affect the shape and mode of the transportation network that ties these various land uses and activities together.

The overwhelming evidence is that the resulting urban system will tend more and more towards the full motorization archetype symbolized by Los Angeles. But this does not mean that this archetype will eventually rule the world. On the contrary: the most recent evidence suggests that Los Angeles seems to be corresponding less and less to its own archetype: its original CBD has approximately doubled its total volume of activity and employment in the course of two decades, its planners are busy promoting subcentres such as Century City, and the city now seems poised to begin construction of a rapid transit system. In significant respects, Los Angeles is more and more conforming to the notions of Kevin Lynch: it may cease to be a full motor-ization city and instead become the prototype for a new type of polycentric city region tied together partly by freeways, partly by different kinds of mass transit connecting its centres along high-density corridors. And this may be a model not merely for the cities of the developed world, but also – as the plans for Mexico City have shown – for the sprawling cities of the still-developing world.

In developing such a model, planners in the world cities will find that they still have open to them a wide range of options. If they are traditionalists, they can ring existing suburbs ·by a green belt and concentrate subsequent development in planned satellite cities outside this belt, as in London and Moscow. They can also try to limit the demands which suburban sprawl makes on land by developing new suburbs or satellites at high densities – as is done, for different reasons but with similar sweeping powers, in Moscow and in Hong Kong. Or they can encourage growth along main radial trans-portation lines so as to provide high-speed access from the CBD to suburban subcentres, so forming a star-shaped pattern as in the plans for Copenhagen – or, on a much larger scale, in the Paris new towns and their linkages to the express rail system. If, on the other hand, the CBD is relatively weak and the highway system follows a grid pattern, then equally planners can develop selected lines for high-intensity development, with improved public transport, connecting selected subcentres which would be encouraged to expand: the pattern now being followed in Los Angeles and Mexico City. Alternatively, if very anti-traditional, they may encourage almost uniform low-density development with a scatter of service and employment nodes, as Frank Lloyd Wright suggested in the 1930s in his plan for Broadacre City. And – most importantly – they can provide various combinations of any and all of these, dependent on the precise geography of their city and its potential for further development: archetypes, whether of existing cities or of planned ones, are always abstractions never to be found in pure form in reality.

Towards a choice

The odd fact about these options is that, despite some heroic attempts, notably in the 1960s, there has never been a really successful attempt to evaluate them in any rigorous or precise way. The truth probably is that the task is impossible: the reality of great cities is too rich and too complex to be caught in fixed, quantifiable categories. All planners can hope to do is to set down some leading heads of the balance sheet, and then to exercise the best judgement they can. Kevin Lynch tried to do this in the 1960s; his analysis holds good in the changed world of the 1980s.

At one extreme, high-density development gives good spontaneous communication, high accessibility and short distances between places; it can produce a strong visual image and, more questionably, a good community sense; it will probably have quite low running costs. But it will be relatively crowded and therefore uncomfortable, housing choice might be limited, and its initial costs are likely to be high. The real trouble with it, both when Lynch wrote and today, is that it goes against the trends and against the grain. In countries with a free and varied housing market – the United States, Great Britain, many nations of western Europe – the evidence strongly shows that the great majority of the metropolitan population, provided they can exercise choice, will opt for a single-family dwelling at a medium or even low density. Therefore, high-density compact development is an option only where – for good reason or bad – individual choice is restricted.

The satellite or new town arangement avoids many of these snags. It offers flexibility, it can provide a choice of housing, it can achieve a good visual image, it allows local participation, it can provide a choice of public and private transport, and it allows spontaneous communication because local service centres are near at hand. But it is less flexible than a really low-density solution, while accessibility to higher-level jobs and services, in the regional CBD, may still be restricted by long travel distances. The urban star (or finger plan) arrangement has some of the same advantages and disadvantages: it gives fast radial movement and the possibility of a wide range of housing, as well as good visual image; but there are difficulties of circumferential movement, of possible congestion on the radials, and increasing communication costs as the pattern develops outwards from the regional centre. The Paris plan of 1965, interestingly, minimizes some of these problems through a combination of finger and satellite arrangements.

Finally, low-density fully-motorized sprawl has more advantages than many European planners would at first accept: it encourages flexibility, it can provide a choice of housing, it allows local participation, it reduces congestion and thus increases accessibility by car. But it is expensive, it entails long travel distances by car, it does not readily encourage accidental contact between people, it may not give a visually satisfying identity or any sense of communal political involvement. Further – as already seen in the Thomson archetype – it may actually reduce accessibility for non-car owners, by making maintenance of a good public transportation system difficult, if not impossible.

All this suggests the age-old wisdom: that there is no such thing as a perfect solution to any problem. None of these archetypes will prove to be the planner's Holy Grail. It will always be necessary to weigh the different costs and benefits that accompany alternative ways of organizing urban space. But, by combining elements of each, it may be possible to guide the growth of the metropolitan region in such a way that its citizens – young and old, rich and poor, car-owning and car-less – are allowed to make those trade-offs for themselves. The best we can hope for, in this process, is to use planning not as a way of imposing designs and life styles on people, but of freeing them to make unconstrained choices for themselves. That is all that planning can finally achieve, and all that planners should ever want to achieve.

Bibliography

1 The metropolitan explosion

On population growth, the viewpoint of experts in the 1930s is set out in Alexander Carr-Saunders, *World Population: Past Growth and Present Trends*, Oxford, 1936. Shorter texts on population geography include John I. Clarke, *Population Geography*, Oxford, 1972; M.G.A. Wilson, *Population Geography*, Melbourne, 1968; and Wilbur Zelinsky, *A Prologue to Population Geography*, Englewood Cliffs, New Jersey, 1966. Important works by French demographers which analyse world patterns of population growth are: Alfred Sauvy, *Fertility and Survival*, London, 1961; Sauvy, *General Theory of Population*, London, 1969; Pierre George, *Questions de géographie de la population*, Institut national d'études démographiques, Cahier No. 34, Paris, 1959; and Germaine Veyret-Verner, *Population: mouvements, structures, répartition*, Paris, 1959.

Adna Ferrin Weber's *The Growth of Cities in the Nineteenth Century* has been republished as one of Cornell Reprints in Urban Studies, Ithaca, 1963. Tertius Chandler and Gerald Fox have updated and vastly extended his work in *3000 Years of Urban Growth*, New York and London, 1974, an invaluable work of scholarly reference. Comparative figures of populations of urban areas are found in United Nations (Statistical Office of the Department of Economic and Social Affairs), *Demographic Yearbook*, New York, annual. Definitions of international metropolitan areas, with their 1955 estimated populations, are in International Urban Research (Director, Kingsley Davis), *The World's Metropolitan Areas*, Berkeley and Los Angeles, 1959. On this basis, the growth of metropolitan areas has been analysed by Jack F. Gibbs and Leo F. Schnore in 'Metropolitan Growth: An International Study', *The American Journal of Sociology*, 66, 160–70, Chicago, 1960. Updated analyses are: Kingsley Davis, *World Urbanization 1950–1970*, Vol. 1 *Basic Data for Cities, Countries and Regions*, Berkeley, 1969; Richard L. Forstall and Victor Jones, 'Selected Demographic, Economic and Governmental Aspects of the World's Major Metropolitan Areas', in Simon Miles (ed.), *Metropolitan Problems*, Toronto, 1970; and United Nations, Department of International

Economic and Social Affairs, *Patterns of Urban and Regional Population Growth* (*Population Studies*, 68), New York, 1980. Daniel Vining's hypothesis of the 'Clean Break' is found in his papers: 'Recent Dispersal from the World's Industrial Core Regions', in Tatsuhiro Kawashima (ed.), *Urbanization Processes: Experiences of Eastern and Western Countries*, Oxford, 1982; (with A. Strauss), 'A Demonstration that the Current Deconcentration of Population in the United States is a Clean Break with the Past', *Environment and Planning*, *A*, *9*, 751-8, 1977; and (with T. Kontuly) 'Increasing Returns to City Size in the Face of an Impending Decline in the Size of large Cities: Which is the Bogus Fact?', *Environment and Planning*, *A*, *9*, 59-62, 1977.

On the palaeotechnic and neotechnic eras see: Patrick Geddes, *Cities in Evolution*, London, 1915; Lewis Mumford, *Technics and Civilization*, New York and London, 1932, and *The Culture of Cities*, New York and London, 1938; Jean-François Gravier, *Paris et le désert français*, Paris, 1947, 1958, and *Mise en valeur de la France*, Paris, 1948.

On the changes in economic organization during the nineteenth century, important sources are: J.A. Hobson, *The Evolution of Modern Capitalism*, London, 1894, 1926; Thorstein Veblen, *The Theory of Business Enterprise*, New York, 1904; Werner Sombart, *Der moderne Kapitalismus*, München, Leipzig, 1916-27, Vol. 3; T.C. Cochran and W. Miller, *The Age of Enterprise: A Social History of Industrial America*, New York, 1942. R.M. Haig's analysis is 'Toward an Understanding of the Metropolis', *Quarterly Journal of Economics*, 40, 179-208, 402-34, Cambridge, Mass., 1925.

Good general comparative introductions to urban problems include: William A. Robson and D.E. Regan, *Great Cities of the World*, London, 1972; Brian J.L. Berry, *The Human Consequences of Urbanization*, London, 1973; Lloyd Rodwin, *Nations and Cities*, Boston, 1970; L.S. Bourne, *Urban Systems: Strategies for Regulation*, Oxford, 1975; H. Wentworth Eldredge, *Taming Megalopolis*, 2 vols., New York, 1967; and P. Self, *Planning the Urban Region*, London, 1982.

2 London

The physical development of London is described in J.T. Coppock and Hugh Prince (edd.), *Greater London*, London, 1964, especially chapters 3-6 inclusive. S.E. Rasmussen, *London the Unique City*, London, 1934, 1937, Harmondsworth, 1960, first distinguished the unique form of London's development. Peter Hall, *London 2000*, London, 1963, examines the planning problems of London in detail and argues that further growth is inevitable. Useful recent guides to London planning include Peter Hall, *Urban and*

Regional Planning, Harmondsworth, 1975, Chapter 7, and John M. Hall, *London: Metropolis and Region*, Oxford, 1976. *The South East Study 1961-1981*, London, Stationery Office, 1964, outlined the government's suggested strategy for the whole region including London on the basis of continued growth. The *Greater London Development Plan* (GLDP) consists essentially of the *Statement*, the *Report of Studies*, and *Movement in London*, all London, 1969, plus many supplementary reports. *Tomorrow's London*, London, 1970, is a popular official exposition. *London under Stress*, London, 1970, and *Region in Crisis: An independent view of the GLDP*, London, 1971, are independent analyses by the Town and Country Planning Association; Judy Hillman (ed.) *Planning for London*, London, 1971, offers further independent views. *The Greater London Development Plan Report of the Panel of Inquiry*, London, 1973, gives a definitive verdict on the plan. Greater London Council, *Modified Greater London Development Plan*, London, 1975, is the end-result.

The *Strategic Plan for the South East*, London, 1970, is accompanied by five supplementary reports, London, 1971, with detailed statistical analyses. It is updated by *Strategy for the South East: 1976 Review*, London, Stationery Office, 1976; *Strategic Plan for the South East: Review: Government Statement*, London, Stationery Office, 1978; Standing Conference on London and South East Regional Planning, *South East Regional Planning: the 1980s*, London, 1981; and *Development Trends in the South East Region*, London, annual from 1981.

On office decentralization, see P. Cowan, *The Office: A Facet of Urban Growth*, London, 1969, and the review by R.K. Hall, 'The Movement of Offices from Central London', *Regional Studies*, 6, 385-92, 1972. For factory decentralization, cf. D.E. Keeble and D.P. Hauser, 'Spatial Analysis of Manufacturing Growth in South-East England, 1960-1967', *Regional Studies*, 5, 229-62, 1971, and 6, 11-36, 1972. D.E.C. Eversley, 'Rising Costs and Static Incomes: some Economic Consequences of Regional Planning in London', *Urban Studies*, 9, 347-69, 1972, is a challenging analysis of some of the consequences; G. Lomas, *The Inner City*, London, 1975; Department of the Environment, *Inner City Studies: Liverpool, Birmingham and Lambeth*, London, Stationery Office, 1977; P. Hall (ed.), *The Inner City in Context*, London, 1981; P. Lawless, *Britain's Inner Cities: Problems and Policies*, London, 1981; and R.K. Home, *Inner City Regeneration*, London, 1982, take the analysis further.

The most comprehensive review of London's social planning problems is D. Donnison and D. Eversley (edd.), *London: Urban Patterns, Problems, and Policies*, London, 1973.

3 Paris

The best introductions to an understanding of Paris are historical and geographical. Pierre Lavedan's *Histoire de Paris* (new edition, Paris, 1960) deserves to become a classic. For the recent period it can usefully be supplemented by the same author's *Histoire de l'urbanisme: époque contemporaine*, Paris, 1952, and D.H. Pinkney's *Napoleon III and the Rebuilding of Paris*, Princeton, 1958. The standard introduction in geography is Pierre George and Pierre Randet's *La Région parisienne*, Paris, 1959; for the morphology of Paris, see also the early introductory chapters of P.-H. Chombart de Lauwe (and others), *Paris et l'Agglomération Parisienne*, 2 vols., Paris, 1952. Good recent British texts are: I.B. Thompson, *The Paris Basin*, Oxford, 1973, and Hugh Clout, *The Geography of Postwar France*, Oxford, 1972. Perhaps the most useful general introduction in English, including planning aspects, is N. Evenson, *Paris: A Century of Change, 1878–1978*, New Haven, 1979.

Two useful general accounts of French planning are Niles M. Hansen, *French Regional Planning*, Edinburgh, 1968, and Lloyd Rodwin, *Nations and Cities*, Boston, 1970, Chapter 6. M. Moseley, 'Strategic Planning and the Paris Agglomeration in the 1960s and 1970s: The Quest for Balance and Structure', *Geoforum*, 11, 179–223, 1980, is the most important recent account.

J.-F. Gravier's *Paris et le désert français* was first published in Paris in 1947; a fully-revised edition was issued in Paris in 1958. The Paris Regional Plan, *Plan d'Aménagement et d'Organisation Générale de la Région Parisienne*, was published by the Ministère de la Construction in 1960. An important analysis and criticism of the PADOG plan is contained in G. Pilliet, *L'Avenir de Paris*, Paris, 1961. The 'Livre Blanc' on the future of the Paris region is called *Avant-Projet de Programme Duodécennal pour la Région de Paris*; it was issued by the Premier Ministre: Délégation Générale au District de la Région de Paris, and published by the Imprimerie Municipale, Hôtel de Ville, Paris, in 1963. The revised 1965 plan, *Schéma Directeur d'Aménagement et d'Urbanisme de la Région Parisienne*, Paris, 1965, is a very important document. For the new towns, see J.M. Rubenstein, *The French New Towns*, Baltimore, 1978; J. Tuppen, 'New Towns in the Paris Region: An Appraisal', *Town Planning Review*, 50, 55–70, 1979; and M. Carmona, 'Les Plans d'aménagement de la Région Parisienne', *Acta Geographica*, 3, 14–46, 1975.

The series published by the Institut d'Aménagement et d'Urbanisme de la Région Parisienne, *Cahiers de l'Aménagement de la Région Île de France*, contains many useful analyses.

4 Randstad Holland

The early history of the Randstad cities is well written up in the following: the introduction to Baedeker's *Holland/Benelux/Luxembourg*, London, 1982; H. van Werveke, 'The Rise of the Towns', in *Cambridge Economic History of Europe*, Vol. III, Chapter 1, Cambridge, 1963; and the Supplementary Notes (*Toelichting*) to the report *De ontwikkeling van het westen des lands* (see below). Two books of especial interest and importance are by Gerald L. Burke, *The Making of Dutch Towns*, London, 1956, and *Greenheart Metropolis*, London, 1966. G.R.P. Lawrence, *Randstad Holland*, Oxford, 1973, is a useful introduction. The most useful source book is from the Information and Documentation Centre for the Geography of the Netherlands, *Randstad Holland*, Utrecht and the Hague, 1980; it can be updated from the same Centre's excellent annual *Bulletin*.

The official reports on the regional planning problems of the Netherlands are published by the Government Physical Planning Service (*Rijksdienst voor het nationale plan*) in the Hague. The first important official report to deal with the problem was *De verspreiding van de Bevolking in Nederland* (with English summary and maps), Publication No. 3 of the *Rijksdienst*, 1949. *Het Westen en overig Nederland*, Publication No. 11 of the *Rijksdienst*, 1956, was a policy report on the broad regional problem which suggested that the net migration between the west and the remainder of the country should be reduced to zero. The most important detailed report on the future of the west is *De ontwikkeling van het westen des lands*, in two volumes (1. *rapport*; 2. *toelichting*), 1958. This laid down the basic principles for planning the Randstad. Its themes were taken up and developed in the *Nota inzake de ruimtelijke ordening in Nederland*, 1960, which has been translated in full into German (*Der Regierungsbericht über die Raumordnung in den Niederlanden*, Materialien zur Landesplanung V, Institut für Raumforschung, Bad Godesberg, 1961), and in a condensed form into English (*Report on Physical Planning in the Netherlands*) and French. The *Second Report on Physical Planning in the Netherlands*, the Hague, 1966, was a condensed English language version in 2 volumes: I. Main outline of *National Physical Planning Policies* and II. *Future Pattern of Development*. The *Third Report* appeared in three parts, summarized in English: the *Orientation Report* (Orienteringsnota), the Hague, 1974, the *Report on Urbanisation* (Verstedelijkingsnota), the Hague, 1976, and the *Rural Areas Report* (*Landelijk Gebiedsnota*), the Hague, 1977.

For current developments, the annual report (*Jaarverstag*) of the Government Physical Planning Service is invaluable. It can be supplemented by the extremely useful series from the Information and Documentation Centre for the Geography of the Netherlands, *Bulletin*, annual and the periodical, *Plan-*

ning and Development in the Netherlands, Assen, twice-yearly. J.A. van Ginkel's important work on the Randstad, cited in the chapter, is 'Suburbanisatie en recente woonmilieus', *Utrechte geografische studies*, 16, 1979 (in Dutch).

5 Moscow

Useful books and articles on Soviet city planning, by British and American authors, include: P.M. White, *Soviet Urban and Regional Planning: A Bibliography with Abstracts*, London, Mansell, 1979: R.A. French and F.E.I. Hamilton, *The Socialist City: Spatial Structure and Urban Policy*. Chichester, 1979; M.F. Hamm (ed.), *The City in Business History*, Lexington, 1976; and J. Pallot and D.J.R. Shaw, *Planning in the Soviet Union*, London, 1981; F.E. Ian Hamilton, *The Moscow City Region*, Oxford, 1976; G. Lappo, A. Chikishev and A. Bekker, *Moscow, Capital of the Soviet Union: a Short Geographical Survey*, Moscow, 1976, V.V. Pokshisherskiy, 'Soviet Cities: Progress in Urbanization in the Seventies', *GeoJournal*, 1, 35–44, 1980; and G.M. Lappo, 'The City of Moscow and the Moscow Agglomeration', *GeoJournal*, 1, 45–52, 1980. Many important Soviet academic articles about cities and regional development appear in translation. Particularly important is *Soviet Geography* (*SG*), published ten times a year in New York, with the following translations from the volume *Goroda-Sputniki*, V.G. Davidovich and B.S. Khorev (edd.), Moscow, 1961: V.G. Davidovich, 'Satellite Cities and Towns of the U.S.S.R.', *SG*, 3, No. 3, 3–35, 1962; and G. Ye Mishchenko, 'Satellite cities and towns of Moscow', *ibid.*, 35–43. The periodical also contains useful news notes on recent events in the Soviet Union, notably: T. Shabad, 'Preliminary Results of the 1979 Soviet Census', *SG*, 2, 440–76, 1979; A.R. Bond and E. Lydolph, 'Soviet Population Change and City Growth 1970–79: A Preliminary Report', *SG*, 20, 461–88, 1979; R. Wixman and P. Caro, 'Territorial Differences in Population Growth in the U.S.S.R, 1970–79', *SG*, 22, 155–62, 1981; and O.A. Konstantinov and A.A. Yepikhin, 'Some Shifts in the Population of the U.S.S.R', *SG*, 20, 407–19, 1981.

The most useful source of all for current Soviet planning is the *Current Digest of the Soviet Press*, Washington (weekly), which reprints important articles from *Pravda* and *Izvestia* verbatim or in summary, as well as articles of general economic interest from academic journals. Much of the information in this chapter has come from this source. Two sources of special value for Soviet planning are the collections of translations from Soviet authorities published in *Recherches Internationales à la Lumière du Marxisme*, vols. 20–21, 208–29, Paris, 1960, including an article on Kryukovo by G. Dukelski, 'Les Premières Microrayons de la première Ville satellite', pages 237–45; and in the

Soviet Review, vol. 2, No. 4, New York, 1961, with an article by A. Zhuravlyev and M.B. Fyedorov, 'The Micro-District and new living Conditions', pp. 37-40. S. Strumilin's description of Soviet society under full communism, 'Family and Community in the Society of the Future', is translated in *Soviet Review*, 2, No. 2, 3-29, 1961. An exceptionally useful review of Soviet thinking on new towns, especially around Moscow, is *Urbanisme et Villes Nouvelles en Union Soviétique*, Cahiers de l'IAURP, 38, 1975.

6 New York

No chapter on the New York region could fail to draw heavily upon the publications of the Regional Plan Association of New York. An essential basis for all study of the contemporary New York region is the *New York Metropolitan Region Study* (Raymond Vernon, director), carried out for the Regional Plan Association by the Graduate School of Public Administration, Harvard University, between 1956 and 1961. It is published in nine volumes, all published in Cambridge, Mass.: *Anatomy of a Metropolis*, 1959, by Edgar Hoover and Raymond Vernon; *Made in New York*, 1959, by Roy B. Helfgott, W. Eric Gustafson and James M. Hund; *The Newcomers*, 1959, by Oscar Handlin; *Wages in the Metropolis*, 1960, by Martin Segal; *Money Metropolis*, 1960, by Sidney M. Robbins and Nestor E. Terleckyj, with the collaboration of Ira O. Scott, Jr.; *Freight and the Metropolis*, 1960, by Benjamin Chinitz; *One-Tenth of a Nation*, 1960, by Robert M. Lichtenberg, with supplements by Edgar M. Hoover and Louise P. Lerday; *1,400 Governments*, 1961, by Robert C. Wood, with Vladimir V. Almendinger; and *Metropolis 1985*, 1960, by Raymond Vernon. The economic projection to 1958, *Projection of a Metropolis*, 1960, by Barbara R. Berman, Benjamin Chinitz and Edgar M. Hoover, was published as a technical supplement. M. Ostow and A.B. Dutka, *Work and Welfare in New York City*, Baltimore, 1975, is a useful recent account. Benjamin J. Klebaner (ed.) *New York City's Changing Economic Base*, New York, 1981, and Masha Sinnreich, *New York - World City*, Cambridge, Mass., 1980, are useful recent sources.

Other important sources from the Regional Plan Association are *Goals for the Region Project*, New York, 1963, a series of five booklets summarizing present trends and planning choices; *Hub-Bound Travel in the Tri-State New York Metropolitan Region*, Bulletin No. 99, New York, 1961; *Spread City: Projections of Development Trends and the Issues they pose: the Tri-State New York Metropolitan Region, 1960-1985*, Bulletin No. 100, New York, 1962; *The Region's Growth*, New York, 1967; *Jamaica Center*, New York, 1968; *The Second Regional Plan: A Draft for Discussion*, New York, 1969; *Urban*

Design Manhattan, New York, 1969; *The Office Industry*, New York. 1972; and *The State of the Region*, New York, 1977.

These should be supplemented by the massive five-volume Plan for New York City by the City Planning Commission, New York, 1969, which is usefully summarized in *Plan for New York City 1969: A Proposal*, New York, 1969; and by the important review by the First National City Bank (introduced by Nathan Glazer), *Profile of a City*, New York, 1972.

The Tri-State Transportation Commission has published a series of major reports including *An Interim Plan*, New York, 1966; *Regional Development Alternatives*, New York, 1967; *Measure of a Region*, New York, 1967; and *Regional Forecast 1985*, New York, 1967.

On transportation planning an important source is: Port of New York Authority, Comprehensive Planning Office, *Metropolitan Transportation 1980: A Framework for the long-range planning of transportation facilities to serve the New York–New Jersey Metropolitan Region*, New York, 1963.

A useful historical account of New York is Alan Nevins and John A. Krout (edd.), *The Greater City: New York, 1898-1948*, New York, 1948.

For the concept of Megalopolis, see Jean Gottmann, *Megalopolis: The urbanized northeastern seaboard of the United States*, Twentieth Century Fund, New York, 1961. Chapter 8 on urban land uses is especially pertinent, as also Chapters 9-12 on the economy. It should be supplemented by Irene B. and Conrad Taeuber, 'The Great Concentration: S.M.S.A.'s from Boston to Washington', *Population Index*, 30, 3-29, Princeton, 1964, Regional Plan Association, *The Region's Growth* (above), and Marion Clawson, *Suburban Land Conversion in the United States: An Economic and Governmental Process*, Baltimore, 1971.

On the New York economy, see: B. Chinitz (ed.), *The Declining Northeast: Demographic and Economic Analysis*, New York, 1978; R.B. Armstrong, *Regional Accounts: Structure and Performance of the New York Region's Economy in the Seventies*, Bloomington, 1980; B.A. Weinstein, 'The Demographics and Politics of Economic Decline in New York City', *Annals of Regional Science*, 11/2, 65-73, 1977; and P.D. McClelland and A.L. Magdovitz, *Crisis in the Making: The Political Economy of New York State since 1945*, New York, 1981.

On the New York City fiscal crisis, see: Congressional Budget Office, 'The Causes of New York's Fiscal Crisis', *Political Science Quarterly*, 90, 1974; the special issues of the journals *Dissent* (23/1 of 1975, with articles by Bensman and Muchnick), *Society* (13/4 of 1976, with articles by Fainstein and Fainstein, Sternlieb and Hughes, and Gerad and Starr) and *Liberation* (19/8 and 9, 1976, with contributions from Zevin, Charlop and Piven); Dick Netzer, 'The New York City Fiscal Crisis', in Chinitz, *op. cit.*; McClelland

and Magdovitz, *op. cit.*; and William K. Tabb, *The Long Default: New York City and the Urban Fiscal Crisis*, New York, 1982.

7 Tokyo

The economic development of Japan from early times up to 1960 is comprehensively treated by G.C. Allen, *A Short Economic History of Modern Japan*, revised edition, London, 1962. Basic geographical accounts are: Ryuziro Isida, *Geography of Japan*, Tokyo, 1961; Shinzo Kiuchi, *A Brief Survey of Japanese Geography*, Tokyo, 1964; Teizo Murata and Shinzo Kiuchi (edd.), *Reconnaissance Geography of Tokyo*, Tokyo, 1957. More recent accounts are found in the Special Publications of the Association of Japanese Geographers, especially No. 3, *Geography in Japan*, Tokyo, 1976 (edited by Kiuchi Shinzo) and No. 4, *Geography of Japan*, Tokyo, 1980. Particularly useful in the latter are K. Murata on 'The Formation of Industrial Areas' and T. Ishimizu and H. Ishihara on 'The Distribution and Movement of the Population in Japan's three major Metropolitan Areas'. See also the special issue of *L'Espace géographique*, 9, 81–172, 1980, and *GeoJournal*, 4, 191–272, 1980. For Japanese cities see D. Kornhauser, *Urban Japan: Its Foundations and Growth*, London, 1976. The Tokyo Metropolitan Government produces the excellent *Tokyo Municipal Library* including No. 4 on *Pollution* (revised 1977), No. 11 on *The Scheme for Revenue Sources* (1976), No. 12 on *Land in the Tokyo Metropolis* (1976), and No. 13 on *City Planning of Tokyo* (1978). Important official reports include: *Report on Tokyo Metropolitan Government* by Professor William A. Robson, Tokyo, 1967, and *Second Report on Tokyo Metropolitan Government*, by Professor William A. Robson, Tokyo, 1969; *Master Plan for the National Capital Region*, by the National Capital Planning Region Development Corporation, Tokyo, 1966; *Sizing up Tokyo: A Report on Tokyo under the Administration of Governor Ryokichi Minobi*, Tokyo, 1969; and TMG, *Planning of Tokyo 1975*, Tokyo, 1975. The monthly *Tokyo Municipal News*, from the TMG, is another rich information source in English. Recent sources include Y. Santo, 'Regional Planning and the Future Development of the Megalopolis in Japan', *Habitat*, 1, 165–73, 1976; S. Kiuchi and N. Inouchi, 'New Towns in Japan', *Geoforum*, 7, 1–12, 1980; and T. Ito, 'Tokaido – Megalopolis of Japan', *GeoJournal*, 4, 231–46, 1980.

8 Hong Kong

A basic source book is the excellent official Handbook, *Hong Kong 1983* (etc., annual), Hong Kong, with statistical supplement. There are a number of excellent books on the economy, especially T.-B. Lin, R.P.L. Lee, U.-E. Simonis (edd.), *Hong Kong: Economic, Social and Political Studies in Development*, Folkestone, 1979; T. and F.M. Geiger, *The Development Process in Hong Kong and Singapore*, London, 1975; W.F. Beazer, *The Commercial Future of Hong Kong*, New York, 1978; R. Hsia and L. Chau, *Industrialization, Employment and Income Distribution: A Case Study of Hong Kong*, London, 1978; D.G. Lethbridge (ed.), *The Business Environment in Hong Kong*, Hong Kong, 1980; and T.-B. Lin, V. Mok and Y.-P. Ho, *Manufactured Exports and Employment in Hong Kong*, Hong Kong, 1980. A. Rabushka, *Hong Kong: A Study in Economic Freedom*, Chicago, 1979, is useful though partisan. On small factories see V.F.S. Sit, 'Hong Kong's Approach to the Development of Small Manufacturing Enterprises', *U.N. Economic and Social Council, Small Industry Bulletin for Asia and the Pacific*, 15, 89-98, 1978, and V.F.S. Sit, 'Factories in Domestic Premises: An Anatomy of an Urban Informal Sector in Hong Kong', *Asian Profile*, 7, 209-29, 1979. The best general source for the urban geography of Hong Kong is F. Leeming, *Street Studies in Hong Kong: Localities in a Chinese City*, Hong Kong, 1977, with excellent case studies. Studies of housing include A.B. Mountjoy, '500,000 Squatters in Hong Kong', *Geographical Magazine*, 53, 119-25, 1980; C.Y. Choi, Y.K. Chan, 'Housing Development and Housing Policy in Hong Kong', in Lin et al., *op. cit.*; E.G. Prior, 'Redeveloping Public Housing in Hong Kong', *Ekistics*, 44, 96-9, 1977; and Y.-M. Yeung, D.W. Drakakis-Smith, 'Public Housing in the City States of Hong Kong and Singapore', in J.L. Taylor and D.G. Williams, *Urban Planning Practice in Developing Countries*, Oxford, 1982.

9 Mexico City

Useful introductions to Mexico City, in English, include: P. Ward, 'Mexico City' in M. Pacione (ed.), *Problems and Planning in Third World Cities*, London, 1981; G. Garza and M. Schteingart, 'Mexico City: The Emerging Megalopolis', in W.A. Cornelius and R.V. Kemper (edd.), *Latin American Urban Research*, Vol. 6, *Metropolitan Latin America: The Challenge and the Response*, Beverly Hills and London, 1978; F. Violich, 'Mexico City and Mexico: Two Cultural Worlds in Perspective', *Third World Planning Review*,

3, 361-86, Liverpool, 1981; and R.A. Fried, 'Mexico City', in W.A. Robson and D.E. Regan (edd.), *Great Cities of the World: Their Government, Politics and Planning*, II, pp. 647-87, London, 1972. D. Butterworth and J.K. Chance, *Latin American Urbanization*, Cambridge, 1981, and I. Scott, *Urban Spatial Development in Mexico*, Baltimore, 1982, are general studies with much useful information and bibliographies.

On the growth of the city, see the standard work, C. Bataillon and H. Riviere d'Arc, *La Ciudad de Mexico*, Mexico, 1979, also available in French original; and L. Unikel, 'La Dinamica de Crecimiento de la Ciudad de Mexico', *Ensayos sobre el Desarrollo urbano de Mexico*, 143, Mexico, 1974.

On housing, in addition to the above, see especially K. Stephens-Rioja, 'Land and Shelter: Important Issues for a Growing Metropolis', *Built Environment*, 8, 108-16, London, 1983; M. Schteingart, 'El Processo de Formacion y Consolidacion de un Asentiamento popular en Mexico: El Caso de la Ciudad de Nezahualcoyotl', *Revista Interamericana de Planificacion*, 15, No. 57, Mexico, 1981; W. Cornelius, 'The Impacts of Cityward Migration on Urban Land and Housing Markets', in J. Walton and L. Masotti, *The City in Community Perspective*, Beverly Hills, 1976; and L.A. Lomnitz, *Networks and Marginality: Life in a Mexican Shanty Town*, New York, 1977. Specifically on the urban land issue, there are two important World Bank Publications, *Land Reform in Latin America: Bolivia, Chile, Mexico, Peru and Venezuela* (Working Paper 275), and *Urban Land Policy Issues and Opportunities* (Working Paper 283), both Washington DC, 1978. On provision of services, see T. Campbell, *Food Water and Energy in the Valley of Mexico* (Institute of Urban and Regional Development, Working Paper 370), Berkeley, 1982.

For plans for the city and its region, consult the Mexican official documents: Secretaria de Asentamientos Humanos y Obras Publicos (SAHOP), *Plan Nacional de Desarrollo Urbano*, Mexico City, 1979; Departamento del Distrito Federal, *Urban Development Plan: Abbreviated Version* (in English), Mexico City, 1980, and *Sistema de Planificacion Urbana del Distrito Federal*, Mexico City, 1982; and Comision de Conurbacion del Centro del Pais, *Plan de Ordenacion de la Zona de Conurbacion del Centro del Pais*, Mexico City, 1981. For a useful general review of these plans, see T. Campbell, *Review of Plans for Urban development in the Valley of Mexico* (Institute of Urban and Regional Development, Working Paper 404), Berkeley, 1983.

10 The future metropolis

On the growth of the suburbs, particularly clear evidence is available from the United States: Donald J. Bogue, 'Urbanism in the United States, 1950',

American Journal of Sociology, 60, 471–86, Chicago, 1954–5; Amos K. Hawley, *The Changing Shape of Metropolitan America: Deconcentration since 1920*, Glencoe, 1956; and G.A. Wissink, *American Cities in Perspective: with Special Reference to the Development of their Fringe Areas*, Assen, Netherlands, 1962, with a comprehensive bibliography. International statistics are assembled in International Urban Research (Director, Kingsley Davis), *The World's Metropolitan Areas*, Berkeley and Los Angeles, 1959. The relation between transportation techniques and city growth is documented in Harlan W. Gilmore, *Transportation and the Growth of Cities*, Glencoe, 1953 and Colin Clark, 'Transport - Maker and Breaker of Cities', *Town Planning Review*, 28, 237–50, Liverpool, 1957–8. For the functions of the central city, see Robert M. Haig, 'Toward an Understanding of the Metropolis', *Quarterly Journal of Economics*, 40, 179–208 and 402–34, Cambridge, Mass., 1925–6; P. Sargant Florence, 'Economic efficiency in the metropolis', in R.M. Fisher (ed.), *The Metropolis in Modern Life*, pp. 85–124, New York, 1955; Raymond Vernon, 'Production and Distribution in the large Metropolis', *Annals of the American Academy of Political and Social Science*, 314, 15–29, Philadelphia, 1957; Committee for Economic Development, *The Changing Economic Function of the Central City*, New York, 1961; Peter Cowan et al., *The Office: A Facet of Urban Growth*, London, 1969; John Goddard, *Office Location in Urban and Regional Development*, Oxford, 1975; Peter W. Daniels, *Office Location*, London, 1975; and Allen Pred, *City-Systems in Advanced Economies*, London, 1977. For the role of communications see Richard L. Meier, *A Communications Theory of Urban Growth*, Cambridge, Mass., 1962; Aaron Fleischer, 'The Influence of Technology on Urban Forms', *Daedalus*, 90, 48–60, Cambridge, Mass., 1961; Karl W. Deutsch. 'On social Communication and the Metropolis', *ibid.*, 99–100; Bertil Thorngren, 'How do contact systems affect regional development?', *Environment and Planning*, 2, 409–29, 1970; John Goddard, *Office Linkages and Location: a Study of Communications and Spatial Patterns in Central London*, Oxford, 1973; and Alex Reid, 'What Telecommunication Implies', *New Society*, 1284–6, 1971. For theories of future development: Kevin Lynch, 'The Pattern of the Metropolis', *ibid.*, 79–98; Melvin M. Webber, 'Order in Diversity: Community without Propinquity', in Lowdon Wingo, Jr. (ed.), *Cities and Space: The Future Use of Urban Land*, Resources for the Future, pp. 23–54, Baltimore, 1963; and 'The Urban Place and the Nonplace Urban Realm', in Webber et al., *Explorations into Urban Structure*, pp. 79–153, Philadelphia, 1964. For the recent counter-urbanisation trends, see B.J.L. Berry (ed.), *Urbanization and Counter-Urbanization*, Urban Affairs Annual Reviews, 11, London, 1976. For the 'concentric' theory of urban growth, see Ernest W. Burgess, 'The Growth of the City: an Introduction to a Research Project', in Robert E. Park, Ernest W. Burgess and Roderick D. McKenzie, *The City*, pp. 47–62, Chicago,

1925; for the 'sector' theory, see Homer Hoyt, *The Structure and Growth of residential Neighbourhoods in American Cities*, Washington, 1939. Michael Thomson, *Great Cities and their Traffic*, London, 1977, has a useful typology of different city forms and their consequences for transport.

B.J.L. Berry, *The Human Consequences of Urbanization*, London, 1973, is the best general introduction to the divergent paths of cities in the advanced and developing world.

Also useful are Lloyd Rodwin, *Nations and Cities: A Comparison of Strategies for Urban Growth*, New York, 1970, and Larry S. Bourne, *Urban Systems: Strategies for Regulation*, Oxford, 1975. Peter Hall and Dennis Hay, *Growth Centres in the European Urban System*, London, 1980, have useful comparative material on trends in Europe, the United States and Japan. For the developing world, useful sources are: Michael Pacione (ed.), *Problems and Planning in Third World Cities*, London, 1981; John Walton and Louis Masoti, *The City in Comparative Perspective*, New York, 1976; John L. Taylor and David G. Williams, *Urban Planning Practice in Developing Countries*, Oxford, 1982; Janet Abu-Lughod and Richard Hay, Jr., *Third World Urbanization*, London, 1977; and Bernard Renaud, *National Urbanization Policy in Developing Countries*, Washington DC, 1982.

Index

267